The face of the city

Civic portraiture and civic identity in early modern England

ROBERT TITTLER

Manchester
University Press
Manchester and New York

distributed exclusively in the USA by Palgrave

Published by Manchester University Press
Oxford Road, Manchester M13 9NR, UK
and Room 400, 175 Fifth Avenue, New York, NY 10010, USA
www.manchesteruniversitypress.co.uk

Distributed exclusively in the USA by
Palgrave, 175 Fifth Avenue, New York, NY 10010, USA

Distributed exclusively in Canada by
UBC Press, University of British Columbia, 2029 West Mall,
Vancouver, BC, Canada V6T 1Z2

British Library Cataloguing-in-Publication Data
A catalogue record for this book is available from the British Library

Library of Congress Cataloging-in-Publication Data applied for

ISBN 978 0 7190 7501 8 *hardback*

First published 2007

16 15 14 13 12 11 10 09 08 07   10 9 8 7 6 5 4 3 2 1

Typeset in Scala with Pastonchi display
by Koinonia Ltd, Manchester

Printed in Great Britain
by Biddles, King's Lynn

The face of the city

MANCHESTER
1824

Manchester University Press

Politics, culture and society in early modern Britain

General editors

PROFESSOR ANN HUGHES
DR ANTHONY MILTON
PROFESSOR PETER LAKE

This important series publishes monographs that take a fresh and challenging look at the interactions between politics, culture and society in Britain between 1500 and the mid-eighteenth century. It counteracts the fragmentation of current historiography through encouraging a variety of approaches which attempt to redefine the political, social and cultural worlds, and to explore their interconnection in a flexible and creative fashion. All the volumes in the series question and transcend traditional interdisciplinary boundaries, such as those between political history and literary studies, social history and divinity, urban history and anthropology. They contribute to a broader understanding of crucial developments in early modern Britain.

Already published in the series

Leicester and the Court   SIMON ADAMS

Ambition and failure in Stuart England   IAN ATHERTON

The 1630s   IAN ATHERTON AND JULIE SANDERS (*eds*)

Literature and politics in the English Reformation   TOM BETTERIDGE

'No historie so meete'   JAN BROADWAY

Republican learning   JUSTIN CHAMPION

Home divisions   THOMAS COGSWELL

A religion of the Word   CATHARINE DAVIES

Cromwell's major-generals   CHRISTOPHER DURSTON

The English sermon revised   LORI ANNE FERRELL *and* PETER MCCULLOUGH (*eds*)

The spoken word   ADAM FOX *and* DANIEL WOOLF (*eds*)

Reading Ireland   RAYMOND GILLESPIE

Londinopolis   PAUL GRIFFITHS *and* MARK JENNER (*eds*)

Inventing a republic   SEAN KELSEY

The boxmaker's revenge   PETER LAKE

Theatre and empire   TRISTAN MARSHALL

The social world of early modern Westminster   J.F. MERRITT

Courtship and constraint   DIANA O'HARA

The origins of the Scottish Reformation   ALEC RYRIE

Catholics and the 'Protestant nation'   ETHAN SHAGAN (*ed.*)

Communities in early modern England   ALEXANDRA SHEPARD *and* PHILIP WITHINGTON (*eds*)

Aspects of English Protestantism, c. 1530–1700   NICHOLAS TYACKE

Charitable hatred   ALEXANDRA WALSHAM

Crowds and popular politics in early modern England   JOHN WALTER

Political passions   RACHEL WEIL

Brave community   JOHN GURNEY

'He is Venerable in his gowne ... wherewith he setts not forth so much his owne, as the face of a City ... His Scarlet gowne is a Monument, and lasts from generation to generation'. (Description of a London alderman by John Earle, in *Microcosmographie, or a Peece of the World Discovered* (1622), part 5.)

Contents

List of figures

Preface

If this book belonged to the animal kingdom, it would constitute one of the wonders of science that such a long gestation period produced such a small volume. Suffice it to say that the path of discovery in what is to me the new field of art history, along with other distractions of employment and life, has not made for expedition in its completion.

The subject of civic portraiture first occurred to me in the course of research, conducted through the mid- and late 1980s, on the role of town halls in the political life of English towns and cities in the wake of the Reformation. Both the halls and the portraits displayed in them suggested to me that political institutions, even at the most local levels, developed images of rule and found ways of projecting those images through the visual media of the day. My reading of the essays collected by Andrew Moore and Charlotte Crawley, published in 1992 as *Family & Friends: A Regional Survey of British Portraiture*, and especially Victor Morgan's short essay therein on the Norwich civic portraits, opened further to me the possibilities of local portrait traditions.[1] Though in the end I could not agree with all their contentions, they provided timely impetus for what followed. Indulgent hosts at Clare Hall and Jesus College, Cambridge, allowed me to try out my early thoughts in papers offered in 1995, as did programme directors of the North American and North East Conferences on British Studies in meetings of those associations. My first attempt to publish on the subject came in 1998. But distractions then took their toll, and the amount of field research I was able to undertake in frequent but necessarily short research trips to the UK thereafter meant that I could only drink the required primary research down in small sips over an extended period of time, hoping the cup would stay warm as I did so.

Through these years the privilege of working in appropriate research libraries and archives remained critically important. London's Guildhall Library, the National Portrait Gallery's Heinz Archive, the British Library, McGill University's Blackader-Lauterman Library, London University's Institute of Historical Research, and the Courtauld Institute's Witt Library, allowed me to augment the resources available in my home university. Concordia University librarians unfailingly made up in their courtesy and efficiency for what the collection in their care lacked in content. Though I am grateful to virtually the entire staff especially of Concordia'a Vanier Library, special thanks should go to Judy Appleby, Maria-Helena Bairos, Ursula Hakein, Wendy Knechtel, Sonya

Poulin, Luigina Vileno, and the late Nikki Celluci. Charles Belanger of Concordia's IITS centre has also been especially helpful with visual images as has Prof. Lionel Sanders with Latin translations. I thank the Editors of *Costume* for permission to publish material on the symbolism of freemen's gloves, which first appeared in volume 40 (2006), pp. 13–20 of that journal.

But the nature of this subject also requires a great deal of work in local museums, galleries and specialized archives. And in the perpetually rushed circumstances in which the overseas visiting researcher finds himself, the help of the knowledgeable curator, archivist or local historian proves exceptionally valuable. I am indebted to the staffs of the Berkshire County Record Office, Birmingham Public Library, Bristol Record Office and City Museum and Art Gallery, Chester Record Office, Christ's Hospital (Abingdon) Archives, Gloucester Record Office, Devon County Record Office (Exeter), Norfolk County Record Office (King's Lynn), St John's College (Oxford) archives, Shrewsbury School Library, and the Wiltshire County Record Office.

I have had the good fortune to have been assisted at such times, and often in follow-up by correspondence, by a host of specialists. Ron Aquila Clarke of the Herbert Art Gallery and Museum, Coventry; Frances Willmoth and Rod Mengham of Jesus College, Cambridge; Susan Pratt of the Courtauld Institute Library; John Blatchley of Ipswich; Ross Turl of the Hampshire Record Office; Susan North, Curator of Fashion at the Victoria and Albert Museum; Rhona Mitchell, formerly of Christ's Hospital, Horsham; Erin Blake of the Folger Shakespeare Library; Sheena Stoddard, Curator of Art at the City Museum and Art Gallery in Bristol; Nigel Hammond, Hon. Archivist of Christ's Hospital, Abingdon; David Pitcher of King's Lynn; Elaine Blake, Curator of Art and Ethnography, Reading Museums Service; Peter Boughton, Keeper of Art and Architecture at Chester's Grosvenor Museum; Paul Cox, Erika Ingham and Antonia Leak at the Heinz Archive of the National Portrait Gallery; Jane Baker and her successors at the Royal Albert Memorial Museum of Exeter; Michael MacCarthy-Morrogh and James Lawson of Shrewsbury School.

None of this would have been remotely possible without the funding I have received from Canada's Social Science and Humanities Research Council, in the form both of an individual research grant and a share of the Major Collaborative Research Initiative grant awarded to the 'Making Publics' project in the latter stages of my labours. I am delighted to be able to express my thanks to SSHRC, and to those involved in the award of these research grants.

With this support, and when not buried in English archives and museums, I was able to engage at a somewhat more leisurely pace with the field of art history. When Dr Catherine MacKenzie, then chair of Concordia's Art History Department, invited me to share my new-found enthusiasms for the visual arts of Renaissance England with undergraduates, I had run out of excuses for learning the subject in its appropriate extent. I consequently began to read more systematically in the contextual area of visual arts in Renaissance England. I am grateful to her and to her successor as Chair, Dr Loren Lerner, for the continuing privilege of teaching in that Department, and for the warm welcome which they and their colleagues have extended to me.

This welcoming attitude to the earnest novice seems to be endemic in that field itself. Christy Anderson patiently encouraged me in a term at Yale, as did Joanna Woodall over coffee in London. She, Tarnya Cooper, Anne Thackray, Elizabeth Goldring and Andrea Galdy have patiently and very constructively read all or parts of the manuscript and diplomatically showed me where balloons were most likely to burst under the pressure of hot air. None of the remaining flaws should be laid at their doorsteps. I am equally indebted to Tarnya Cooper for letting me read and discuss her pioneering doctoral thesis and for myriad suggestions and encouragement in my own work; to Maurice Howard, Karen Hearn and Susan Foister for responding generously to numerous questions and for affirming the importance of the subject itself; to Anne Thackray again for serving as my interpreter to that initially foreign country of Art History. David Dean, Norman Jones, Sally-Beth MacLean, Stephen Porter, Joe Ward, Bronwen Wilson, Daniel Woolf, and Paul Yachnin have also pitched in at one point or another with helpful suggestions and thought-provoking observations. Even given these most fruitful contacts and interchanges, it is impossible to keep up with relevant scholarship: something new and important always appears on the eve of publication. Phil Withington's *The Politics of Commonwealth* (Cambridge, 2005) proves the point. I regret that such an imaginative and provocative work appeared too late to receive due consideration.

Having an amenable and quiet place to work has proven a frequent concern over the duration of this project. I am grateful to Pauline Croft and Geoff New for the loan of their London flat (surely the most wonderful place to write and with a working kitchen to match) over part of two summers and to Concordia Vice-Rector Bob Roy, who extended me the privilege of a post-retirement office where I could work on a daily basis on campus. Sincere thanks to Sue Womersley, copy-editor extraordinaire, for her work on this manuscript.

The final thanks, of an entirely unprofessional kind, must go to my wife Anne, who has heard it all (and all too often) and always patiently, and to my extended family. The recent addition of grandsons Daniel Alexandrovitch Drojjine and Peter Irving Tittler has added an entire new dimension to life's joys. They are the rightful dedicatees of this book.

NOTE

1 Victor Morgan, 'The Norwich Guildhall Portraits: Images in Context', in Andrew Moore and Charlotte Crawley, eds, *Family & Friends: A Regional Survey of British Portraiture* (1992), pp. 21–30.

Introduction

This book derives from my long-standing interest in the political life and culture of English provincial towns in the wake of the Reformation, and in the material and visual expressions of that milieu. It follows my study of the English town hall as the seat and symbol of civic authority in the provincial towns of this era, and builds upon my understanding of post-Reformation politics and political culture in the same urban milieu.[1] I take as my starting point here the broad questions which emerge from those earlier investigations: 'what is the role of visual culture in the political and social discourse of the local community in early modern England?' and, more specifically, 'what did particular forms of visual culture mean in the life of an English provincial urban community following the Reformation?'.

Pursuing these themes somewhat further, this book moves from one form of visual culture to another, and from town halls to portraits. It expands its scope from provincial towns and cities to take in the London metropolis as well as other types of communities and institutions altogether. This reflects the recognition that schools and other charitable foundations, university colleges, and London livery companies also constituted civic communities, that they experienced challenges in these years which were very similar to those experienced in towns and cities, and that they responded in very similar ways. Finally, it considers a much broader context than was provided by the Reformation alone.

The aim is not simply to round out previous work on the political life of local communities in these years. It is to contribute to the broad picture of how communities and institutions of all types in this era, whose corporate identities and values had long been articulated in visual as well as other terms, coped with the large-scale destruction of a traditional, substantially internalized visual culture which had evolved in and around traditional Roman Catholic belief over the course of a millennium. It is also to ask how they did so at a time also marked by rapid change in other aspects of English life: the emergence of the Tudor state, the dramatic rise in population and the cost of living, the burgeoning of a new and more mature form of capitalist free enterprise, the disestablishment and frequent re-establishment of myriad social and civic institutions cashiered by the Reformation, and the emerging fears of crime, rootlessness and unrest. Were older visual traditions swept entirely away, or did they adapt over time to meet new circumstances? Did new forms of visual expression emerge to fill some of the consequent void? Did both the meaning and the vocabulary of visual imagery change as well, and in what ways might they have done so? What part did visual discourse, especially in the form of portraiture, play in the broader development of a post-Reformation political culture in the civic bodies at hand? How did it contribute to the definition, or to the promulgation, of civic identity and purpose which were so urgently required by the ruling elites of contemporary institutions? How may we understand the consumption of such portraiture as a political and social commodity: who will have produced it; to what audiences might it have been directed; by what 'publics' will it have been consumed; what will they have understood by that experience?

As the first of its two prime objectives, this study investigates the meaning and role of portraiture in the political and social discourse of the day. It does so not by examining the familiar milieu of the royal court and country house, but rather by considering the civic context of urban, pedagogical and occupational institutions.

It is this objective which principally determines the time-frame at hand, c. 1500–c. 1640. The former date, which is entirely approximate, allows us to see the emergence of civic portraiture from its pre-Reformation roots, and identifies the elements of continuity which spanned the Reformation era to follow. Among its other effects, the Reformation itself, along with the sweeping social, economic and political changes of the same era, created problems, even crises, of identity and legitimacy for all sorts of civic bodies, as well as for particular social status groups and for the monarchy itself.

These related issues raised critical questions about political relationships and the exercise of authority, questions which would dominate English political discourse for decades to come. How were the newly empowered elites (whether individual people newly risen in the social pyramid, or civic officials of newly chartered institutions in their political roles) to act in fulfilling their new roles, and how could they learn to do so? How should the civic body (whether livery company or university college, endowed school or charity, town or city government institution) be regarded by those over whom its officials presided? To whom or what should respect and deference be paid, and why? The resolution of these issues would determine the extent of administrative efficacy, political authority, moral integrity, and legal responsibility of governing authorities the realm over. As the Tudor monarchy itself understood right from its inception, they could be neither denied or ignored. No wonder that the culture of English politics at all levels reflected this central concern for defining identities, encouraging legitimation and behaving appropriately through these years.

As we now know, the terminal date of 1640 marks the eve of yet more serious crises. In addition, it marks an approximate point by which civic portraiture had become a widely employed strategy for defining the identity and projecting the legitimacy of myriad civic bodies at all levels. It also more or less marks the widespread establishment of civic patronage for professionally trained and highly skilful portrait painters who had come by that time to set the aesthetic standard for the portrait genre.

That point begs the question of the book's second chief objective: to flesh out the contours of this unfamiliar 'civic' portrait type, and to place it appropriately in the early and wider history of English portraiture as a genre of cultural expression. This aim raises a separate set of questions, ones which emphasize the text as much as the context, the practitioners as much as the patrons. What were the implications of the Reformation and associated events for the development of easel portraiture in England as it applied to the civic portrait? What may we make of the relations between foreign and native-born, London-based and provincial, practitioners of that genre, and how did those relationships affect the genre itself? How did the distinctive imagery of the civic portrait reflect the didactic requirements of the patron, and how then did civic portraits differ from the more familiar and courtly portrait forms? What sort of publics did these works address, and in what spatial environments did they do so?

The first of these principal objectives may contribute somewhat more to the fields of social, urban and political history; the second, more to the field of art history in its broadest sense. Such a study gains encouragement from the continual weakening of traditional disciplinary boundaries; it seems a subject whose time has come.

'Civic' portraiture has been so largely overlooked by even the best of conventional art historical scholarship that it still requires a full definition, carefully constructed. At least at the outset of my labours I thought I knew what I meant myself by the term: the portraits of officers in, or benefactors to, or heroes and heroines of, civic institutions. These bodies included individual towns and cities, but also London livery companies, charitable foundations, schools and (taking a broad view of the notion of 'civic' bodies) colleges, and similar communities bound by formal governing structures and common purpose. Officials of these bodies, who often became the subjects of civic portraits, might hold the titles of 'mayor', 'alderman', 'master', 'founder', and so forth. Benefactors might be those who secured a charter of foundation, incorporation, privilege, or similar boon, or those who contributed substantial lands or sums of money. They might even include those who had given a building for use as the common hall of the company, as was the case with Henry VIII's Sergeant Painter Sir John Browne who gave a building to be used as the Painter-Stainers' Hall in 1532.[2] And heroes and heroines might include such semi-folkloric figures as Dick Whittington and Lady Godiva, who had contributed, or were thought to have contributed, in important ways to the identity of particular communities or institutions.

The face of the city

Because I was especially concerned to understand the meaning of such portraits in their civic context, it seemed important to focus on paintings which had been commissioned or purchased by the civic institution itself. My reading in the archives of all sorts of civic institutions, especially provincial towns and London livery companies, had turned up a surprising number of references to the commissioning or display of such portraits by those bodies. Those references led me to assume that a portrait commissioned by the civic body rather than by the sitter would naturally represent the motives of that civic body rather than the person, and that they would therefore provide direct and perhaps telling insights into the civic and corporate mentality of the era. This became a further element in my initial working definition: a true civic portrait had to be commissioned or purchased by the civic body and not by the sitter. In addition, I reasoned that in order to fulfil the intention of the commissioning institution, such portraits would have to be displayed in a civic space specific to it: college and company halls, borough court rooms, council chambers, mayors' parlours, and so forth. The archives of town, school, college and company yield many references to such displays.

But early on in my labours I came upon the portrait of John Vernon (d. 1616) in the Merchant Taylors' Hall, and looked into what that Company's archives had to say about its provenance. A long-time member of the Merchant Taylors' Company of London who had served as its master and become its benefactor, Vernon had certainly earned a rightful place in the Company's pantheon of worthies. Towards the end of his life he had his own portrait painted for his own gratification, a sure sign, or so it appeared, of a 'personal' rather than a civic portrait. But then in July of 1616, 'to the end that his faythfull true love borne to the Company might be had in remembrance', he donated it to the Merchant Taylors, asking (perhaps a bit coyly) whether they thought his friendship to the Company might entitle him to have his picture hung along-side other such heroes. The Company took the hint – they could hardly have done otherwise – and hung the painting. One may still see it displayed in their hall.[3] In the same year of 1616 Vernon made a similar gift to the city of Chester, the place of his birth and object of his several generous benefactions, along with 'a case ... to houlde and carry the same from London, to be hung in the pendice'.[4] But given the origins of these paintings, commissioned by Vernon and not by his Company or his native city, how far could I take them as true civic portraits as I had initially defined them, and how common were such benefactions?

In the event, Vernon's case proved far from unique. Many other such figures were painted by their own order, or that of their families, and then given during or shortly after the sitter's lifetime to his or her favourite charity, native town, university college or livery company. Some of these were, and some just as clearly were not, initially intended for such donations resulting

4

in civic display. Similarly, numerous civic portraits turned out to be copies, commissioned by the civic institutions, of personal portraits originally done for the family or sitter.

In some few cases, ironically, the sitter or family commissioned a painting for *private* display which emphasized the sitter's civic role. These were intended to exhibit his or her virtuous character or civic spirit, thus giving the work an even greater affinity with true civic portraits. Many of these were later given to or purchased by the civic institution, and then more often than not hung in that central, quasi-public space common in one form or another to all institutional types and known universally as 'the hall'. This new place of display and even the act of acquisition itself then imparted to such works most of the defining characteristics of civic portraits. They became part of the ceremonial landscape of the civic building and the mnemonic record of the institutional identity. Often they were also painted over in places, or had inscriptions or civic arms added to them, so as to make them conform more closely to civic purposes.

This recognition required me to loosen up my initial definition. I came to accept that, though the purest variety of the species would have been purposely commissioned by the civic body, civic portraits could also have been painted at the sitter's request, and then acquired by the civic body through donation, imitation or purchase. Then, too, while not necessarily seeking to deny the personal achievements of the subject, they had in some manner, by elements either of content, labelling or place of display, to show the sitter's relationship and contribution to the civic body, and to be displayed by that institution. Typically, as we'll see in chapter 5, their emblematic programmes prominently featured those attributes, virtues and achievements which contributed to that body and enhanced its identity and reputation. They often bore the institution's coat of arms along with the sitter's own. The objects or implements held by or displayed near the subject, his or her form of dress, and the inscriptions on the painting or its frame, further privileged civic over personal objectives.

The definitional requirement that civic portraits be displayed in civic spaces remains inviolate. One like Vernon's, first done at the sitter's commission and later given to the institution, would no doubt have been viewed by his family and friends in the setting of his own home quite differently than by members of the livery in the Company Hall. But the fact of its display in that hall, identifying him as a benefactor of the Company, in close proximity to other Company memorabilia and seen by members of that livery, would surely allow it to serve as a 'civic' portrait in every practical sense.

I also came to recognize that both the place of display and (rare though surviving originals may be) the choice of frame may have been worked out so as to make a new acquisition conform visually to the pattern and meaning of other portraits already on hand. This is most obviously the case in the rare

English examples of the extensive portrait series, as may be found in Norwich or Peterhouse, Cambridge. Even literal verisimilitude of appearance may have been less important than in personal portraits. A large number of civic portraits prove to have been done posthumously, several decades or even more than a century after the death of the subject, making it impossible to achieve a true likeness. And finally, very few civic portraits in the sense of easel paintings have come to light in England prior to the break from Rome and the early stages of the ensuing Reformation, only appearing a generation or so after personal portraits emerged in England, and more than a century at least after they became established elsewhere in Western Europe.

Even this looser, more inclusive, definition provided reasonably firm lines of demarcation between civic and that more conventional and common type which might be called 'personal' portraits. The latter were principally done to make certain statements about the sitter him or herself: about his or her faith, character, achievements, fame, family ties, heritage, social status and so forth. It is entirely appropriate to think of them as statements of self-affirmation and personal legitimation. Emblematic and iconographic programmes will have been worked out accordingly. Heraldic achievements and personal mottoes; spouses, children or even pets; background scenes of landscape or estates; fashionably personal rather than civic dress; reference to military prowess; and a variety of other touches and props were commonly included to serve those ends. Save perhaps for heraldic devices intended to identify the sitter, it is extremely unusual to find any of these devices in their civic counterparts.

Especially prior to the early seventeenth century, personal portraits more often than civic portraits attempted to recapture a reasonable verisimilitude of the sitter's appearance. Most were painted literally from life or at least during the sitter's lifetime; and many came to be executed by a more skilful class of painter. Finally, personal portraits will have been displayed in private, usually domestic, locations specific to the sitter's person, family or close friends. Such locations ranged from the long galleries of the great country houses to the more modest halls or chambers of the middling sorts of people and even to the closed locket of the intimate portrait miniature. Most of those which have survived long-remained in such spaces, though some of them came into institutional hands at some substantially later date, right up to modern times.

Early English civic portraits differ from personal or courtly portraits in one other important respect which must be noted at the outset. The general neglect which this subject has met among art historians and others, a quite different reception than has met English *personal* portraiture of the same era or *civic* portraiture in many other parts of Europe, remains striking and problematic. From classic twentieth-century surveys by, e.g., Erna Auerbach, Eric Mercer and Ellis Waterhouse, through much of the huge contribution of Sir Roy Strong and even beyond, the scholarly discussion of English portraiture of

IOANNES MASONVS EQVES AVRATVS

GVLIELMVS BOSTOCK HANC TABVLAM POSVIT . 16

1 'Sir John Mason', Christ's Hospital, Abingdon; Sampson Strong, 1607.

this era has not been particularly concerned with portraits of non-elite social groups or of those outside the canonical mainstream, especially of royalty or the landed classes.[5]

Perhaps this relative neglect merely echoes the views of contemporaries themselves in valuing portraits more for the status and identity of the sitter than for the context or authorship of the work. It seems also to stem from deep-rooted traditions of art historical scholarship and connoisseurship which privileged concerns for appearance and artistry over content and context, and which measured the worth of a portrait by its success in conveying formal, essentially neo-classical, style. And part of this scholarly neglect must also be due to the tardy and slow appearance of civic portraiture itself in England at a time when, by contrast, civic bodies in, e.g., the Italian Peninsula, the Holy Roman Empire and especially the Netherlands were producing such portraits in considerable abundance. Had English institutions produced them as early, and in similar abundance, art historians would no doubt have taken more note. But England's civic institutions, and especially its town and city governments, never developed the same degree of political autonomy or (with the obvious exception of London) population levels as scores of their continental cousins in this era, and thus they lacked the strength of civic indentity and patronage which would have produced such a comparable flowering.

Whatever the explanation, the prime focus has more often than not (and perhaps especially for pre and post-Elizabethan works) remained on portraits as works of art, and on the effort to understand, interpret, and display them accordingly. The consequent scholarly agenda has therefore been taken up until very recently with questions about artistic technique and skill, attribution, influence of one formal school or painter upon another, and the nature and extent of foreign influence (especially in its neo-classical dimensions) on the English experience. From Lucas Hornebolte and Hans Holbein to Peter Paul Rubens and beyond, much of the canon of early English portraiture staked out in this literature derives from the brush of foreign artists, schooled in formal aesthetic principles and highly specialized techniques, and lured to England by the promise of courtly patronage.

On the other hand, traditional scholarship has largely overlooked those post-Reformation paintings, including a large number of our civic portraits, which are more obviously 'vernacular' and even 'naive' and certainly native English in form and workmanship.[6] In the context of this study I take the term 'vernacular' to mean painting which does not conform to the accepted conventions of a particular formal or polite style, but which demonstrates some distinct familiarity with the technical aspects of painting on board or canvas as such. Sampson Strong's early seventeenth-century portrait of Sir John Mason, founder and benefactor of Christ's Hospital, Abingdon, provides a useful example of contemporary vernacular portraiture (fig. 1). It shows a reasonably adept handling of technique in the texture of the fur-lined robe, and at least some effort to depict shading by the use of delicately contrasting flesh tones rather than linear outlines on the face, and in the colouration of hair and eyes. This work characteristically remains essentially two-dimensional and lifeless, fails to achieve a natural look of the hands or other features, and could not readily be pigeon-holed in any of the established formal styles of the day.

The late sixteenth-century portrait of John Falkner (fig. 2), described on

MASTER, IOHN FALKNER,
T:TIMES MAIOER OF THE
CITY OF GLOCESTER

2 'John Falkner, Mayor of Gloucester'; anon., c. 1600.

the canvas as '3: TIMES MAIOER OF THE CITY OF GLOCESTER' (*sic*), or the double portrait of John and Joan Cooke, also of Gloucester (fig. 3), are also anonymous and vernacular works, but they must be considered 'naive' as well. They also remain entirely two-dimensional, lack specialized technique or perspective, and may not be categorized in any contemporary formal style. But in contrast to the Mason portrait, which is by no means lacking in skill, they also demonstrate a marked inability to depict accurate bodily proportions (especially in Falkner's arms and hands) or facial features. They do not demonstrate a skilful handling of paint or mastery of technique in its application. The lack of formal training in the art of portraiture has allowed their creators to produce works which may hold a certain degree of charm for the modern eye,

M[r] IOHN COOKE, MAIOR OF THE CITIE OF GLOCESTER 4. TIMES.

3 'John and Joan Cooke, Mayor and Mayoress of Gloucester'; anon., c. 1590s–c. 1620.

but which nevertheless remain truly artless in most other respects. Sir Roy Strong's view that 'Hans Holbein the Younger ... had an influence directly or otherwise on all artists working in England in the sixteenth century' holds water (if, indeed, at all) only if his use of the term 'artists' excludes painters working in this vernacular mode.[7]

There have been a few exceptions to this general neglect of works outside the bounds of canonical interest. One of them has come in discussions devoted to the largest and most familiar collection of civic portraits from this era, which is in Norwich, though even here attention has been paid as much by historians as art historians.[8] Then, too, art historians specializing in the English as well as other traditions have considerably broadened the range of their interests and approaches in recent years, reaching out to other disciplines and working their craft in ever-broader interpretive circles. Exemplary practitioners of this 'new art history' as it applies to early modern England appear among students of, e.g., architecture,[9] funeral monuments[10] and other visual forms even more than of portraiture. But the pioneering contributions of, e.g., Susan Foister, examining the ownership of paintings by a study of household inventories,[11] Lucy Gent and her collaborators exploring the interface of classical and native English traditions of visual arts in general,[12] and Tarnya Cooper, examining portraits of some middling, non-elite, sorts of people as statements of Protestant affirmation, brilliantly exemplify the potential of a broader perspective on portraiture.[13] Taken together, these suggest the benefits of looking at what a historian might well term 'portraiture from below', or at least from half-way down. A substantial proportion of English civic portraits done prior to the early seventeenth century, and a good many thereafter, would qualify for this designation.

I have approached the civic portraits under scrutiny here, most of them well out of the canonical mainstream, not so much as works of art, but rather as cultural and political artefacts of their time. Save for some of those done especially for the wealthier livery companies and in the last two or three decades of the chosen period, they do not much exhibit (nor were they particularly intended to exhibit) many of the aesthetic qualities, especially linked with classical form, which have traditionally dominated the conventional art historical agenda. For example, while much of that agenda has dealt with questions of the attribution of works to particular artists, and to the styles, training and influences of those artists, far fewer of these civic portraits have been signed than of the more polite and familiar canon of the era. Most of those who produced civic portraits and other vernacular portraits of the era were more craftsmen ('painter-stainers' especially) than artists, more often engaged in painting objects ranging from inn signs and pageant scenery to stair-railings, ships' prows and coaches, than they were in producing portraits. It can be scant exaggeration to state that most of them would no more have signed their names to a painting than a brick-maker would have signed a brick. Even the word 'painting' itself was taken in many more and broader senses than we would use it today. Not until the early decades of the seventeenth century, when theoretical writings about painting became more current in England, did the terminology become more refined and specific.[14]

Admittedly, the civic portraiture of this era is not an easy subject to explore. Historians, as opposed to art historians, of this era, are used to having at hand an enormous secondary literature on any aspect of their chosen subject: the history of Tudor and early Stuart England must surely be one of the most thoroughly investigated and described periods of any national history anywhere. Because the historians' conventional sources come in the form of archives, they are used to the facilities of the National Register of Archives, and the indexes of scores of national, county and local record offices, most of them now on-line, to locate the grist for their mill. By contrast, and despite the long and honourable labours of the Heinz Archive of the National Portrait Gallery, the Courtauld's Witt Library and the photographic archive of the Paul Mellon Centre, there is as yet no central and truly comprehensive register or listing of English portraits and their location for this era, especially for those, including most civic portraits, which were done anonymously rather than by known painters, or those held in civic institutions. Nor, for that matter, do any of these valuable research archives systematically list portraits by their location or holding institution.

This is not so much a problem for university portraits, as the catalogues compiled for Oxford by Rachel Poole in the early twentieth century, and for Cambridge University and at least some of its colleges by J.W. Goodison, provide valuable entrées.[15] But it remains a high hurdle for anyone investigating portraits held in provincial towns, London livery companies, and endowed charitable institutions. Though even remote and local museums may be expected to have accessible listings of their collections, relatively few galleries of art and only a smattering of museums of local history now hold the early civic portraits produced for the communities which they serve. Indeed, many such paintings which can be identified archivally have simply perished or otherwise disappeared. When town museums do have one or two in their collections, the aesthetic limitations of many of those works render them at least as likely to be in storage as on pubic display. Not much beyond the name of the sitter, and sometimes not even that, tends to be known, nor do invariably overworked and under-supported staff have the time to investigate what might be learned about them. Published histories of livery companies do sometimes identify portraits, and those compiled prior to the Second World War sometimes record those which would soon be destroyed in that conflict. But rare is the company which has anything like a curator for its collections who might carry out fundamental research.

Ideally, such research could utilize archival sources to identify portraits which have not survived as well as those which have, since accounts for payment or inventories of institutional possessions often reveal crucial information. Without such research it is often difficult to verify the date, provenance or subject of many portraits which do exist, and impossible to learn of those which have not survived.

Two portraits held by the Merchant Taylors' Company exemplify the potential of such archival research: the example is especially instructive because the Merchant Taylors have taken particularly good care of their portrait collection, because their Company archives are among the fullest of all the London livery companies, and because the Company has been especially well served by its historians through the years. And yet it is only very recently that two of the

Company's portraits, of Robert Dowe and Sir Thomas White, have been identified as the work of the prominent early seventeenth-century portraitist John de Critz. Laconic and unambiguous references to payment for these paintings to de Critz, in the fiscal year 1606–7, have been found in the Company's unpublished accounts, but this had not been noticed before.[16]

Even when research has been possible, it does not always provide full information. Inscriptions on paintings, for example, often accurately identify the sitter by name and date, and sometimes by office as well. But inscriptions cannot always be trusted. Dates and other wording were sometimes added on sometime after the completion of the painting, and not always accurately so.

Odd as it may seem, there are even paintings on which an inscribed date is too early to represent the year in which the painting will have been done. The double portrait of Degory Wartur and his wife, done for the Shrewsbury Drapers' Guild and still held in the building (now a restaurant) which long served as that Company's hall, provides a case in point. This intriguing work, first mentioned in an inventory of 1654 and noted in several local histories and inventories down to modern times, is inscribed and dated 1404 ('*Degory Watur et Uxor*. Burgess of Shrewsbury AD 1404'), which would make it very much earlier than the earliest civic panel portrait which has yet come to light. Wartur, who lived from sometime around 1382 to about 1477, was Master of the Drapers' Guild of Shrewsbury and founder of St Mary's Almshouses in that town. He certainly had a prime claim to being a civic hero of his community. But can this panel really have been done as early as 1404, when Wartur himself was barely out of his teens, as the inscription suggests? And if this is an implausible date for the work, why is it there?

One look at the painting itself gives the lie to a 1404 creation. It shows the two subjects in the severe black dress of a seventeenth-century Puritan couple (odd and intriguing in itself), and in styles appropriate to that time. The date of 1404 turns out to be when Wartur, his father, and his three brothers were admitted to the Drapers' Guild, as noted in a guild roll of that year. The 1654 inventory also notes a painting of the King, Henry IV, who granted the Company its charter in the 1440s. Judging by their style and the style of the sitters' dress, both works were very likely completed close to the date of the 1654 inventory, and displayed in the Shrewsbury Drapers' Hall from that time. Though undoubtedly a civic portrait, in that it was commissioned by the Drapers' Guild of Shrewsbury for display in the Company Hall, and certainly an interesting one from an aesthetic perspective, this is surely not a civic portrait of our period or of the year 1404.[17] In working out the provenance of this work, the inscribed date must be ignored.

Of course, even more serious difficulties of identification arise when portraits are not inscribed or dated. Some provincially produced portraits allow the sitter's dress to identify him as a mayor or alderman, but his precise identity and dates may remain unknown. One such portrait rests in Bristol, where a reliable catalogue of local portraits has been unable to determine an identity.[18]

Even when a painting is accurately inscribed and dated, the question of the painting's provenance and date of acquisition, critical factors in determining whether a portrait may have been intended as civic or personal, often remains problematical. Such was the case with John Vernon's gift of his portrait to the Merchant Taylors which has been noted above. But more emphatic examples of these dilemmas arise in the city of Canterbury. We know that Canterbury placed a portrait of the Merchant Taylor Sir Thomas White, a substantial benefactor though not an officer of that city, in its Guildhall in the year 1608. It must obviously be labelled as a civic portrait in the fullest sense. On the other side of the ledger, we also know that a portrait of the Canterbury alderman John Colfe, done around 1600 when Colfe would have been about fifty years old, came in to the city's hands only in 1772, which rules it out as a civic portrait of our period.

So far, so good; these are clear-cut cases. But what are we to make of that city's 1602 portrait of alderman Leonard Cotton (1526–1605, mayor in 1580) which was first recorded as being in the Guildhall only in 1929, though it may have come into the city's hands, and remained unrecorded, at any time before this? And what of Canterbury's painting of John Watson (1559–1633, mayor in 1615) which was done in the 1620s, but of whose acquisition or commissioning we also have no record? We know whose faces these images represent, but the provenance of the paintings remains murky, and they cannot be considered civic portraits under the strict definition of that term.[19]

Especially for those portraits which have not been photographed for the research files of the Heinz and other archives, on-site visits prove critically important. When not in local museums, civic portraits may still be held by the civic body for which they were produced, sometimes in the very court rooms, company or college halls, and mayor's parlours in which they were first displayed. While my visits to view such works have usually met with genuine interest, encouragement and unfailing courtesy (including offers of coffee after long journeys, ladders to view high-hung works, and revelations of other local portraits previously unknown to me), ease of access is not always possible. Civic bodies do not necessarily list their holdings with museums or archives so that the researcher may learn of them. Portraits are not by any means always conveniently accessible to the public, and sometimes cannot be made available even on appointment. Nor is it always even obvious to whom preliminary enquiries about viewing may be directed. Perhaps most surprisingly, some of these portraits have not been photographed even for insurance purposes, and in some cases no images of them may be had for copying or purchase.

So it is that we have a distinct and definable corpus of early English portraiture, well outside the stylistic mainstream, largely neglected by conventional art historical research or museum display, and for which the very sources themselves are often not easily discovered or viewed. Yet these obstacles should not obscure the value of the subject or impede its investigation. On the one hand, civic portraiture proves a very important aspect of institutional, civic and urban political cultures in this era. It has much to tell us, not only about the sitters who look out at us over the centuries, but especially about the identities, collective memories, goals and actual operation of the institutions which hold these images. These institutional patrons, constituting 'publics' of a certain sort and creating a demand for a particular class of material object, have yet to be investigated. It seems essential to do so now.

Equally important, this subject also reveals a great deal about portraiture in England generally in this era, considerably expanding the range of portrait types with which we are already familiar. The provincial provenance of many civic portraits raises the question of authorship and cultural expression outside the London metropolis. It invites an examination of the cultural relations between London at the centre and the provincial towns and regions at the periphery. Can we assume that almost all civic portraits done for institutions outside of London were commissioned from London-based practitioners, whether foreign or native-born? Or will we discover that, as with the performance of plays in this same era, there were parallel traditions of local portrait painters, part-time if not necessarily full-time, either based away from London or itinerant as well? Were some civic portraits done outside of London influenced by continental conventions through a process of percolation downwards from the metropolis, or were there more direct contacts with foreign-born artists? What is the nature of cultural interchange not only between places, but between formal/polite notions of style and informal/vernacular traditions which were often regional in nature?

Investigating the cultural geography of English civic portraiture also begs the question of the relationship between English and continental portraiture, between the native and neo-classical idioms, and thus the comparative study of visual culture itself. Why is it that the numerous foreign-born and trained portraitists working in England, painting in widely understood, formal traditions at least from the time of Henry VII, took so long to implant in England conventions which had long since been adopted in most of the rest of Europe?

We also need to know more about civic patronage for portraiture and the institutional bodies which extended it. What did civic patrons want their portraits to express? How much control, if any at all, did sitters wield over the final image? What role did the resulting paintings play in the social and political discourse of the time, and in those particular civic bodies to which

they pertained? Finally, how did the civic portrait contribute to the civic identity, and to the collective memory, of civic institutions?

These questions suggest an agenda which addresses some traditional art
historical issues as well as some which are less traditional. The discussion
begins (chapter 1) with a general description of civic portraiture which will flesh
out the bare definition given above, suggest the geographic and chronological
patterns by which such works appeared, and identify precursor portrait forms.
It moves on in chapter 2 to consider the civic institutions which commissioned and displayed such works (university colleges, provincial town governments, London livery companies, schools and charitable institutions) and the
chronology by which they did so. If, applying a now-familiar metaphor, we
think of portraits as texts or statements, this chapter identifies their authors: it
asks 'Who was speaking?'.

While a few of our civic portraits emanate from known, professionally
trained portrait painters working in the formal and polite, heavily neo-classical,
traditions of their time, most were done by artisan/craftsmen or 'painter-
stainers' working in essentially vernacular traditions and substantially isolated
from those formal and polite modes. Chapter 3 investigates both traditions,
considers the relations between them over the era at hand, and reflects on
the circumstances of the painter's occupation in both traditions. It answers
the question 'Who were the messengers?'. A consideration of the timing and
circumstances in which civic portraiture appeared in England, and the conditions which prompted its distinctive formulations, follows in chapter 4. As we
will see, the political and cultural implications of the Henrician Reformation,
and especially their significance for particular civic institutions, play a large
role here, as do several underlying forces of economic and social change operating at the same time. These ambient circumstances beg the central question
of the content and meaning of our civic portraits. Chapter 5 explores the visual
vocabulary employed by civic as opposed to personal portraiture, and thus it
addresses the imagery, inscriptions, and mnemonic content of the images at
hand.

The discussion to that point will have considered the production of civic
portraits: who commissioned them, when and why they did so, who painted
them and in what occupational and aesthetic circumstances, and how the
finished works spoke to the patronal agendas of civic institutions. But any
consideration of portraits as political or social artefacts must also consider the
other side of the cultural equation, the consumers as well as the producers. We
must also ask who saw these paintings, in what circumstances they did so, and
what they were meant to come away with from that experience. This becomes
the subject of chapter 6: it asks where these texts were displayed, who was
meant to read them, and for what ends. Two appendices round out the work:
one (A) presents a census of civic portraits which have provided the data base

for this study. The second (B) summarizes the known cost of portraits in the era at hand.

NOTES

1 Robert Tittler, *Architecture and Power: The Town Hall and the English Urban Community, c. 1500–1640* (Oxford, 1991); Tittler, *The Reformation and the Towns in England: Politics and Political Culture, c. 1540–1640* (Oxford, 1998).

2 W.A.D. Englefield, *The History of the Painter-Stainers' Company of London* (1923), p. 63.

3 Court Minutes, Merchant Taylors' Company, Guildhall Library microfilm, 328/7, fols, 244–6; Frederick M. Fry, ed., *A Historical Catalogue of the Pictures, Herse-Cloths and Tapestry at Merchant Taylors' Hall* (1907), pp. 67–8.

4 BL Harleian MS 2150, fols 180r and 181r. The 'pendice' or 'pentice' was one of the city's civic buildings in which the mayor and council met, and in which some of those civic portraits were displayed.

5 Erna Auerbach, *Tudor Artists: A Study of Painters in the Royal Service and of Portraiture on Illuminated Documents from the Accession of Henry VIII to the Death of Elizabeth* (1954) and especially *Nicholas Hilliard* (Boston, 1961); Eric Mercer, *English Art, 1553–1625* (Oxford, 1962); Ellis Waterhouse, *Painting in Britain, 1530 to 1790* (4th edn, 1978); Roy Strong, *Holbein and Henry VIII* (1967), *Tudor and Jacobean Portraits* (2 vols, 1969), *The English Icon: Elizabethan and Jacobean Portraiture* (1969), *The Elizabethan Image: Painting in England, 1540–1620* (1970), *The Cult of Elizabeth: Elizabethan Portraiture and Pageantry* (Berkeley and Los Angeles, 1977), *Artists of the Tudor Court: The Portrait Miniature Rediscovered, 1520–1620* (1983), and *The Tudor and Stuart Monarchy* (3 vols, Woodbridge, Suffolk, 1995–98, especially vol. II, 'Elizabethan').

6 An important exception is the landmark collection edited by Lucy Gent, *Albion's Classicism: The Visual Arts in Britain, 1550–1660* (London and New Haven, 1995).

7 Strong, *Tudor and Jacobean Portraits*, I, pp. ix–x.

8 See especially Virginia Tillyard, 'Civic Portraits Painted for, or Donated to, the Council Chamber of Norwich Guildhall before 1687 with Documentary Evidence relating to the Artistic Background of the City' (MA thesis, Courtauld Institute, 1978); Victor Morgan, 'The Norwich Guildhall Portraits: Images in Context' in Andrew Moore and Charlotte Crawley, eds, *Family & Friends: A Regional Survey of British Portraiture* (1992), pp. 21–30.

9 Benefiting enormously from their close association with the burgeoning field of building history, it may not be surprising that architectural historians in particular have come to the fore in reaching out to other disciplines and considering the social context of their subject. The tardiness with which art historians have entertained a similarly deliberate study of vernacular painting stands in contrast to this scholarship. Though the literature here is simply too large to list in any comprehensive manner, the following works exemplify the appropriate breadth of recent architectural history: Eric Mercer, *English Vernacular Houses* (1975); Malcolm Airs, *The Making of the English Country House, 1500–1640* (1975); Mark Girouard, *Life in the English Country House: A Social and Architectural History* (London and New Haven, 1978); R.W. Brunskill, *Traditional Buildings of Britain: An Introduction to Vernacular Architecture* (1981); Maurice Howard, *The Early Tudor Country House: Architecture and Politics, 1490–1550* (1987); Tittler, *Architecture and Power*; John Bold, 'Privacy and the Plan', in John Bold and Edward Chaney, eds, *English*

Architecture Public and Private: Essays for Kerry Downs (1993); Nicholas Cooper, *Houses of the Gentry, 1480–1680* (London and New Haven, 1999); and chapters by Maurice Howard and Christy Anderson in Gent, *Albion's Classicism*.

10 Especially the seminal work of Nigel Llewellyn, *Funeral Monuments in Post-Reformation England* (Cambridge, 2000).

11 Susan Foister, 'Paintings and Other Works of Art in Sixteenth Century English Inventories', *Burlington Magazine*, 123:938 (May, 1981), pp. 273–82 and, despite its canonical subject, her masterful *Holbein and England* (London and New Haven, 2004).

12 Gent, *Albion's Classicism*, especially the editor's introduction.

13 Tarnya Cooper, '*Memento Mori* Portraiture: Painting, Protestant Culture and the Patronage of Middle Elites in England and Wales' (Ph.D thesis, University of Sussex, 2001).

14 See, for example, Lucy Gent, *Picture and Poetry, 1560–1620: Relations between Literature and the Visual Arts in the English Renaissance* (Leamington Spa, 1981), chapter 2, and further discussion of terminology below in pp. 28–9 amd 71–3.

15 R.L. Poole, ed., *Catalogue of Portraits in the Possession of the University, Colleges, City and County of Oxford* (3 vols, Oxford Historical Society Publications, vols 57, 1912; 81, 1926; and 82, 1926); Poole, ed., *Catalogue of Portraits Exhibited in the Reading Room and Gallery of the Bodleian Library* (Oxford, 1920); J.W. Goodison, ed., *Catalogue of Cambridge Portraits*, I, *The University Collection* (Cambridge, 1955); Goodison, ed., *Catalogue of the Portraits in Christ's, Clare and Sidney Sussex Colleges* (Cambridge, 1985); Goodison, *Portraits and other Pictures at King's College, Cambridge* (Cambridge, 1933).

16 The full story may be found in Robert Tittler, 'Three Portraits by John de Critz for the Merchant Taylors' Company', *Burlington Magazine*, 147:1228 (July, 2005), pp. 491–3.

17 Hugh Owen and John Brickdale Blakeway, *A History of Shrewsbury*,(2 vols, 1825), II, pp. 334–7; Michael Peele, 'Medieval Deeds of the Shrewsbury Drapers Company', *Transactions of the Shropshire Archeological Society*, 52 (1947–48), pp. 238–40. I am grateful to James Lawson and Michael MacCarthy-Morrogh for help in sorting this out.

18 R. Quick, ed., *Catalogue of the Second Loan Collection of Pictures held in the Bristol Art Gallery* (Bristol, 1905), no. 227.

19 Heinz Archive, National Portrait Gallery, *vide* 'Canterbury Collection' (1964); J. Ogden, *A Descriptive List of the Pictures ... of the Corporation of the City of Canterbury* (2nd edn, 1912), *passim*.

Chapter 1

English portrait traditions

One of the central themes of Lorne Campbell's definitive survey of Renaissance portraiture is that there was very little new in the typology of European portraiture in the sixteenth century: 'almost all the types of portrait produced during the sixteenth century were already being painted during the fifteenth century, if not earlier'.[1] In this, as in many other aspects of visual culture, the English experience with portraits in general proved something of an exception to the norm.

If we take portraiture, as Campbell does, to mean easel paintings, and even if we make due allowance for physical attrition over the centuries, evidence for its production in England remains distinctly meagre prior to the Tudor era, and even more so when compared to the portrait traditions of much of the rest of Europe. And if we restrict our comparison to civic, as opposed to personal, portraiture, the contrast proves even sharper. A very few English examples of this idiom appear to have been produced prior to the mid-sixteenth century. But it is nevertheless fair to say that civic portraits as easel paintings were indeed virtually new to England in the sixteenth century.

This is not to deny that some 'portraits' of civic figures (which, as will become evident below, is not quite the same thing as 'civic portraits') certainly existed in the forms of funeral monuments and brasses,[2] heraldic drawings,[3] manuscript illuminations,[4] and stained glass windows in earlier times.[5] Yet these examples bore characteristics and aims which set them apart from the easel portraits (and one exceptional fresco series) under the lens here. They certainly served as precursors to them, but cannot be equated with them.

Even that is more than may be said for the genre of engraved prints which emerged as a viable portrait form in England only shortly after civic easel portraits themselves. It is only towards the latter decades of the sixteenth century, with the work of the Englishman William Rogers and a number of Dutch engravers especially, that engraved portraits became widespread. Even

4 'Simon Eyre, Alderman of London'; Roger Leigh, mid-fifteenth century.

then, and for long afterwards, they were much more often taken from extant easel paintings than the other way round. It was well into the seventeenth century (virtually the Civil War years and Interregnum) before they became a common means of disseminating images of civic leaders to a wider public.[6]

But even if we exclude prints from our discussion, relationships among the various other media, especially as they sometimes served as models or inspirations for civic portraits of the sixteenth century and after, often prove to be both complex and difficult to document. Though the number of his images makes this an unusual case, the several early sixteenth-century 'portraits' of the Humanist founder of St Paul's School, John Colet, illustrates this well.

Matthew Parker, Elizabeth's first Archbishop of Canterbury, left to Cambridge University his copy of an illuminated New Testament which had been produced for Colet by Peter Meghan of Bois-le-Duc around 1506–9, and which shows Colet kneeling before the figure of St Matthew. The Italian sculptor Pietro Torrigiano, who worked in England during the 1510s and early 1520s, did a bust of Colet around 1520 as part of his funeral monument at St Paul's School. Sometime before 1535 Holbein based his drawing of Colet on this bust, and when the Mercers' Company had the St Paul's School statutes rebound in 1585, they used the same drawing for the front cover. Finally, three later panel portraits are recorded of Colet, respectively at Magdalen College Oxford, St Paul's School, and in the Mercer's Hall, London, all based to some extent on Holbein's drawing of Torrigiano's bust. Even without considering the engraved portraits done of Colet later on, this is a full visual record. The three panel paintings meet all the criteria for civic portraits in our sense of the term if not necessarily before 1640. Though few civic figures of their time will have been as well-connected or touched as many bases as Colet, this story serves to illustrate many of the possibilities for producing images which meet (or do not meet) the definitions of the civic portraits at issue here.[7]

Meghan's illuminated image of Colet represents another important precursor form of English portraiture, and one which sometimes alluded to civic figures. The manuscript illumination developed chiefly as a form of pre-Reformation religious art, but in its portrayal of donors and benefactors it also served as an early form of portraiture. With works like the Wilton Diptych, the form of the illumination made the leap from vellum or paper to board, and its content made a similar leap from a religious to secular subject.[8] Other examples of the parchment or paper manuscript serving as a precursor to civic easel portraiture may be found in the illuminated first letters of the annual plea rolls of the Court of King's Bench, and in works depicting civic figures rather than royalty or ecclesiastical benefactors. Roger Leigh's curious 'portraits' on paper of fifteenth-century London aldermen depicted in their official and heraldic context represent perhaps the best known of these[9] (fig. 4), though the generic mayor shown being sworn to office in Robert Ricart's late fifteenth-century

5 'Swearing in the Mayor' from Robert Ricart, 'The Maire of Bristowe ...'; anon., c. 1484.

instruction book for Bristol mayors, 'The Maire of Bristowe is Kalendar' (fig. 5), may be considered in the same category.[10]

Paintings of saints, biblical figures and donors, typically on altar screens and reredos, also served as important precursors. Along with funeral monuments and glass paintings, all of them religious in intent and displayed in religious settings, they are closest in form to civic portraits of the post-Reformation era.

Naturally enough, considering their principally devotional purpose prior to the Reformation, funeral monuments were usually erected in such religious spaces as chapels, churches and churchyards, and cathedrals. As their principal purpose gradually shifted after the Reformation to the commemoration of social status and personal achievement without what might be called the 'purgatorial imperative' to pray for the souls of the departed, those which commemorated civic, as opposed to saintly or biblical, figures came to resemble personal portraits. The tendency of pre-Reformation monuments to be commissioned by such quasi-civic groups as the religious fraternity gave way steadily thereafter to commissioning by the personal patronage of the sitter and his or her family circle rather than by the institution.[11] And though these images often came with heavily moralistic overtones, they tended to express moral codes linked with chivalric or other personal and status-based notions rather than those linked with civic society in its institutional guise. Finally, of course, they were erected in churches, churchyards and chapels rather than in the spaces of civic institutions.

Portraits painted on glass must also be considered a precursor form. The medium itself may be traced back several centuries before the Reformation, with the depiction of generic or specific civic figures, either as patrons and donors of particular devotional images or as civic worthies in their own right. As with funeral monuments, glass portraits emerged chiefly in ecclesiastical settings like churches and the chapels of guilds and fraternities. When, exceptionally, glass paintings appeared in domestic settings the intent was much more likely to be secular than spiritual. Yet especially in pre-Reformation days glass portraits of civic figures in churches did often express civic aims as much as religious, reminding us of how much the two settings could overlap.

Norwich's Cult of the Holy Name and Coventry's Trinity Guild are typical of the myriad religious institutions which encouraged such devotional or commemorative imagery. In the halls of these institutions portraits of local benefactors or civic figures could readily be mixed in with those of saints or biblical scenes. Coventry's St Mary's Hall once held some twenty such glass portraits, including four fifteenth-century mayors.[12] Norwich's Guildhall and some of its larger churches held a number of glass portraits of the city's ruling elite. St Peter Mancroft, for example, displayed portraits of Thomas Elys and his wife Margaret, three times mayor and mayoress, members of the prominent Garnish family, and arms of civic officials from the Elys,

Garnish and Ramsay families.[13] An especially well-preserved and vivid series of merchants' portraits on glass, depicting the Seven Acts of Corporal Mercy, may be found in the windows of All Saints North Street in York, though these appear to be generic rather than specific merchants.[14] The image of William Smarte in the parish church of St Mary-le-Tower, Ipswich (fig. 6) provides another excellent example.

Oddly enough, the various iconoclastic injunctions of the Reformation years did not specifically call for the destruction of stained and painted glass as such, and Queen Elizabeth even tried to protect it.[15] But such injunctions did of course call for the destruction of 'idolatrous' images, a great many of which happened to be on glass. A considerable amount of stained and painted glass therefore fell victim to the Reformation and its aftermath, iconoclasts often failing to distinguish between religious and secular images. The Puritan excesses of the seventeenth century brought yet a second round of destruction, so that the vast majority of medieval glass paintings had been destroyed by the time of the Stuart Restoration of 1660.[16] Glass painting as a craft certainly survived the Reformation in England, but its presence was both diminished and redirected chiefly towards the domestic settings of country houses.

The almost simultaneous emergence of civic portraits on board or before 1600, on canvas may to some degree be considered as a surrogate form for such display, albeit in buildings which were, or had become, strictly secular and civic spaces. There were obvious practical advantages to either board or canvas. Both were arguably less fragile than glass to begin with and less expensive to produce and display. Canvas especially proved cheaper, more easily transported, and more readily suited to larger works. The secular nature of such portraits could be made more emphatic in civic rather than ecclesiastical buildings, where they could be moved around as needed, and visually contextualized with other civic rather than spiritual imagery.

Sometimes this transition of civic imagery from one medium and place to another may be traced quite directly. Early sixteenth-century painted glass images in Norwich included those given by the wealthy Norwich merchants and civic leaders Robert Jannys and Augustine Steward. Though these glass pieces bore moral messages and neither of them actually portrayed their donors, the very fact of their donation nonetheless commemorated the fame of those local worthies. Several decades later actual easel portraits of Jannys and Steward were painted on much more durable oak panel for display in the Norwich Guildhall, where they may be seen today. These two men, both Norwich mayors in their time (Jannys in 1517 and 1524, Steward in 1534, 1546 and 1556), paid for the glass images themselves as statements of devotion and piety, but the panel images seem to have been commissioned by the city after their death. The two successive commissions mark the transition from personal acts of pious benefaction and invocations for prayer in the first

6 'William Smarte' (detail), St Mary-le-Tower Parish Church, Ipswich; anon.,
late sixteenth century.

instance to civic and secular commemoration in the latter: the memories of
Jannys and Steward had been appropriated for the civic domain.[17]

Of course, neither funeral monuments nor glass paintings were part of
that greater tradition of easel portraiture, both personal and civic, which had
already developed so fully and for so long in many other parts of Europe. In
the Italian city-states, whose rulers lusted after legitimacy in any and all forms,
it was not unusual by the end of the fifteenth century for self-made dukes,
popes and cardinals, quondam *condottieri* and other *signori*, to collect literally
hundreds of portraits, most of them of family members past and present and
other contemporary rulers, for display as part of their claims to power and
patrimony. Similar displays, albeit rarely so large, existed throughout the larger
courts and states of the Holy Roman Empire, with its myriad independent and
semi-independent cities and their well-established traditions of autonomy,
and even in some of the French cities. Nor did the English in general as readily
pick up the styles and techniques associated with formal Renaissance portraiture: the use of oil and canvas rather than tempera on gesso-prepared wooden
panels, the more sophisticated use of shading and perspective, the allusion
to classical forms, the sense of harmony and proportion, and the attention
to character-revealing detail which distinguished that newer idiom from the
mainstream of late medieval gothic representation or from the strictly vernacular works which predominated in local areas.[18]

This deliberate pace by which both easel portraiture and these more sophisti-

The face of the city

cated, formal characteristics of technique and style evolved in England remains challenging to explain. English communities of all sorts had long enjoyed a well developed celebratory and ceremonial culture and a rich tradition of pre-Reformation religious painting. Foreign craftsmen working through religious imagery in several media had become reasonably common in England from well before the Reformation.[19] Then, too, at least some English men and women, including Henry Tudor himself in his years of exile, certainly spent enough time on the continent to know about its traditions of portraiture. Some had had their portraits painted on panel while on such visits well before Bosworth Field. The fine Northern Renaissance portrait of the English gentleman Edward Grimston, done in Flanders by Petrus Christus as far back as 1446,[20] is but one of the portraits of Englishmen done abroad as early as the mid-fifteenth century.

Part of the explanation for this chronology no doubt lies with the attitudes of the native English towards foreign craftsmen. Certainly the evidence of myriad foreign (mostly Dutch and Flemish) glaziers and other craftsmen working in England right up to the Henrician Reformation, added to the circles of patronage which Holbein and others like him came quickly to command thereafter, puts the lie to any suggestion that English patrons necessarily resisted foreign craftsmen who could bring such skills with them to England.[21] 'The well-to-do, both lay and clerical', as Richard Marks reminds us, 'had no qualms about acquiring or commissioning works of art from abroad or from foreign artists.'[22] But English patrons had quite different interests than the English craftsmen who had to vie with foreigners for their commissions.

On the whole, and especially in the sixteenth century, foreign glaziers, painters and others were intensely resented by native-English competitors. London liveries both large and small as well as their counterparts in provincial guilds fought a continuing battle with the crown and parliament over the occupational rights of foreigners throughout the sixteenth century. Pressure for more restrictive legislation did not always get through parliament, but it took some considerable time before the two groups mixed at all easily with each other, apprenticed each others' children, or otherwise learned directly from each other.[23]

In addition, English court and urban cultures in the years leading up to about the 1530s remained both financially and culturally impoverished when compared with some continental counterparts. In practice, if not in theory, meaningful political authority remained widely dispersed through numerous rural and regional centres of late feudal authority rather than centralized at Westminster as it would become especially in the southern parts of their dominions under the Tudors.[24] The aristocracy over much of the nation could still count on their authority, based heavily on custom, lineage, tenantry and 'good lordship', as the effective law in their regions of influence. As a whole

26

they travelled but little abroad save for military expeditions up to the close of the Hundred Years War, remaining relatively innocent of the broader currents of continental culture, visual or otherwise. In the rough and tumble English political world through the 1530s at least, the landed classes remained much more concerned with power than with *politesse*.

Then, too, the sort of urban life most likely to produce cultural patronage also remained far less developed in most of the ways that made for such famously rich cultural patronage abroad. London, by far the largest urban area of the realm at around 55,000 inhabitants at the opening of the sixteenth century, was not yet what it would become even half a century later either in size or sophistication. Its substantial economic importance in Europe belies the relative paucity of its cultural life compared to centres like Bruges, Ghent, Antwerp, Paris, and a host of German and Italian cities. By continental standards all other English cities remained small, politically weak, few in number, and lacking that prominence in the nation's culture enjoyed by the many more thoroughly urbanized centres of Western and central Europe.[25]

Taken together, these typically English circumstances help to explain why traditions of continental portraiture, whether urban, royal or aristocratic, failed to leap across the Channel and take root in England any sooner than they did. Only by the 1530s and 1540s, with the monarchy more firmly established on the throne and the aristocracy, including numerous new creations, more subservient to it, were the crown and court circle able to take the lead in making portraiture as fashionable in England as it had long been abroad. Patronage opportunities then rapidly broadened, geographically beyond the boundaries of London and Westminster, and socially well beyond the court circle. Those opportunities attracted a number of foreign artists, of whom Hans Holbein the Younger, resident in England from 1526–28 and again from 1532 to his death in 1543, was surely the most prolific and influential. By the time of Holbein's death paintings of particular people further down in the social scale could be commissioned much as they would be in modern times, while paintings of representational types or of the famous figures of the day could also be purchased ready-made from painters' shops or stalls.[26]

One of the most revealing testimonies to this trend lies in the diary of that remarkable patron of portraiture, Thomas Whythorne. In what is conventionally considered the first-known autobiography of an Englishman, Whythorne described how, as a 20- or 21-year-old Oxford drop-out working as a music tutor in London, and thus well below the ranks of those whom Holbein might have painted, he visited a portrait painter's shop and studio around the year 1549. Whythorne saw in that shop numerous portraits in various stages of completion along with some finished portraits and possibly other paintings as well. He fancied one of a woman playing a lute and bought it. Then he commissioned a portrait of himself playing at the virginals.[27] Lacking any further description of the painter or his subjects, we may surmise that most of the other paintings in the shop probably depicted kings, queens, or other members of the elite. But neither the anonymous lutenist nor Whythorne himself (whose recognition even as a minor composer lay well ahead of him in 1549) measured up to that status by a long chalk.

Whythorne must have liked his portrait, or at least liked the idea of having one done of himself, for a year later, after weathering a serious illness, he commissioned a second one. He wanted on that occasion to have a picture to document how his illness had altered his appearance. In so doing, he noted in his autobiography that a looking-glass could show only how one looks at the moment, and not how one had looked before. He continued, using the contemporary term 'counterfeit' for 'portrait', by explaining that:

> diverse do kawz their kownterfetts to bee mad to see how tym doth alter them from tyme to tyme, so thereby they may konsider with them selvz how they owht to alter their Kondisions.[28]

By the end of his life Whythorne had commissioned no fewer than five portraits of himself, as well as one of a widow with whom he became enamoured as a young man, and perhaps still others as well. He wanted a record of his appearance as it changed through the years, and he had an additional aim:

> the which iz for to leav with their frendz, especially with their children, if thei hav any that be yoo[ng] who, when thei do kum to yeerz of diskresion, thoh their fatherz be dead yet may thei see what maner of favor thee had.[29]

When it comes to appearance, we may be fairly certain that portraits of men like Whythorne and others of the middling sort were sharply divided, in style and quality of workmanship, from the standard set by Holbein.[30] The least expensive and least accomplished portraits, undoubtedly still the clear majority of the whole, would have been done by native-born craftsmen, painters-of-all-work, daubing away in the vernacular and even the naive idiom.

These men and occasionally women would have been known as 'painters' or 'painter-stainers' in their time, as opposed to 'limners' (painters on board or canvas but known especially for painting miniatures) or 'picture-makers', the latter designation most nearly referring to our modern usage of an 'artist' who may have painted portraits. The Painter-Stainers Company of London divided its ranks further into Face Painters, History Painters, Heraldic Painters and House Painters, though these terms were not necessarily widely used by others.[31] Painter-stainers from London or elsewhere painted portraits from time to time. They must account for many of the vernacular civic portraits of interest to us here. But they lacked formal training in the elements of contemporary polite style or even in the handling of materials; they exemplified no particular stylistic traditions; unless they were members of 'painter-stainers' guilds, of which the Painter-Stainers' Company of London, formed in 1502, was the most prominent and powerful, they shared no self-conscious professional identity.

At the opposite end of the scale we have the smaller proportion of contemporary portraits which were being carried out by specialists in the portrait genre, still almost always foreign-born, formally trained in and well aware of contemporary conventions of continental portraiture. The majority of them would have migrated to London and been London-based. Yet some were itinerant, and a few also emerged in the ranks of those several colonies of Dutch and Flemish refugees who were permitted to settle in provincial towns and cities as they fled persecution in the 1560s and 1570s especially.[32]

At first glance it seems odd that this burgeoning demand for portraiture, especially at the upper end of the social pyramid, could not have been met by skilled English craftsmen themselves. Manuscript illuminators and heraldic painters, sometimes one in the same person and English as well as foreign-born, seem common enough in fifteenth-century England, though the quality of work produced by the native born had begun a steep decline in its latter decades.[33] The same continuity in occupation, if not always in quality, applied to painters on glass. Glass painting and staining remained entirely viable right into the 1530s,[34] and even in the years of the Marian revival of official Catholicism some such craftspeople could still be found to undo some of the destruction of the previous two decades. The same may be said for those usually anonymous craftsmen who had long painted portraits of a sort on reredos and screen panels in ecclesiastical buildings. Several such skills may be seen in the diverse work of artisans like the John Barbor and his wife who received sundry commissions from the borough of Leicester at that time.[35]

The development of easel portraiture in England affirms that there were two visual traditions at work. Though they overlapped to some extent, they nevertheless remained perceptibly distinct through the sixteenth and (though with diminishing distance between them as assimilation gradually took hold) on into the seventeenth century. Yet only one of them has become familiar to us. This, of course, is that formal or 'polite' and essentially courtly tradition blooming into what may still be called the Renaissance mode – three-dimensional, 'naturalistic', neo-classical and much more sensitively wrought – of Hans Holbein and a few others which came to be seen as the mainstream of polite painting in England by the 1530s and 1540s.

The development of formal styles, connecting the late Gothic manuscript illuminations, religious panels and heraldic images on the one hand with conventions of polite, neo-classical portraiture on the other, constitutes a narrative which belongs to the canon of art historical writing. We see the fruits of these efforts displayed in major portrait galleries, described in mainstream textbooks, and studied in traditional university courses.

True, some of the leading artists (for whom the word 'artists' is indeed an accurate term) working in England in the late sixteenth century occasionally strayed outside the bounds of contemporary polite convention. Portraits of Elizabeth, such as Marcus Gheeraerts the Younger's Ditchley portrait of c. 1592,[36] join with portraits like the Armada series in taking some strikingly idiosyncratic twists and turns in the last years of the century. Gheeraerts was of course a well-trained professional, even something of a celebrity artist of his time,[37] and even the anonymous hands at work on these other portraits demonstrate some skill in the handling of paint, so that we cannot classify them as entirely 'naive'. But they certainly are well off the mainstream of contemporary naturalistic portraiture as practised over most of Europe at that time.

Yet on the whole the more formal works certainly did mirror contemporary trends in continental portraiture and thus did bring those trends to the English scene. Contextually considered, the production of these formal and 'polite' paintings chiefly emanated from the patronage of kings and queens, the court circle, and the 'better sorts of people' drawn very largely from the landed classes. Save for the crown's own agenda of political legitimation and dynastic continuity, it feasted especially on the genteel sitter's intense need for social and political display. The nobility in the rougher and more chaotic conditions of the fifteenth century had satisfied that need by maintaining huge and peripatetic households (geared to providing hospitality as well as housekeeping), armed bands of liveried retainers, and fortified homes or castles to suit. But the more stable and secure conditions of the Tudor age saw such display take more sophisticated and sometimes less costly forms. Household size sharply diminished; indentured retaining became far less tolerated and less frequent; and the country house, with its long galleries for displaying the family portraits and elegant furnishings, replaced the fortified castle as the principal venue for the art of self-fashioning.[38]

This context for the burgeoning of polite and courtly portraiture has nowhere been more aptly stated than in the words of the late Lawrence Stone:

> Noblemen and gentlemen wanted above all formal family portraits, which take their place along with genealogical trees and sumptuous tombs as symptoms of the frenzied status-seeking and ancestor worship of the age. What patrons demanded was evidence of the sitter's position and wealth by opulence of dress, ornament, and background.[39]

Some of the predominantly foreign craftsmen working in the polite and formal manner became itinerant from time to time, thus offering their services more conveniently to provincial patrons who remained isolated from the London scene. But that group as a whole quickly established a strong and enduring beachhead in western parts of London. Parishes like St Leonard Shoreditch, St Giles Cripplegate, St Andrew Holborn, and St Anne's came by the 1570s to host an artisanal community of Dutch, Flemish, and sometimes French or German families devoted to practising their crafts and passing them on to later generations through a complex web of intermarriage and apprenticeship.[40] Two generations later, as the aptly named William Painter noted in the prologue of *Chaucer Newly Painted* (1623), they were still there:

> You curious Painters
> and you limners all,
> from Temple Barre
> along to Charing Cross,
> that your gay pictures
> hang out on the wall[41]

This ethnic and stylistic divide between two types of practitioners was not absolute. There are exceptions to those characteristics just as there were contacts between the two groups; the characteristics associated with each group may be seen as part of a continuum rather than as two poles irrevocably apart. Yet this divide did apply generally throughout the sixteenth and on into the seventeenth century. The reluctance of the foreign artist community to take on native English apprentices, the resentment of native English painters or painter-stainers towards immigrant competitors, and the failure of English men and women to educate their own children in painting and drawing (a prejudice upon which Sir Thomas Elyot ruefully remarked in 1531),[42] all served to sustain it for some time to come.

In addition, and save for those patrons who could come more or less regularly to London, this persistent divide perpetuated the influence of vernacular work outside the metropolis. In the absence of closer interaction between native-born and foreign-born communities in most provincial centres, it appears (as we will see at greater length in chapter 3) that most regional centres of vernacular portraiture therefore continued to operate substantially on their own right into the seventeenth century rather than taking all their cues from London. They appear to have done so especially in towns and cities with strong ecclesiastical traditions, places like Gloucester, Exeter, Chester and Bury St Edmunds, where craftsmen could draw on deeply rooted and sometimes family-based traditions of visual craftsmanship. And, though convincing evidence has been presented for the active presence of Dutch and Flemish refugee painters in Norwich, which boasted by 1600 the largest Netherlandish refugee community in England outside of London, it has been more difficult to show that the two approaches to painting joined forces even there within the era at hand.[43]

These usually anonymous craftsmen drew their patronage from a broader and socially more diverse clientele. They attracted the middling sorts of people, including townspeople and professionals, as well as some members of the gentry and (even fewer) aristocracy. But most important of all for our purposes, they came especially in the latter years of the sixteenth century to attract the patronage of civic institutions: of provincial towns and cities, university colleges and schools, hospitals and other charitable institutions, and the livery companies of London.

Notwithstanding a few of the very first civic paintings, done for the universities by known, court-centred painters, it is substantially within this alternative patronal context that the civic portrait first blossomed as a visual type of its own at that time. Not needing to engage in the social competition rampant among the landed classes of the day, finding it difficult to send to London for commissions, and often financially unable to seek out the best contemporary painters, the governing elites of provincial towns and cities, endowed grammar schools and university colleges usually turned instead to the ranks of 'mere' craftsmen, often locally based.

In consequence, most of the civic portraits which can be dated prior to the seventeenth century, and especially those commissioned by bodies outside London, are more or less vernacular in appearance, and more likely to have been carried out either by local painters-of-all-work or by second-rate, itinerant and foreign-born painters outside the ranks of the dominant, London and family-based painter dynasties. The style and quality of civic portraits in general, especially those commissioned by the London livery companies, would catch up with the formal, polite styles of the de Critzes and Mytenses especially in the opening years of the seventeenth century. Yet for the time being we must recognize the vernacular, local and artisanal provenance of most of them if we are to understand what came later.

The distinctions drawn thus far between personal portraiture on the one hand and civic portraiture on the other have concentrated largely on questions of authorship, style, expertise, and both social and geographic distribution. Yet tempting as it may be to do so, we cannot attribute the chronology of their appearance merely to any 'natural' or inevitable evolution of certain styles or formats from one group of painters to another. Nor can we readily conclude that English civic portraiture evolved for the same reasons or at the same time as its personal and courtly counterpart. Such assumptions would not satisfactorily account for the time lag between English and many continental traditions of portraiture in general, or between personal and civic portraiture within England. But if we treat portraiture as artefact – as both a material object crafted for particular purposes and a text designed to convey certain statements to particular audiences – we may be able to render a more persuasive account of these chronologies. This perspective allows us to consider the civic portrait as part of the social and political discourse of its time. That discourse, in turn, will have been shaped by the institutional experience of English civic institutions at that same time.

NOTES

1 Lorne Campbell, *Renaissance Portraits: European Portrait-Painting in the 14th, 15th and 16th Centuries* (London and New Haven, 1990), p. 41.

2 In general, see Brian Kemp, *English Church Monuments* (1930); K.A. Esdaile, *English Church Monuments, 1510–1640* (1946); and especially Nigel Llewellyn, *Funeral Monuments in Post-Reformation England* (Cambridge, 2000).

3 See especially Erna Auerbach, *Tudor Artists: A Study of Painters in the Royal Service and of Portraiture on Illuminated Documents from the Accession of Henry VIII to the Death of Elizabeth* (1954), pp. 6–9, 56–8, 78–9, 94–5, and 111–15.

4 See, for example, the portraits of London aldermen of the mid-fifteenth century painted in watercolour on paper by Roger Leigh and held in London's Guildhall Library, as in fig. 4 (Guildhall Library reference numbers 32132–52, and 32170–3); similar works on paper of some fifteenth-century Coventry civic figures held in the Aylesford Collection, Birmingham Public Library; Mary Dormer Harris, ed., *The Register of the Guild of the Holy Trinity, St Mary, St John the Baptist and St Katherine of Coventry* (Dugdale Society 13, 1935), as illustrations facing pp. 4, 30, 42, 46, 62, 68, 74, 91, 104 and 108. See also portraits of monarchs in town charters, such as those in Ipswich and Shrewsbury of Richard II, or college charters, or in the opening pages of the annual plea rolls, or in livery company archives such as the portrait of Elizabeth Woodville in the records of the Skinners' Guild and Company of London (as cited in J.L. Laynesmith, *The Last Medieval Queens: English Queenship, 1445–1503* (Oxford, 2004), pp. 52 and 145). See also Auerbach, *Tudor Artists*, pp. 17–46; Richard Marks and Paul Williamson, eds, *Gothic Art for England 1400–1547* (2003), especially chapters VI and VII and catalogue sections 2, 8 and 9; and Kathleen L. Scott, *Later Gothic Manuscripts, 1390–1490* (2 vols, 1996), *passim*.

5 Christopher Woodforde, *English Stained and Painted Glass* (Oxford, 1954) and *The Norwich School of Glass Painting in the Fifteenth Century* (Oxford, 1950); Richard Marks, *Stained Glass in England During the Middle Ages* (London, Buffalo and Toronto, 1993), especially chapters 9 and 11; David King, 'Medieval Glass Painting', in Carole Rawcliffe and Richard Wilson, eds, *Medieval Norwich* (2 vols, London and New York, 2004), I, pp. 121–36; Sarah Brown and David O'Connor, *Glass Painters* (Toronto and Buffalo, 1991), and Bernard Rackham, 'The Glass Paintings of Coventry and its Neighbourhood', *Walpole Society*, 19 (1930–31), pp. 89–110.

6 Arthur M. Hind, *Engraving in England in the Sixteenth and Seventeenth Centuries*, I (Cambridge, 1952), chapter 1; Leonie Rostenberg, *English Publishers in the Graphic Arts, 1599–1700: A Study of the Printsellers, Publishers and Engravers* (New York, 1963), pp. 1–10; Anthony Wells-Cole, *Art and Decoration in Elizabethan and Jacobean England: The Influence of Continental Prints, 1558–1625* (London and New Haven, 1997), Part I, and Antony Griffiths, *The Print in Stuart Britain, 1603–1689* (1998) Introduction and chapter 1.

7 Cambridge University Library, MS Dd.VII.3; Heinz Archive, National Portrait Gallery, *vide* Colet, John; F. Grossmann, 'Holbein, Torrigiano and Portraits of Dean Colet', *Journal of the Warburg and Courtauld Institutes*, 13 (1950), pp. 202–36; *ODNB*, *vide* Colet, John; (2004); Ian Doolittle, *The Mercers' Company, 1579–1959* (1994), plate III, between pp. 40 and 41. It is considered probable but not certain that Magdalen's portrait, said by Rachel Poole to be a 'modern painting' based on a drawing by Holbein, is actually a portrait of Colet. R.L. Poole, ed., *Catalogue of Portraits in the Possession of the University, Colleges, City and County of Oxford* (3 vols, Oxford Historical Society Publications, vols 57, 1912; 81, 1926; and 82, 1926), II, p. 212.

8 William A. Shaw, 'The Early English School of Portraiture', *Burlington Magazine*, 65 (Oct., 1934), pp. 175 and 181.

9 Guildhall Library MSS 32132–52, and 32170–3. Although the specific alderman pictured in each drawing is named, the drawings are themselves not only generic in form, but almost all of them are exactly alike in all details save for the colouring of their clothes.

10 Robert Ricart, *The Maire of Bristowe Is Kalendar* [c. 1484], ed., Lucy Toulmin Smith (Camden Society, NS, 5, 1872), and Bristol Record Office MS 04720(1), fol. 152.

11 Llewellyn, *Funeral Monuments*, pp. 272–82.

12 Rackham, 'The Glass Paintings of Coventry and its Neighbourhood', pp. 94–6. These included as well, on the north wall, a series of nine English kings dating from the mid-fifteenth century; Marks, *Stained Glass*, p. 89.

13 King, 'Glass Painting', pp. 121–36; Woodforde, *The Norwich School of Glass Painting*, pp. 38–41.

14 I am grateful to Professor Alexandra F. Johnston for this observation.

15 Margaret Aston, 'Puritanism and Iconoclasm', in Christopher Durstan and Jacqueline Eales, eds, *The Culture of English Puritanism, 1500–1700* (Basingstoke, 1996), p. 94.

16 Robert Whiting, '"Abominable Idols": Images and Image-breaking under Henry VIII', *Journal of Ecclesiastical History*, 33:1 (Jan., 1982), pp. 30–47; Aston, 'Puritanism and Iconoclasm', pp. 98–9.

17 Woodforde, *The Norwich School of Glass Painting*, p. 196; King, 'Glass Painting', pp. 134–5; Andrew Moore and Charlotte Crawley, eds, *Family & Friends: A Regional Survey of British Portraiture* (1992), pp. 196–7.

18 One now uses the term 'Renaissance' with care and trepidation. It has been taken here and elsewhere to mean those characteristics of essentially three-dimensional, naturalistic and neo-classical imagery prescribed by formal rules of representation typical of the era, and not to make now contentious, finer distinctions between one species of this canonical beast and another.

19 See, for example, John Mitchell, 'Painting in East Anglia around 1500: The Continental Connection', in John Mitchell and Matthew Moran, eds, *England and the Continent in the Middle Ages: Studies in Memory of Andrew Martindale* (Proceedings of the 1996 Harlaxton Symposium, Stamford, 2000), pp. 365–80; and Brigett Corley, 'Historical Links and Artistic Reflections: England and Northern Germany in the Late Middle Ages', in *ibid.*, pp. 189–202.

20 David Piper, *The English Face* (2nd edn, 1992), p. 33.

21 Marks, *Stained Glass*, chapter 10 and Marks, 'An Age of Consumption: Art for England c. 1400–1547', in Marks and Williamson, *Gothic Art for England*, pp. 15–16.

22 Marks, 'An Age of Consumption', p. 15. See also Cecil H. Clough, 'Late Fifteenth Century Monarchs Subject to Italian Renaissance Influence', in Mitchell and Moran, *England and the Continent*, pp. 298–317.

23 D.R. Ransome, 'The Struggle of the Glaziers Company with the Foreign Glaziers, 1500–1550', *Guildhall Miscellany*, 2 (1960), pp. 12–20; Ian W. Archer, *The Pursuit of Stability: Social Relations in Elizabethan London* (Cambridge, 1991), pp. 136–7; Jacob Selwood, '"English-Born Reputed Strangers": Birth and Descent in Seventeenth Century London', *Journal of British Studies*, 44 (Oct., 2005), pp. 728–53. For a somewhat subtler approach which recognizes a growing degree of assimilation after c. 1600 in at least one provin-

cial city, see Victor Morgan, 'The Dutch and Flemish Presence and the Emergence of an Anglo-Dutch Provincial Artistic Tradition in Norwich, c. 1500–1700', in Juliette Roding, et al., *Dutch and Flemish Artists in Britain, 1550–1800* (Leiden, 2002), pp. 57–72.

24 See M.E. James, 'The Concept of Order and the Northern Rising 1569, *Past and Present*, 60 (Aug. 1973), especially pp. 53–7, and James, *Family, Lineage and Civil Society: A Study of Society, Politics and Mortality in the Durham Region, 1500–1640* (Oxford, 1974); Christine Carpenter, 'Henry VII and the English Polity', in Benjamin Thompson, ed., *The Reign of Henry VII* (1993), pp. 11–31; Steven G. Ellis, 'Centre and Periphery in the Tudor State', in Robert Tittler and Norman Jones, eds, *A Companion to Tudor Britain* (Oxford, 2004), pp. 133–50.

25 See Lawrence Manley, *Literature and Culture in Early Modern London* (Cambridge, 1995), chapters 1–2; John McVeagh, *Tradeful Merchants: The Portrayal of the Capitalist in Literature* (1981); Alexander Leggett, *Citizen Comedy in the Age of Shakespeare* (Toronto, 1973); Laura Stevenson O'Connell, 'Anti-Entrepreneurial Attitudes in Elizabethan Sermons and Political Literature', *Journal of British Studies*, 15 (1976), pp. 2–20.

26 This is not to suggest that Holbein himself painted English, as opposed to foreign, subjects much below the level of the landed elite. Susan Foister, 'Paintings and Other Works of Art in Sixteenth Century English Inventories', *Burlington Magazine*, 123:938 (May, 1981), pp. 273–82, especially p. 277, and Foister, *Holbein and England* (London and New Haven, 2004), p. 99.

27 James M. Osborne, ed., *The Autobiography of Thomas Whythorne* (Oxford, 1961), p. 20. I am grateful to Professors David Dean and Norman Jones for bringing this source to my attention.

28 *Ibid.*, p. 134.

29 *Ibid.*, p. 134.

30 The one Whythorne portrait which has survived, dated 1569, is, as we might expect, a vernacular work of no great aesthetic distinction. See Osborne, *Autobiography of Whythorne*, frontispiece.

31 In the later Middle Ages 'limner' usually connoted a manuscript illuminator, but by the early or mid-sixteenth century its meaning had expanded to take in portrait painters and miniaturists. Scott, *Later Gothic Manuscripts*, II, p. 373. For fuller discussions of contemporary terminology see Mary Edmond, 'Limners and Picture-makers: New Light on the Lives of Miniaturists and Large-scale Portrait Painters working in London in the Sixteenth and Seventeenth Centuries', *Walpole Society*, 47 (1978–80), pp. 63–5, and Lucy Gent, *Picture and Poetry, 1560–1620: Relations Between Literature and the Visual Arts in the English Renaissance* (Leamington Spa, 1981), chapter 2. I am grateful to Elizabeth Goldring for this latter reference.

32 See Morgan, 'The Dutch and Flemish Presence', and Maximilian Martens and Natasja Peeters, '"A Tale of Two Cities": Antwerp Artists and Artisans in London in the Sixteenth Century', in Roding, et al., *Dutch and Flemish Artists in Britain, 1550–1800*, pp. 31–42.

33 Richard Marks and Nigel Morgan, *The Golden Age of British Manuscript Painting, 1200–1500* (New York, 1981), pp. 30–2 and Scott, *Later Gothic Manuscripts*, I, 'Introduction' and p. 25.

34 See, for example, evidence for the south-west in Robert Whiting, *The Blind Devotion of the People: Popular Religion and the English Reformation* (Cambridge, 1989), pp. 203–5.

35 Barbor was frequently employed about such work in St Martin's Leicester, between 1554

and his probable death in 1557 or 1558, and his wife received payment in his stead in those last years for regilding the rood figures of Mary and John the Baptist. Thomas North, ed., *The Accounts of the Churchwardens of St Martin's Leicester* (Leicester, 1884), pp. 67, 70, 72, 78 and 79.

36 National Portrait Gallery, London, cat. no. 2561.

37 See Karen Hearn, *Marcus Gheeraerts II: Elizabethan Artist in Focus* (2002), especially pp. 11–16.

38 See Mark Girouard, *Life in the English Country House: A Social and Architectural History* (London and New Haven, 1978), especially chapters 1–3; Maurice Howard, *The Early Tudor Country House: Architecture and Politics, 1490–1550* (1987); C.M. Woolgar, *The Great Household in Late Medieval England* (London and New Haven, 1999), especially chapter 2; and Nicholas Cooper, *Houses of the Gentry, 1480–1680* (London and New Haven, 1999), chapter 1.

39 Lawrence Stone, *The Crisis of the Aristocracy, 1558–1641* (Oxford, 1965), p. 712.

40 Edmond, 'Limners and Picture-makers', pp. 63–5.

41 William Painter, *Chaucer Newly Painted* (1623 edition, STC, 2nd edn, no. 19125.5), Prologue, unpaginated.

42 Sir Thomas Elyot, *The Book Named the Governor* (1531), ed., S.E. Lehmberg (New York, 1962), p. 52.

43 Morgan, 'The Dutch and Flemish Presence', *passim*.

Chapter 2

The evidence: patrons and venues

Almost all civic portraits were commissioned or acquired by one of four types of institution: the two universities and their colleges, provincial towns and cities, London livery companies, and endowed charitable institutions including schools, almshouses and hospitals. The general aims and visual programmes of civic portraiture, as well as the particular contexts in which they emerged, apply more or less to all four types. Yet each institutional type developed its own distinctive emphasis. This chapter seeks to describe the chronological emergence of civic portraits in all of these institutional venues in the era at hand. As an investigation of the main types of patronage for civic portraiture, it presents an overview of the evidence. It considers the question 'Who was speaking?' when such works were commissioned and designed.

THE UNIVERSITIES

Though not everyone will consider universities and their colleges as 'civic' institutions, they share almost all the characteristics of the other institutional types of their time: e.g., a considerable degree of self-government, self-perpetuating and hierarchical social and administrative structures, a physical delineation from their surroundings, a corporate memory and so forth. It is also the universities which demonstrate the smoothest transition from pre-Reformation, religiously-oriented portraits to post-Reformation, secular and civic portraits. Oxford University seems to have come a little later than Cambridge to adding founders' and benefactors' portraits to its ceremonial or mnemonic culture. Yet, unless one is merely misled by the uniquely comprehensive resource of Rachel Poole's three volume catalogue of its portraits, for which no counterpart exists at Cambridge, it is Oxford which proved more prolific than Cambridge in the long run which is to say, for the purposes of this study, up to 1640.[1] Even by the late eighteenth century Cambridge University itself, apart from its colleges, appears to have held only twenty-eight portraits, including sculptures, and few of the individual colleges held more than a handful each. Then, too, and with some obvious exceptions among less skilled painter-stainers noted below, Cambridge does not seem to have hosted for any length of time any resident portrait specialists, as did Oxford with men like Sampson Strong, or to have come to rely on particular London-based portraitists like Richard Greenbury whom it would regularly and frequently commission for its portraits.[2] Save for the unique Peterhouse series, mostly done over a surprisingly brief period, most Cambridge civic portraits of this era seem to have been painted elsewhere and donated rather than commissioned directly.[3]

Oxford and probably Cambridge each hold or held at least one of the very earliest English civic portraits on board or canvas. In that limited sense it was the universities, and not the London livery companies as one might expect, which were the first type of institution to employ such works. This early if very modest institutional beginning allows us the clearest glimpse of that transition from earlier portrait forms and styles to those which are more familiarly civic portraits of the period under study here. With university foundations having been especially rich in pre-Reformation portrait imagery, college portraits, particularly of early founders, exemplify somewhat more clearly than other types the transition from manuscript illuminations, stained glass and even carvings, to easel portraits on board or, eventually, canvas.

If we could be sure that the surviving image of Bishop John Alcock (d. 1500), founder of Jesus College, Cambridge in 1496, was the College's first portrait of Alcock, a dating worked out by its style and content would almost certainly make it the oldest surviving English civic portrait which has yet come to light (fig. 7). It certainly looks every bit as if it had jumped off the page of a late Gothic manuscript illumination of that time. Its lavish use of colours like red and gold; the caption which protrudes, ribbon-like, from Alcock's mouth; the ecclesiastical imagery of his crozier, mitre, prie-dieu and prayer book; his kneeling pose at that prie-dieu; his virtually regal bishop's cloak; and the distinctively Gothic elements of proportion, perspective and shading, all clearly pre-date the mainstream of civic portraiture as it developed in years to come. College tradition suggests that the Hebrew lettering in the upper-left corner has been painted over, or has replaced an earlier image of a crucifix which originally appeared in that space.[4] These indications lead us to wonder if this is truly a work of c. 1500, perhaps strategically repainted to make it politically correct in the post-Reformation world, or whether it is in fact a later work altogether which may have been modelled on an earlier prototype.

College archives first record a payment for a portrait of Alcock in 1598,[5] suggesting that, if this refers to the surviving work, it was a second Alcock portrait, done as a direct and visually literal copy of a Gothic prototype. The

7 'John Alcock, bishop of Ely and founder, Jesus College, Cambridge'; anon., 1598(?).

size of the work, at 38" by 27", which was rather large for a portrait of c. 1500, makes it further unlikely that this was the c. 1500 painting with some over-painting, and more likely that the extant painting is indeed that identified in the archives as a work of 1598. A crucifix may well have appeared in an earlier version, perhaps c. 1500, but by 1598 such a reference would of course have been inappropriate for display in such a public space as a college hall. A hypo-thetical original may or may not have been an easel portrait; it could well have been the illumination which is suggested by the appearance of the surviving, almost certainly later, work.

Another early Cambridge portrait, commissioned for her college by her executors in 1511–12 (but perhaps not completed until 1513), showed Lady Margaret Beaufort, founder of Christ's College. This is no longer extant, though it has been suggested that a 1598 portrait of Lady Margaret by Rowland Lockey is based upon it.[6] If Jesus's 1598 Alcock does not have a portrait precursor, this would probably have been the first Cambridge civic portrait. In any event, the archival evidence for it allows Cambridge to boast of at least one of the earliest civic portraits known to us. In addition, the distinct possibility remains that a number of other founders' portraits, such as one of the Elizabeth Woodville images held at Queens', may also be later copies of earlier, even fifteenth-century, panel portraits.[7]

The fact that Beaufort and Woodville were female should not pass without notice. These works are not only precursors of the bulk of civic portraits in general, but also precursors for female subjects as well as male. But for the fact that civic portraits of females virtually all depict benefactors rather than officials (save for those portraits of reigning queens which may be considered civic), and for obvious differences in dress and adornment, there seems no difference in how men and women would be portrayed in such portraits.

Although the same possibility of lost early portraits exists at Oxford, the first verifiable portrait there seems to be the quite different-looking painting of Richard Fox (1447–1528), bishop of Winchester and founder of Corpus Christi College (fig. 8). This is a somber, even bleak, portrait by the Fleming Jan Rav or Raf (1512–post 1544), better known as Johannes Corvus. It was done sometime between 1518 and 1532 though, if Roy Strong's conjecture about it having been based on a death mask is correct, it would have been sometime after Fox's death in 1528. Five other portraits of Fox have been held at the College, at least two of them acquired by 1604.[8]

But as far as can be determined, a number of decades passed before colleges in either university, much less the universities themselves, commissioned or acquired additional civic portraits. At Cambridge a lapse ensued between the time Christ's acquired its second portrait of Lady Margaret Beaufort, most likely in the 1530s, and the decade of the 1560s, at which time Trinity's Master Henry Beaumont gave a Hans Eworth portrait of Henry VIII to his college. Corpus may have acquired the 1562 portrait of Nicholas Bacon (though it may just as likely have been acquired later), and Peterhouse began its programme of founders' and benefactors' portraits, in the same decade.[9] Aside from these very early examples, and notwithstanding the differences between the various types of patronal institutions, the adoption of the civic portrait as easel painting in the universities seems to have run a course which would be followed shortly thereafter by the London livery companies and the provincial towns and cities.

CLARVS WJNTONIÆ PRÆSVL COGNOIE FOXVS
QVI PIVS HOC OLIM NOBILE STRVXIT OPVS
TALIS ERAT FORMA TALIS DVM VIXIT ÆMICTV
QVALEM SPECTANTI PICTA TABELLA REFERT ·

8 'Richard Fox, bishop of Winchester and founder of Corpus Christi College, Oxford';
Johannes Covus, c. 1528–32.

The number of portraits in either university whose completion and acquisition can confidently be dated seems far smaller than the number of those which cannot, making any comprehensive or definitive listing virtually impossible. But extant evidence suggests that Cambridge colleges were somewhat more likely than Oxford colleges to acquire or commission civic portraits prior to 1600, and Oxford's more likely to do so thereafter.

We may account for Cambridge's early lead in several ways. Cambridge itself enjoyed closer proximity to the Dutch and Flemish traditions which proved so influential in the early going. More Cambridge colleges were founded or substantially expanded in the latter half of the sixteenth century than at Oxford, suggesting a larger number of major founders and benefactors.[10] More of the great figures of court and state, men like William Cecil, Matthew Parker, Nicholas Bacon, Edmund Grindal and Walter Mildmay, were involved as patrons or benefactors in that growth, principally of the Elizabethan era.[11]

Thereafter, and in the years when the influence of Cambridge graduates at court reached its peak under Elizabeth, the pace picked up smartly. The University itself acquired its first civic portraits in 1580 when Edward Grand, headmaster of Westminster School, donated paintings of Robert Dudley, earl of Leicester and Lady Margaret Beaufort. John Parker, son of Elizabeth's first Archbishop of Canterbury, Matthew Parker, gave one of his illustrious father in the same year.[12] The newly founded Emmanuel College acquired three anonymous portraits of its founder, Sir Walter Mildmay (done in 1574, 1579 and 1588 if not necessarily, at first, for the College).[13] By 1590 the newly founded Sidney Sussex had acquired at least two portraits of its foundress (by Steven van de Meulen, c. 1565 and by George Gower, c. 1575), both painted prior to the College's foundation and donated to it shortly thereafter.[14] Lockey's 'Margaret Beaufort', probably copied from an earlier portrait, came in to St John's College[15] in the same year that Jesus acquired its 1598 Alcock.[16] Donated portraits of William Cecil, Lord Burghley; Elizabeth herself (anon., c. 1588–89); and Robert Cecil came in by 1603.[17]

Founders and benefactors below the great figures of state were also celebrated by portrait acquisitions in these years. Gonville and Caius acquired a portrait of its substantial benefactor Joyce Frankland (1586); and Peterhouse added to its extensive series (see below) with a painting of Andrew Perne in 1589.[18] But the pace slackened dramatically after the accession of James I, with but five firmly datable acquisitions between 1603 and 1640: 'James I' by the University in 1611–12 and 'Charles, Prince of Wales' by the University in 1612–13,[19] Robert Slade and John Blythe by Peterhouse in 1616 and 1617 respectively (both additions to the Peterhouse series);[20] and William Perkins by Sidney Sussex in 1639.[21]

In and after the reign of James, that pattern of university and college acquisitions substantially reversed. Oxford had experienced few college foundations or substantial building programmes in the latter decades of the sixteenth century, and arguably remained more distant from the court circle in London and Westminster in those years.[22] Only a dozen or so Oxford portraits aside from Richard Fox's can be dated to before 1600.[23] But the opening decades of the seventeenth century saw enormous growth, in student numbers, new foundations (Wadham, 1610, and Pembroke, 1624–26), building programmes of established colleges (Brasenose, Lincoln, Merton, St John's, Exeter, Jesus, Trinity, Oriel, Queen's, University College, and St Edmund's Hall), and the University itself (the Bodley, 1602 and the Schools).[24] The pace by which portraits were commissioned and acquired by such bodies followed suit, with nearly forty reliably datable, individual (i.e., non-series) portraits being added in those years to 1640.

Over and above those conventional paintings which appear in these totals for both universities, large and strikingly anomalous portrait programmes appeared at both Cambridge and Oxford during the period at hand. The series of founders and benefactors begun at Peterhouse, Cambridge in the mid–1560s, eventually accounted for twenty-five individual portraits. These were laid out in sequence in the two upper rows of wainscoting in the Stone Parlour at the west end of the College's Old Combination Room, the whole scheme being removed to the Master's Lodge in 1748–50.[25] Nineteen of these paintings, including that of Johannes Holbroke (fig. 9) have been attributed to the same hand in and around the year 1565; three (Archbishop John Whitgift, Henry Wilshawe and Andrew Perne) by a second hand probably around 1589, two more (Robert Slade and John Blythe) in 1616 and 1617 by a third hand, and one (Joseph Cosins) done in 1634 by a fourth hand.[26]

The subjects of this remarkable series, unique to its time, are more often founders, stretching back to Hugh de Balsham (d. 1286) and Edward I (1239–1307), than benefactors. Almost all its subjects had died by the time the first paintings appeared in the mid–1560s. Each painting has been done on board, scaled to fit its place in the wainscoting of the room. Most figures originally appeared against a teal-blue background, often painted over in later years, with an inscription in an upper corner and another inscription, in the form of a Latin distich, added soon after on a panel placed just beneath each image.

Given that the subjects of the first nineteen were long since departed by the time they were painted, there is no question of verisimilitude, or any evidence that those who created these earlier works attempted to achieve actual likenesses from such potential sources as funeral monuments or engravings. Yet the six figures which were added between 1589 and 1634 were sufficiently contemporary with the date of their portrayals for their faces to have been familiar. Crude as these vernacular works may be, they must be taken as at least approximately representative of their subjects' actual appearances.

All portraits in the series are vernacular works of their time, showing

9 'Johannes Holbroke', Peterhouse, Cambridge; anon., c. 1565.

none of the features often associated with the formal, polite styles of the day. Figures remain essentially two-dimensional, outlines are linear rather than tonal, shading remains sparse and crude, colour ranges are limited (probably a factor of cost as much as style), facial features are generally coarse and, especially in the earlier works, somewhat stereotypical; fingers are stiff and anatomical proportions in general crudely rendered. As we might expect, they seem to have been done not by portrait specialists, but by painter-stainers local to the Cambridge area. One of them, John Newman or Newton, is known to us at least by name, and received payment for work on the Slade and Blythe portraits of 1616–18.[27]

As if to symbolize the shift of portrait activity from Cambridge to Oxford with the advent of the Stuart dynasty, a somewhat analogous but much grander portrait series took shape as the 'Bodley Frieze' at Oxford half a century after Peterhouse began its series in the mid–1560s. This much larger and ambitious production came to light in 1949, when workers in the Bodleian Library began to uncover from under a thick layer of plaster what proved to be a continuous frieze in fresco of 202 portraits, 201 men plus the poetess Sappho, done in the

10 'Geoffrey Chaucer', from the Bodley Frieze, Oxford; anon., c. 1618–20.

early seventeenth century. When fully revealed, the Frieze extended without a break, along the walls and just below the ceiling of three contiguous rooms: the Picture Gallery, the Tower Room and the Upper Reading Room. Subsequent research shows that the whole had been carried out around the years 1618 to 1620 and repaired or restored several times thereafter until water damage to the roof and walls caused it to be plastered over entirely in the 1830s, there to remain concealed for over a century.[28]

Each portrait head in the Frieze, including that of Geoffrey Chaucer (fig. 10), is enclosed in a painted oval medallion and, somewhat like their Peterhouse predecessors, has been set against a blue background. In contrast to the Peterhouse heads, however, which were done on board and eventually framed as individual pieces, each of the Bodley fresco portraits has been separated from its neighbours by a variety of painted devices – hour-glasses, skulls, books, inkpots, scrolls, sundials, manuscripts and so forth – generally symbolizing themes of learning and mortality. The figures depicted in this extraordinary creation fall roughly into the four faculties served by the Bodley at its founding in 1602: Law, Medicine, Theology and the Arts. Most were historic figures: worthies from Greek and Roman (though, curiously, not biblical) antiquity; early Christian saints; medieval and Renaissance scholars; some of the leading Protestant reformers of the sixteenth century; and a mixture of scholars, jurists, scientists and literary men of the Tudor and early Stuart age. These last include a few Oxford figures like John Rainolds, President of Corpus, and

Lawrence Humphrey, who was, among his other accomplishments, tutor to Thomas Bodley, but no one portrayed was still alive in 1618 when the work is thought to have commenced.[29]

Obviously almost none of these 202 figures could have been founders, benefactors or donors to Oxford or its colleges: another point which sets these subjects apart from their distant cousins at Peterhouse. With that common motive for selection off the table, the meaning of this assembled pantheon, and of the Frieze itself, has been much debated. Their original interpreter, Bodleian Librarian J.N.L. Myres, argued that they were meant to represent major authors in the Bodley's initial collection, which was even then being catalogued by the first Bodley Librarian, Thomas James.[30] But several of the portrait subjects were not authors, while there are of course many authors in that catalogue-in-progress who were not represented in the Frieze. More likely, the chosen subjects were meant to stand as a collective statement of the value of learning, of the deep, western traditions of scholarship, and of the Bodley's prime purpose in representing and sustaining that intellectual heritage for all time. This approach picks up steam from the fact that the Frieze, like the opening of the Bodley itself, came at a critical time in both the physical expansion and intellectual blossoming of the University. We may consider it as a visual declaration of what Charles Webster has termed that 'great instauration' just then getting underway at Oxford.[31]

Though this remarkable series may not share quite all the characteristics of most contemporary civic portraits – its fresco form in particular sets it apart – we must make an exception here to the definitional rule that civic portraits were always easel paintings. They were, after all, created to honour those whose work both benefited and exemplified, in the broadest sense, the pedagogical role of the University and its Library. They were commissioned specifically for those institutions. They were obviously displayed in what must be construed as a civic building where they would be seen on a daily basis by those who frequented that academic sanctum. Like a growing number of civic portraits done posthumously, their creators do appear to have paid at least some attention to replicating what they considered to be the actual appearance of their subjects, employing books available to them which carried engraved 'virtual' images of many of the Frieze's subjects.[32]

But of course this process could not have captured the literal verisimilitude of that vast majority of subjects who had long passed on. The very concerted effort to find and employ such documentary models as recent engravings, while not recognizing that they, too, were mere modern approximations of verisimilitude, remains ironic. It suggests that the creators of the Frieze had absorbed some, but not all, of what Peter Burke has called the 'Renaissance Sense of the Past' making its way slowly but steadily into the mind's eye of scholars in England and the rest of Europe.[33]

And who were those creators? The participation of Thomas James, Bodley's first Librarian, can hardly be denied,[34] but there is also evidence that Thomas Bodley himself expressed his wish to have such a series, and that his close friends and fellow-Oxfordians Ralph Winwood and Sir Henry Savile played commanding roles in selecting the subjects to be included and seeing the project to its completion after Bodley's death. Savile in particular, already a generous Oxford benefactor, an early English admirer of Vitruvius, and apparently familiar with similar displays at the Uffizi and elsewhere in Italy, seems to have been in an excellent position to undertake the task. It is highly fitting that his own portrait would hang in the University by 1622.[35]

The Bodley Frieze represents a unique visual artefact in England. Curiously, none of those who have written about it have noted the likely influence of the Peterhouse achievement at Cambridge as a home-grown precedent for a civic portrait series, though this must surely be considered as a probable and accessible influence. It has, on the other hand, been likened to continental examples of such portrait series which may have served to inspire it, works like Paolo Giovio's mid-sixteenth-century collection of portraits at Como,[36] or the early seventeenth-century collection in the civic library of Augsburg.[37] Then, too, there may be influences outside the realm of visual artefacts. The contemporary interest in historical biography, running from the popularity of Plutarch's *Lives* (five editions of which were published in England before 1618)[38] to the efforts of writers like William Jaggard and John Stow briefly to 'portray' former mayors of London in their turn-of-the-century works,[39] and to the contemporary Protestant interest in recording benefactors,[40] must surely have created something of an intellectual context for this sort of biographical display. And, to look forward from the time of its creation rather than backwards, the Frieze may very well have served to inspire further English examples of such work in years to come: busts of Roman worthies in the Cotton Library, the 1668 frieze of thirty-three heads in Bishop Cosin's Library at Durham, Bishop Morton's collection at Auckland Castle, or the Marquis of Bath's at Longleat.[41]

PROVINCIAL TOWNS AND CITIES

It seems fair to say that civic portraits commissioned by formal institutions of local, civil government derive almost exclusively from provincial towns and cities rather than from the governing structures of the London metropolis. This is because the practical governance of the City of London was so completely dominated by the livery companies and by leading liverymen themselves, that the portraits of its mayors, leading dignitaries, and the occasional folkloric figure were commissioned by and for the liveries with which such figures were associated rather than by the City's formal, institutional structures in which liverymen served. They were then displayed in the halls of those companies rather than in the London Guildhall or other such 'City' buildings. Though Lady Godiva could be portrayed at the commission of the city of Coventry, for example, Dick Whittington would be visually recalled by the Mercers' Company of London and by the commercial engraver Richard Elstrack, rather than by the City itself.[42] Not only did London not become a formally corporate entity until the turn of the seventeenth century, it also did not begin to commission its own portraits until the year 1670, when the City deemed it important to have portraits of the justices of the Fire Court after the momentous conflagration of 1666.[43] In this, of course, London stands in sharp contrast to myriad continental cities whose greater degree of civic autonomy fostered an earlier and more substantial civic portrait tradition.

English provincial towns and cities worked somewhat differently. Guilds in many towns had substantial influence on the governing process; numerous borough governments of the post-Reformation era traced their institutional roots to pre-Reformation guilds and religious fraternities. But though the governing structures of provincial towns and cities, usually consisting of a mayor and two concentric aldermanic councils, may conventionally have been staffed by guild members, the governing authority rested with the combination of those offices and not with the guilds. Therefore the civic portraits commissioned in provincial towns and cities were commissioned by the governing bodies and not the guilds to which their officials may have belonged.

Many towns and cities, including Norwich, King's Lynn, Leicester and Exeter, continue even to the present day to display their civic portraits in the council chambers, courtrooms and mayors' parlours for which they were initially intended. In other cases they are displayed in the more modern analogues to such rooms and spaces. One of Bristol's early civic portraits hangs today in a court building to be sure, but it is the late twentieth-century Crown Court building, where the image of John Whitson hangs high over the stairwell leading from the main lobby.[44] The single largest group of civic portraits from our period, roughly nineteen so far as they can reliably be dated, remains in Norwich, where they are now divided between the old Guildhall and the Blackfriars Hall. Some civic portraits elsewhere have been moved to local museums, though these tend more often to be museums of local history or of folklore than museums of art. Eleven of the twelve civic portraits of Gloucester done before 1640 fit into this category.[45]

Once again the fragmentary nature of the evidence makes precise dating uncertain, but it appears unlikely that civic portraits in provincial towns even pre-date the Reformation. It has recently been suggested that the 1616 portrait of the fifteenth-century Bury St Edmunds benefactor Jankyn Smyth, inscribed with the date 1473, is a Jacobean copy of a work of that earlier date in which the painter simply and literally copied everything, date and all, on to the new work.[46] Though as we have seen, the temptation to count Shrewsbury's portrait of Degory Wartur as a work of 1404, the date which appears upon it, must be dismissed,[47] this suggestion regarding the Bury St Edmunds work raises the possibility of at least one civic portrait completed well before the sixteenth century. Yet though the 1616 portrait may indeed be a copy of an older work, even a work of 1473, it is by no means clear what sort of earlier work this may have been. It could, after all, have been a heraldic drawing in manuscript form, such as has survived for civic leaders in Coventry and London;[48] a stained glass or funerary portrait from a church window; a brass or stone funeral monument; or a commemorative wood carving on a rood loft or screen, all of which were quite common in earlier times. Although an earlier, 1473 panel portrait of Smyth cannot definitively be ruled out, there seems no particular reason to assume that a putative 1473 prototype for a 1616 Smyth portrait had itself been a civic portrait, on board or canvas, in the sense employed here. And given the many decades between 1473 and the first verifiable civic portrait on panel, it would take stronger evidence than has surfaced so far to cinch the point.

But if the earliest English provincial municipal portrait is probably not one of Jankyn Smyth from 1473, neither is civic portraiture a practice which, as has been suggested elsewhere, 'starts in Norwich in the late sixteenth century'.[49] It is much more likely that the earliest panel portraits of civic figures commissioned by the governing body of a town or city and intended for display in a civic place were those of the brothers Nicholas (1496–1546)[50] and Robert Thorne the Younger (1492–1532)[51] of Bristol. If the dates on these oak panel paintings accurately record the date of the painting, these were done in 1530 and 1536 respectively, with two copies made of each virtually a century later. Both the style of the works and the context for those dates provided by the men's careers make 1530 and 1536 entirely plausible dates for the completion of these portraits. It is unlikely that such early dates for a civic portrait would have been added on after an even earlier completion of the works themselves. In short, there is much less reason to anticipate here the risks of dating encountered in Shrewsbury's portrait of Wartur and his wife or Bury St Edmunds's Jankyn Smyth.

By the 1530s both Thorne brothers counted among the most successful and adventurous overseas merchants in all of England and certainly among the leading Bristolians of the day. Both served in high civic office. Both were extremely generous benefactors to their native Bristol. Among numerous benefactions of note, Robert Thorne had purchased the Hospital of St Bartholomew in Bristol in 1532 with the intention of turning it into a grammar school and even appointed the first master, but he died in that year (providing an obvious occasion for a commemorative portrait) before his intentions could be completed. Nicholas completed the establishment of the school and contributed further to its endowment.[52] With its wealthy merchant dynasties like the

11 'Lady Godiva of Coventry'; Adam van Noort (?), 1586.

Thornes, its obvious and close contacts with continental cities and customs, and well-established traditions of civic life (marked, for example, by the completion of Robert Ricart's very early manual for civic governance),[33] Bristol is precisely that sort of community which we might expect to be precocious in such matters as civic portraiture.

Of similarly well-positioned cities, it is Norwich which seems next to have taken up the practice of civic portraiture on panel. If its 1549 portrait of Alan Percy, former priest and prominent benefactor, is not the first English civic portrait of all as has been claimed,[54] it is at least one of the first, and it does seem to have inaugurated that largest and most remarkable series of early civic portraits of any English town or city.[55] Percy was one of ten or so major benefactors to the rebuilding and extension of the Norwich Guildhall undertaken in the late 1530s, four of whom (Robert Jannys, Augustine Steward and John Marsham as well as Percy) were also eventually honoured with portraits that were hung, and still hang, in that very building.[56]

So far as one can tell from reliably datable evidence, Percy's portrait failed to create any more immediate interest in producing others portraits like it in the city of Norwich. Though a few undated and undatable paintings may have followed on its heels, some two decades passed before we find the next portraits which can be dated with some certainty. Both Bristol and Exeter commissioned portraits of Sir Thomas White in 1566,[57] either or both of which may be copies of a White portrait likely to have been done for the Merchant Taylors' Company in the same year. Exeter also commemorated three more of its benefactors, William Hurst, John Blackaller and Joan Tuckfield, very shortly thereafter.[58] Assuming again that the date of its inscription refers to the date of the painting, Norwich commissioned its second civic portrait, this of the local benefactor Sir Peter Rede, in 1568, and one of his wife probably at the same time.[59] And at roughly this time we find a portrait of the local bailiff and sheriff, Gregory Stonyng, commissioned by the city of Lichfield.[60] From the end of the 1560s there is again something of a gap in known and dated civic portraits until Bristol seems to have commissioned another civic portrait, of an unidentified mayor,[61] and Coventry commissioned its striking and important portrait of Lady Godiva (fig. 11), its semi-mythical heroine and protector, both in the 1580s.[62] Norwich had one done of the jurist Sir Edward Coke in 1587 during the time of his service as Recorder to that city.[63] In the 1590s Exeter added the figure of its benefactor Lawrence Atwell to the walls of its Guildhall,[64] and several more towns commissioned easel portraits of the remarkable benefactor Sir Thomas White.

A virtual score of White portraits done prior to 1640 have been identified in all, almost certainly making him the most widely portrayed man of his age outside the ranks of royalty and the court circle. These were mostly done for or by the provincial towns and cities (including Bristol, Canterbury, Chester, Coventry, Exeter, Gloucester, Lincoln, Norwich, Oxford (2), Reading, Salisbury, and Winchester) which were beneficiaries of his famous loan-scheme to journeymen in the clothing trades, but also for the borough of Leicester, St John's College, Oxford (at least four) of which he was the founder, and the Merchant Taylors' Company (at least one and probably two) of which he served as Master. Most cannot be dated precisely, but at least one appears to have been done in 1566 or 1567 and those in the provincial locales of Chester, Coventry and Oxford may confidently be assigned to the 1590s.[65]

At least on the evidence of datable portraits, we must wait until these last years of the sixteenth century before we find towns and cities commissioning portraits of actual civic officials, as opposed to benefactors, monarchs, contemporary statesmen or mythological figures, with any regularity. But from that point on the practice became sustained without further interruption. The important series of twelve civic portraits at Gloucester seems to have begun in the latter decades of the century, most likely in the 1590s.[66] Norwich resumed its interest with two more (its sometime sheriff and mayor, Robert Yarham, and its benefactor Joanna Smith) in 1594.[67]

Some of these works coincided with salient events in the life of their patronal towns, or in their civic halls. In addition to the early portraits in the Norwich series, done at least in part to commemorate benefactions to support the extension of its Guildhall in the 1530s, Bristol's 1566 portrait of White coincided with his arrangement with that city to administer his rotating charity scheme;[68] Exeter most likely added its Atwell portrait to coincide with and celebrate the extensive additions and renovations to its historic Guildhall in these same years.[69] The turn of the century and early seventeenth century saw the creation of civic portraits in ever-increasing numbers and places, so that by c. 1640 there are close to two dozen towns and cities, having among them some ninety portraits which may be identified with some considerable confidence.[70]

LONDON LIVERY COMPANIES

As noted above, and in contrast to the experience of provincial towns and cities, the London-based patronage for civic portraiture did not yet derive from the offices of City government itself. Instead it was the wealthy merchants and craftsmen of the livery companies, and the companies themselves, which supplied London's civic portraiture. In this activity they acted more in their capacities as liverymen than as City officials. Their patronage contributed to the honour of their companies before that of the City itself; their commissioned works adorned their company halls rather than the City Guildhall.

One would expect that many senior London liverymen, especially those engaged in foreign trade, would have had earlier, more regular, and more extensive contacts with their continental counterparts, and thus have become aware of the virtues of civic portraiture well before their country cousins. One might also expect that the interest in portraiture in general among people beyond the aristocracy and the court circle would have arisen sooner in London than elsewhere. London held the highest concentration of wealthy merchants and professionals. It was proximate to the royal court, parliament, courts of law, and other institutions of national government, and to the clientele attracted to them. It enjoyed more extensive contacts with foreign cities, and their already well-established traditions of such patronage, than any other English town or city.

Then, too, London's livery companies as well as the City itself had already enjoyed a long and rich history of civic celebration, extending back to well before the Reformation and often to origins in religious guilds and fraternities. Lavish company feasts and other celebrations were legendary even in their own time, and opposition to their excesses had already become a frequent cause for complaint by the Reformation era. Food and drink were served to famous excess, one livery trying each year to outdo others as part of its honour and reputation, and the convivial event itself serving, at least in theory, as an

12 'Henry VIII granting the Charter to the Barber-Surgeons';
Hans Holbein the Younger, 1543.

important bonding experience for livery members across lines of rank and status. Company halls were festooned with all sorts of celebratory objects – banners, birches, company plate, tapestry hangings, and eventually, of course, portraits of the company worthies, past and present.[71]

Similar expectations of livery company precocity in portrait patronage arise from the efforts of Hans Holbein the Younger and a few others like him in responding to London and court-based patronage and producing accordingly. Holbein especially made his mark among the social elites and at court as is well known, but he also found patronage beyond those circles. And indeed Holbein's commission to portray Henry VIII granting his charter to the newly amalgamated Barber-Surgeons' Company in 1541, an arrangement wrought by statute (32 Henry VIII, c. 42), brought images of both royalty and at least some prominent Londoners on to the same large (305 × 177 cm) tableau (fig. 12). Though the possibility has now been raised that this was a work done at least in part by Holbein's assistants rather than by the master himself,[72] it nevertheless results from Holbein's design and his ability to attract the commission for it. On either side of the enthroned King the scene portrays some eighteen other identifiable figures present at the occasion. They include John Chambre, Royal Physician and canon of Windsor; Thomas Vicary, Sergeant-Surgeon, receiving the charter on the Company's behalf; Sir William Butts, also a royal physician; Thomas Alsop, the King's Apothecary; surgeons Sir John Ayliffe and Richard Ferris in addition to Vicary; and royal barbers Nicholas Simpson, John Pen and Edmund Harmon.[73]

The Barber-Surgeons' painting is significant in several ways. It does seem to have planted a seed for the patronage of portraiture among the Barber-Surgeons, albeit one which would take a few decades to germinate. Later on it struck the fancy of James I and Charles I in turn, both of whom borrowed it from the Company Hall at one time or another so that it could be copied.[74] It seems to have been one of a very few mid-century civic group portraits primarily intended to document the receipt of charters of incorporation, and of the rights and privileges contained in such charters, at times of political uncertainty.

It may eventually have served as the ancestor, at least in the British tradition, of those group portraits, especially in the eighteenth and nineteenth centuries and extending to the British colonial experience as well, which documented milestone constitutional occasions. One thinks of Christ's Hospital, now in Horsham, with its huge (27' × 13') painting of Edward VI granting the foundation charter, and the even larger one of William and Mary granting a charter to the same foundation following the Glorious Revolution.[75] One might well also think ahead to John Turnbull's large group painting of the signing of the American Declaration of Independence in 1776, or Robert Harris's equally important rendering of the Fathers of Canadian Confederation at the Charlottetown Conference in 1864, which was destroyed by fire in 1916.

But in the short term neither the considerable historic significance of the Barber-Surgeons' charter picture, nor the spectacular impression it must have made at the time of its creation, should mask the fact of its isolated position in the chronology of English civic portraits. It failed to have as much of an immediate influence in that vein as one might have anticipated for such a large and dramatic work, done by such a prominent painter (or, if that be the case, by his workshop), and which was so novel to England in producing a painstakingly detailed painting of a large group rather than one or two individuals.

So far as one can tell on the basis of secure attributions, it did not lead Holbein to further patronage among the London merchant elite, nor did it establish easel portraiture as a notable tradition in the livery companies in general, a development which was still several decades away. (A possible exception to this may be the portrait of Sebastian Cabot said to have been commissioned by the Muscovy Company of which Cabot was the first governor, and of which engravings and copies survive. But the Company, which was founded in 1555, cannot have commissioned it of Holbein, who died in 1543, as has been claimed, and the destruction of the Company records in the Great Fire of 1666 makes it impossible to determine whether it purchased a Holbein portrait, commissioned independently, at some later time.[76]) Two or three other near-contemporary charter portraits aside, it had little immediate effect in introducing the group portrait as part of the visual vocabulary of civic bodies in England: another contrast with the Dutch, Flemish and other continental traditions in which Holbein had been reared.

This is by no means to deny that London merchants and other 'middling elites' did come to embrace portraiture in Holbein's time and ever since. Thomas Whythorne's experiences in commissioning portraits of himself from the 1540s on must surely represent a much wider practice among those even of his modest social standing. Personal portraits of prominent Londoners like the goldsmith and Lord Mayor Sir Thomas Exmewe,[77] the Lord Mayor Sir William Gerrard,[78] or of that pre-eminent Londoner of his age Sir Thomas Gresham,[79] do appear around or shortly after the mid-century.

But even in the face of all this activity, and in the presence of all these possible influences, the livery companies and other civic bodies themselves proved surprisingly slow to adopt the easel portrait, whether formal or vernacular in style, as part of their celebratory or mnemonic vocabulary. Though problems of dating and documentation may once again camouflage for us some of the earlier paintings, and though there are indications of earlier livery company portraits in glass windows or on paper,[80] a list of over forty well-documented livery company easel portraits produces a chronology which neither pre-dates nor much differs from civic portraiture elsewhere.[81] In fact, what is probably the earliest livery company portrait of a single individual which can be precisely dated, Thomas Lovell's portrait which appears in the Grocers' Company Hall by 1566/67,[82] comes well after both the Bristol portraits of the Thornes and Norwich's Alan Percy and much later than the university portraits of Beaufort, Fox, and possibly Alcock or Woodville. Very few indeed may be dated to the period c. 1566–96. Portraits done of prominent Londoners like Exmewe and Gresham done prior to that time prove almost always to have started out as 'personal' portraits commissioned by the sitter even if they were sometimes acquired by civic bodies later on.

Numerous passing archival references to portraits or, more frequently, other paintings or 'pictures' in general hanging on livery company walls do not become common before the opening of the seventeenth century. A great many of these references, probably the majority, fail to identify the sitter or even the medium, so that they could conceivably refer to drawings, cloth banners, works on paper or parchment, or even stained glass. In this plethora of veiled or imprecise references, most of which turn up in company accounts for payment, we can only assume that the chronology of identified portraits fairly accurately reflects the emergence of civic portraiture as easel paintings in London's liveries.

Of those livery companies which commissioned datable easel portraits of their governors and benefactors, the Haberdashers got into the act fairly early. In July 1598 the Company's 'court' or ruling body ordered that the Company's Wardens have ten paintings of the Company's 'ancient benefactors to be made and set up in the hall' though only five of these are known to have been completed.[83] The Haberdashers' example was followed in the next decade by both the Ironmongers and the Merchant Taylors.[84] The 1610s saw portraits added by the Drapers,[85] Brewers[86] and Grocers,[87] and another by the Merchant Taylors,[88] with the Grocers in particular consciously emulating the earlier example of the Haberdashers' display. The Grocers' council specifically instructed the committee struck for this purpose to report concerning 'the pictures of famous worthy magistrates & Benefactors of this company [which were] to be made and placed in most fitt and convenyent places in this hall' (as in Haberdashers Hall).[89]

The 1620s saw portraits by the Barber-Surgeons,[90] Painter-Stainers,[91] Carpenters[92] and Goldsmiths.[93] In the following decade new portraits were commissioned by the Painter-Stainers,[94] Leathersellers,[95] Merchant Taylors,[96] Salters,[97] and Ironmongers,[98] with the Salters adding one[99] and the Ironmongers seven, all but one of these last by 'Mr. Cocke' or 'Cooke' (presumably Edward Cooke, about whom little is known), in or just prior to the year 1640.[100] Most of the figures depicted in this substantial corpus are former distinguished masters of their companies. Some others, including some women, were benefactors.

In addition, companies seem frequently in these years to have added portraits of kings and queens, both living and deceased, as well as narrative biblical scenes with moralistic themes. Laurels for the grandest and most imaginative of these must go to the Carpenters' Company, which hired a local man named John Baker in 1571 and provided him with eleven yards of canvas to make a large mural of what the archives call 'The Story' on the walls of the Company Hall. Uncovered by workmen in 1845, this turns out to be a tableau of four biblical scenes highlighting the historical role of the Carpenters' craft: 'Noah building the Ark', 'King Josiah rebuilding the temple in Jerusalem', 'Christ in the Carpenters' Shop', and 'Christ teaching in the Synagogue'.[101] While not civic portraits themselves, narrative paintings of this type do appear from time to time in both personal or institutional collections of this era, and they frequently included what must be taken as portraits, real or imagined, of the figures involved.

There is one way in which the London-based civic portraits clearly outdid their country cousins. For reasons of affluence and proximity as well as bragging rights in inter-company rivalries, livery companies were more likely than provincial town governments to employ the fashionable painters of the day, most of them foreign-born and/or trained, and at an earlier time. These included the likes of Daniel Mytens (now credited with the Ironmongers' portrait of Nicholas Leate),[102] Cornelius Johnson or Janssen (of Sir Hugh Myddleton, 1628; possibly Robert Gray, 1633; Pargeter, Peacock and Babb in 1623/24 and Thomas Thorold, 1637)[103] and John de Critz, who accepted commissions from the Merchant Taylors (Robert Dowe, Sir Thomas White, Prince Charles and Nowell Southern), as we have seen, and probably also the Barber-Surgeons.[104]

These painters relied mainly on patronage from courtly or aristocratic patrons and did very well with it, but they carried out work for livery companies and sometimes for university colleges as well. These works tend to be far more skilfully rendered than what were often still the work of local painters-of-all-work toiling in the provinces or in most university colleges.

SCHOOLS AND CHARITABLE INSTITUTIONS

Given that many grammar schools and charitable institutions were founded or refounded after the Dissolutions, and that the initiatives in such activities were often taken by members of the contemporary merchant elite, it follows readily that many or even most of the portraits we find in schools and charitable institutions depict men and women of that social group. The portraits themselves are often copies of those done for the London livery companies, whose members were extremely active in the foundation of provincial schools, especially in their native towns and cities.[105] Some were personal portraits commissioned by the sitter or his family for residential display and presented later on to the institution. Aldenham Grammar School's portrait of its founder Richard Platt, Master of the Brewers' Company and sometime Lord Mayor of London (fig. 13), illustrates both practices. First painted in 1600, possibly as a copy of one done for the Brewers' Hall in that year, it was given by his son to the school in 1611.[106]

There are other possibilities as well. In 1625 the corporation of Bristol commissioned copies of the Thorne brothers' portraits done just the year before for the Council House so that they might have another set to hang in the grammar school which the brothers had founded. They hung them there, fastened with chains to the wall, in that year.[107] So far as we know, John and Joan Cooke of Gloucester (fig. 3) had only been visually commemorated in a funeral brass (probably of their own devise) when the corporation of Gloucester commissioned their portraits as founders of the local grammar school, hanging them in the school where they remained for centuries to come.[108] The civic pride of a provincial town sometimes showed itself in odd ways when it came to portraiture. Though we usually think of London-based cultural artefacts moving outwards, it was the mayor of Lincoln, in 1622, who gave to the Charterhouse in London a portrait of its founder, Sir Thomas Sutton, and not the other way round. Sutton had made his very considerable fortune in London, but remained a Lincoln man in the eyes of his native city.[109]

There are even cases in which that most common sequence, whereby school and hospital portraits were modelled on others, came to be reversed. The National Portrait Gallery's portrait of George Abbot, which remained in family and private hands until its acquisition by the Gallery, derives from an original done for Abbot's Hospital in Guildford in 1623; Emmanuel College

13 'Richard Platt, founder of Aldenham School'; anon., 1600.

Cambridge's portrait of Sir Wolstan Dixie derives from an original in Christ's Hospital.[110]

It remains possible that some very few schools and charitable institutions' founders' and benefactors' portraits were completed as civic portraits prior to Henry VIII's break from Rome and the subsequent events of the early

Reformation. But for the most part, civic portraits began to appear with some frequency in such institutions only when dissolved monastic institutions were refounded as grammar schools or alms institutions under lay patronage, or when their premises were adopted for that purpose, especially in and after the reign of Edward VI. Both Christ's Hospital, Abingdon, and its namesake originally in the City of London and now in Horsham, are two such institutions. Both depended right from the start on private benefactions for much of their income and on personal political influence for their establishment.[111] Benefactors of Christ's Hospital, Abingdon, included Lionel Bostock, Robert Orpwood, Maud Teasdale, and John Parkins, and the Marian privy councillor Sir John Mason (fig. 1); their portraits will be discussed in chapter 6. Those of the latter Christ's Hospital were the London Lord Mayors Sir Richard Dobbs, Sir John Leman, and Sir Wolstan Dixie, plus Lady Mary Ramsay, wife of an early president and benefactress in her own right. All of these figures were commemorated with portraits, mostly between 1593 and the 1620s.[112]

As these examples suggest, most portraits for this sort of institution depict founders, benefactors (of both genders) and, less often, headmasters or other officials drawn from society's middling elites and mostly from urban rather than landed backgrounds. Whether merchant leaders of provincial towns like the Thornes of Bristol and the Cookes of Gloucester, or those who came to London to make their fortunes like the Gloucester-born Richard Pate, the Lincolnshire-born Richard Platt or the Reading-born Sir Thomas White, or those born in London to begin with, it is they more than any other group who established civic portraiture in England at this time. This observation applies to civic portraiture in all four of the institutional types considered here. Especially if we take the word 'gentry' in its conventional sense as a reference to an agrarian-based grouping, we must surely think twice about the assumption that 'Portraiture during the sixteenth and early seventeenth centuries was almost entirely the prerogative of the gentry classes and upwards.'[113]

A later chapter will explore the motivations for this patronage more closely, but it seems obvious even now that these patrons acted out of a concern to establish the legitimacy and role of their institutions just as much as of themselves. And they needed to do so. Most of these institutions, and a great many of these individual portrait patrons and subjects, very consciously dwelt in a world which was still in many ways dominated by traditional, agrarian and feudal values, and which remained sceptical of what these institutions stood for: schools providing education as a means of social advancement; provincial town governments asserting their autonomous identity against the traditional perquisites of feudal lordship; trade and craft guilds serving to inculcate responsible civic leadership; and the very legitimacy and moral rectitude of civic and post-feudal society itself.

NOTES

1 R.L. Poole, ed., *Catalogue of Portraits in the Possession of the University, Colleges, City and County of Oxford* (3 vols, Oxford Historical Society Publications, vols 57, 1912; 81, 1926; and 82, 1926). The enormous utility of this work should not lull us to a neglect of its frequent errors and inaccuracies, or the appearance of further research, published and unpublished, since its appearance.

2 For Strong and Greenbury, see below, chapter 3.

3 J.W. Goodison, ed., *Catalogue of Cambridge Portraits*, I, *The University Collection* (Cambridge, 1955), pp. xvii–xxi.

4 Conveyed to me by Professor Keith Wrightson, former Fellow of Jesus College, to whom I am grateful.

5 The manuscript reference is to a payment of 26s 8d for the painting 'of our founder' in 1598; Jesus College, Cambridge, Audit Book, MS ACC 1.2, unfoliated, but arranged by year. See also the unpublished catalogue of Jesus portraits compiled by Frederick Brittain and held in the College Archives. I am very grateful to Ms Frances Willmoth, Archivist of Jesus College, for these references, and to Dr Rod Mengham, Fellow and Curator of Pictures at Jesus for further help on this portrait. The suggestion on the College's website that the painting was acquired in 1570 cannot reliably be credited.

6 Goodison, ed., *Catalogue of Cambridge Portraits*, I, p. xvii; Goodison, ed., *Catalogue of the Portraits in Christ's, Clare and Sidney Sussex Colleges* (Cambridge, 1985), pp. 35–6; Roy Strong, *Tudor and Jacobean Portraits* (2 vols, 1969), I, p. 20. Beaufort died in 1509, and was painted c. 1512 when her executors commissioned a portrait of her by 'Maynerde, payntor'. This refers to Maynarde Vewicke or Wewycke, employed by both Henry VII and Henry VIII. This earliest of several portraits commissioned in the years after her death does not survive. It was long confused with another, extant, version, held by the College since 1927. This is still sometimes referred to as 'after Maynard Vewicke, early 16th century' though a little-cited tree-ring analysis of its panel shows it to have been done between 1558 and 1580. John Fletcher, 'Tree Ring Dates for some Panel Paintings in England', *Burlington Magazine*, 116:854 (May, 1974), p. 255–6; Frederick Hepburn, 'The Portraiture of Lady Margaret Beaufort', *Antiquaries Journal*, 72 (1992), pp. 118–20, and 130; Janet Backhouse, 'Lady Margaret Beaufort', in Richard Marks and Paul Williamson, eds, *Gothic Art for England 1400–1547* (2003), pp. 246–9; Susan Foister, *Holbein and England* (London and New Haven, 2004), pp. 16 and 19–20. Backhouse overlooks Fletcher's tree-ring analysis.

7 An early, probably fifteenth-century, panel portrait of Elizabeth Woodville, thought to be by John Stratford or John Searle, King's Sergeant Painters both, hangs at Queens' College, Cambridge, but attribution and dating appear to rest more on College tradition than any more specific evidence. A.D. Browne and C.T. Stedman, *A Pictoral History of the Queens' College of Saint Margaret and Saint Bernard, commonly called Queens' College, Cambridge, 1448–1948* (Cambridge, 1951), plate 8 and accompanying text. However, another, in the Royal Collection, proves to have been done on a panel dated by tree-ring analysis to the 1470s, and may have served as a model for the Queens' picture. Fletcher, 'Tree Ring Dates for some Panel Paintings in England', p. 256.

8 One of the two was presented by John Vowell, alias Hooker, the Exeter MP and historian, in 1579 and the other was painted by Sampson Strong in 1604. Poole, ed., *Catalogue of Portraits*, II, pp. 261–5; Jane Turner, ed., *The Dictionary of Art* (34 vols, 1996), 26, p. 30;

Erna Auerbach, *Tudor Artists: A Study of Painters in the Royal Service and of Portraiture on Illuminated Documents from the Accession of Henry VII to the death of Elizabeth* (1954), p. 53; Strong, *Tudor and Jacobean Portraits*, I, pp. 124–6 and plate 249.

9 Goodison, ed., *Catalogue of Cambridge Portraits*, I, p. xviii; Hepburn, 'Portraiture of Lady Margaret Beaufort', p. 131 and fig. 7; *ODNB*, *vide* Bacon, Nicholas.

10 C.N.L. Brooke, ed., *A History of the University of Cambridge* (4 vols, 1988–2004), II, chapter 2.

11 The definitive statement of the superior influence of Cambridge, as opposed to Oxford, men in Elizabethan government may be found in Winthrop S. Hudson, *The Cambridge Connection and the Elizabethan Settlement of 1559* (Durham, N. Carolina, 1982).

12 Goodison, ed., *Catalogue of Cambridge Portraits*, I, p. xvii; Henry Bradshaw, 'On the Collection of Portraits Belonging to the University before the Civil War' [1872], *Collected Papers of Henry Bradshaw* (Cambridge, 1889), pp. 286–96.

13 Heinz Archive, National Portrait Gallery, *vide* Mildmay, Walter; *ODNB*, *vide* Mildmay, Sir Walter.

14 Goodison, ed., *Catalogue of the Portraits in Christ's, Clare and Sidney Sussex Colleges*, pp. 86–7.

15 Strong, *Tudor and Jacobean Portraits*, I, pp. 20–1; *ODNB*, *vide* Lockey, Rowland.

16 See above, n. 4.

17 Goodison, ed., *Catalogue of Cambridge Portraits*, I, p. xx; Bradshaw, 'On the Collection of Portraits', pp. 291–2.

18 *ODNB*, *vide* Frankland, Joyce; Heinz Archive, *vide* Frankland, Joyce; Poole, ed., *Catalogue of Portraits*, II, pp. 248–9; F. Thompson, *Newport Free Grammar School: A Brief History* (Newport, 1987), p. xix.

19 Bradshaw, 'On the Collection of Portraits', pp. 291–2.

20 Robert Willis, ed., *The Architectural History of the University of Cambridge* (3 vols, Cambridge, 1886, ed., John Willis Clark, repr. 1988), I, pp. 68–9; T.A. Walker, *A Biographical Register of Peterhouse Men* (2 vols, Cambridge, 1927 and 1930), II, p. 294; Heinz Archive, *vide* 'Collections for Peterhouse'.

21 Goodison, ed., *Catalogue of the Portraits in Christ's, Clare and Sidney Sussex Colleges*, p. 84.

22 See especially Kenneth Fincham, 'Oxford and the Early Stuart Polity', in Nicholas Tyacke, ed., *The History of the University of Oxford*, IV, *Seventeenth Century Oxford* (Oxford, 1997).

23 Lady Devorguilla at Balliol, two for certain of Joyce Frankland at Brasenose, four of Sir Thomas White at St John's and one each of Richard Pate (Corpus Christi), Sir William Petre (Exeter), Thomas Pope (Trinity), Cardinal Wolsey (Christ Church) in mid-century, Elizabeth Woodville (Queen's College), and William of Wyckham (New College); see Appendix A.

24 Nicholas Tyacke, ed., *The History of the University of Oxford*, IV, *Seventeenth Century Oxford* (Oxford, 1997), pp. 1–2 and map, p. xx.

25 Willis, ed., *Architectural History*, I, pp. 63–7; R.J. Skaer, 'The Panel Portrait of Andrew Perne', *Peterhouse: A Record* (volume for 1997–98, published 1999), pp. 38, 41; S. Rees Jones, 'Five Portraits from Peterhouse, Cambridge' (Courtauld Institute of Art Research

Report no. 152 [typescript] 1951), p. 2. I am very grateful to Ms Susan Pratt for retrieving this typescript report from the Courtauld archives.

26 This and the following two paragraphs based on Willis, ed., *Architectural History*, I, pp. 63–7; Heinz Archive, *vide* 'Collection for Peterhouse'; Rees Jones, 'Five Portraits from Peterhouse, Cambridge', pp. 1–2.

27 Walker, *Biographical Register*, II, p. 294. For more on Newman, see below, chapter 3.

28 J.N.L. Myres, 'The Painted Frieze in the Picture Gallery', *Bodleian Library Record*, 3 (1950–51), pp. 82–90.

29 *Ibid.*, pp. 83–5; Myers and E. Clive Rouse, 'Further Notes on the Painted Frieze and Other Discoveries in the Upper Reading Room and the Tower Room', *Bodleian Library Record*, 5 (Oct., 1956), pp. 290–308.

30 J.N.L. Myres, 'Thomas James and the Painted Frieze', *Bodleian Library Record*, 4 (1952–53), pp. 30–51.

31 Tyacke, ed., *History of the University of Oxford*, IV, pp. 1–4; M.R.A. Bullard, 'Talking Heads: The Bodleian Frieze, its Inspiration, Sources, Design and Significance', *Bodleian Library Record*, 14:6 (Apr., 1994), pp. 461–83. Charles Webster, *The Great Instauration: Science, Medecine and Reform, 1626–1660* (London, 1975).

32 Bullard, 'Talking Heads', pp. 465–7.

33 Peter Burke, *The Renaissance Sense of the Past* (1969), chapter 2.

34 Myres, 'Thomas James and the Painted Frieze', *passim*.

35 Bullard, 'Talking Heads', pp. 475–7; *ODNB*, *vide* Savile, Henry; Anon., *Portraits of the Sixteenth and Early Seventeenth Centuries* (Oxford, 1952), p. 5, cat. 14.

36 I am grateful for this reference to Dr Andrea Galdy; see also Linda Klinger Aleci, 'Images of Identity: Italian Portrait Collections of the Fifteenth and Sixteenth Centuries', in Nicholas Mann and Luke Syson, eds, *The Image of the Individual: Portraits in the Renaissance* (1998), pp. 67–80.

37 Myres, 'The Painted Frieze', p. 84, n. 2.

38 See A.W. Pollard and G.R. Redgrave, eds, *A Short-Title Catalogue of Books Printed in England, Scotland and Ireland, and of English Books Printed Abroad, 1475–1640* (2nd edn, 2 vols, 1976), II, p. 242.

39 William Jaggard, *A View of all the Right Honourable the Lord Mayors of this Honourable City of London* (STC 14343, 1601), and John Stow, *A Survey of London* (1598, 2nd edn, 1603), of which the standard modern edition is Charles Lethbridge Kingsford, ed., *A Survey of London by John Stow, reprinted from the Text of 1603* (2 vols, Oxford, 1908). Jaggard attempted woodcut portraits in his book, though he had but three woodcuts in all to deploy. He solved this dilemma by simply repeatedly recycling them in turn to 'depict' each of the lord mayors he described. Stow omitted visual images, but see especially parts on 'Honor of Citizens, and worthiness of men in the same', I, pp. 104–17, and his list of mayors in 'The temporall Gouernment of this City … ', II, pp. 147–86.

40 Ian Archer, 'The Arts and Acts of Memorialization in Early Modern London', in J.F. Merritt, ed., *Imagining Early Modern London* (Cambridge, 2001), pp. 89–113.

41 Myres, 'The Painted Frieze', p. 84, n. 2; Bullard, 'Talking Heads', p. 461, n. 2, and, more generally, André Masson, *The Pictorial Catalogue: Mural Decoration in Libraries* (1981).

42 For Godiva, see n. 60 below. The Mercers' Company to which Whittington had belonged,

commissioned a glass painting of him in the 1440s, and the fashionable engraver Richard Elstrack did an engraving in the early seventeenth century for commercial distribution, but no easel portrait is known to have been done of him in this era; *ODNB*, *vide* Whittington, Richard.

43 The decision, taken 19 April 1670, had an almost immediate effect. By the end of 1671 portraits of fourteen Fire Court judges, King Charles II and James, Duke of York, undertaken by John Michael Wright and Peter Lely, hung in the Great Hall of the London Guildhall. Vivien Knight, ed., *The Works of Art of the Corporation of London* (1986), p. 3.

44 John Whitson served as a Bristol MP in 1625. Though painted c. 1629, there are indications that this portrait may not have been acquired until the early twentieth century.

45 Brian Frith, *Twelve Portraits of Gloucester Benefactors* (Gloucester, 1972). These are paintings of John Falkner, Sir Thomas Bell, Richard Pate, Sir Thomas White, John Haydon, William Goldston, Joan Goldston, Gregory Willsheire, Isabel Wetherstone, Thomas Poulton and John Thorne.

46 Margaret Statham, ed., *Accounts of the Feoffees of the Town Lands of Bury St Edmunds, 1569–1622* (Suffolk Record Society 46, 2003), pp. lii, 239, and plate I.

47 See p. 13 in the Introduction.

48 Depicted in what may well be fifteenth-century manuscript portraits in the 'Portraits volume' held in the Aylesford Collection of the Birmingham Reference Library (no reference number), and reprinted in Mary Dormer Harris, ed., *The Register of the Guild of the Holy Trinity, St Mary, St John the Baptist and St Katherine of Coventry* (Dugdale Society 13, 1935), illustrations facing pp. 4, 14, 30, 42, 46, 64, 68, 74, 91, 104, 108; and the Aldermen of London series, Guildhall Library, London, MS nos. 32132–52 and 32170–3. See also Kathleen Scott, *Later Gothic Manuscripts, 1390–1490* (2 vols, 1996), I, plate 333; and Richard Marks and Paul Williamson, eds, *Gothic Art for England, 1400–1547* (London, 2003), pp. 268–9.

49 Victor Morgan, 'The Norwich Guildhall Portraits: Images in Context', in Andrew Moore and Charlotte Crawley, eds, *Family & Friends: A Regional Survey of British Portraiture* (1992), p. 21.

50 Three portraits of Nicholas Thorne were completed before 1640: one in 1530, inscribed with that date right on the oak panel; a second, to be hung in the Council Chamber, as recorded in the Borough Audit Book in 1624; and a third, to be hung in the Grammar School, and recorded in the Audit Book in 1625. The first of these paintings was copied by the local watercolourist Edward Cashin in 1825, and is described shortly thereafter in 'Alderman Haythorne's Manuscript' (*vide* Bristol City Museum catalogue entry E 183; registration number M2537), held in the Bristol City Museum, as bearing the date 1530 over the sitter's head. For the 1624 painting, see Richard Quick, ed., *Catalogue of the Second Loan Collection of Pictures held in the Bristol Art Gallery* (Bristol, 1905), no. 202, and Bristol Record Office, Audit Book, MS F/Au/1/19 (1624), pp. 294 and 296. For the 1625 painting, see MS F/Au/1/20 (1625), p. 25. Cashin's copies, made in miniature and in watercolour, may be found in the 'Catalogue of the Braithwaite Topographical Collection', held in the Bristol City Museum, assigned the reference numbers M2536 and M2537. My thanks to Ms Sheena Stoddart, Curator of the Bristol City Museum, and Dr Evan Jones of the University of Bristol for helping me interpret evidence of this and other Bristol portraits.

51 Dated and presumably painted in 1536. Quick, ed., *Catalogue of Pictures*, no. 201, currently catalogued in the Bristol City Museum as K4462. Photographs of it have

been published in Jean Vanes, *Education and Apprenticeship in Sixteenth Century Bristol* (Bristol, 1982), plate I, and C.P. Hill, *A History of Bristol Grammar School* (Gloucester, 1951), frontispiece. True to form, the painting is an anonymous, vernacular work, characteristic of its time.

52 *ODNB*, *vide* Thorne, Robert, the younger, and Thorne, Nicholas.

53 Robert Ricart, *The Maire of Bristowe Is Kalendar* [c. 1484], ed., Lucy Toulmin Smith (Camden Society, NS, 5, 1872).

54 Morgan, 'Norwich Guildhall Portraits', p. 21.

55 Virginia Tillyard, 'Civic Portraits Painted for, or Donated to the Council Chamber of Norwich Guildhall before 1687, with Documentary Evidence relating to the Artistic Background of the City' (MA thesis, Courtauld Institute, 1978), catalogue no. 90, p. 52; Norwich Castle Museum (NWHCM) civic portrait no. 65:F. Their function as a series is enhanced by the similar (though not exactly the same) size and framing of each portrait, and by their display in the same room or (currently) two rooms.

56 Tillyard, 'Civic Portraits', p. 12 and, closely following Tillyard's account, Morgan, 'Norwich Guildhall Portraits', p. 24. Both authorities consider the Marsham, Steward and Jannys portraits to have been painted considerably later, probably in the early seventeenth century, although Tillyard feels, plausibly enough, that the latter portrait may have been based on an earlier model, perhaps a tomb erected in 1533. Tillyard, p. 23. NWCHM accession nos. 68:F (Jannys); 75:F (Steward); 70:F (Marsham).

57 Quick, ed., *Catalogue of Pictures*, no. 206; Hugh Lloyd Parry, *The History of the Exeter Guildhall and the Life Within* (Exeter, 1936), pp. 152–3; Robert Tittler, 'Three Portraits by John de Critz for the Merchant Taylors' Company', *Burlington Magazine*, 147:1228 (July, 2005), p. 493.

58 On-site examinations. Lloyd Parry, *Exeter Guildhall*, p. 152–3; George Oliver, *History of the City of Exeter* (1861), p. 218; S.T. Bindoff, ed., *The House of Commons 1509–1558* (History of Parliament Trust, 3 vols, 1982), I, p. 439.

59 Tillyard, 'Civic Portraits' pp. 45–6; Moore and Crawley, eds, *Family & Friends* p. 197; NWCHM accession nos. 76:F (Sir Peter Rede) and 78:F (Mrs Anne Rede).

60 M.W. Greenslade, ed., *Victoria History of the County of Stafford* 14 (1990), plate 21 (b), pp. 78, 83, 129.

61 Quick, ed., *Catalogue of Pictures*, no. 227.

62 Coventry City Record Office, MS A7, 'Book of Yearly Accounts', p. 142; Thomas Sharp, *Illustrative Papers on the History and Antiquities of the City of Coventry* (Birmingham, 1871), p. 219; Ronald Aquila Clarke and P.A.E. Day, *Lady Godiva: Images of a Legend in Art and Society* (Coventry, 1982), pp. 12, 30. My thanks to Mr Clarke for showing me the painting and discussing it with me.

63 Moore and Crawley, eds, *Family & Friends*, p. 199.

64 The painting seems to have been done in 1588 and purchased by the corporation in 1599. Exeter Corporation Act Book no. 5, Devon County Record Office (Exeter Branch), p. 432, entry of 12 December 1599; Lloyd Parry, *Exeter Guildhall*, p. 153. Atwell had made his fortune as a member of the Skinners' Company of London, but remembered his place of origin in his benefactions. In 1606 the Corporation agreed to pay for portraits of another of its worthies, Laurence Seldon, and of his wife, to be hung in its Council Chamber; Exeter Corporation Act Book no. 5, Devon County Record Office (Exeter Branch), entry of 20 June, 3 James I, p. 172.

65 See Appendix A, White, Sir Thomas and, in general, Robert Tittler, 'Sir Thomas White of London: Civic Philanthropy and the Making of the Merchant Hero', in *Townspeople and Nation: English Urban Experiences, 1540–1640* (Stanford, 2001), pp. 100–20.

66 Best described in Frith, *Gloucester Benefactors*, though his tentative suggestions about dating, which takes no account of the costumes in which these figures have been rendered, seems unreliable. Both evidence of dress, and the fact that Gloucester City Chamberlains' Accounts, in which one would expect a record of payment, are missing for the years 1597–1627, suggest a date in the early years of that hiatus. My thanks to Susan North, Senior Curator of Fashion at the Victoria and Albert Museum, for her thoughts about dating some of these portraits based on costume.

67 Moore and Crawley, eds, *Family & Friends*, pp. 198–9.

68 Tittler, 'Sir Thomas White', pp. 106–8.

69 Lloyd Parry, *Exeter Guildhall*, pp. 76–7 and 153.

70 See Appendix A .

71 The scholarly literature on this is of course very extensive, but the following present a fair sampling of these activities: George Unwin, *The Gilds and Companies of London* (4th edn, 1963), especially chapters 12, 13 and 16; Ian W. Archer, *The History of the Haberdashers' Company* (Chichester, 1991), especially pp. 126–32; Matthew Davies and Ann Saunders, *The History of the Merchant Taylors' Company* (Leeds, 2004), pp. 9, 31–2, 36, 73.

72 Foister, *Holbein and England*, pp. 59, 65–7 and 191. Infra-red photography has shown the faces as much more distinct in the original version, before repainting. Foister warns us that many of the details may have been completed by others.

73 Francis Weston, 'Some Account of the Barbers' Company and the Plate, Pictures and Charters at Barber-Surgeons' Hall', *Journal of the British Archaeological Association*, NS, 21 (1915), pp. 35–7; Jessie Dobson and R. Milnes Walker, *Barbers and Barber-Surgeons: A History of the Barbers and Barber-Surgeons Company* (Oxford, 1979), pp. 118–22; Roy Strong, 'A Preliminary Cartoon for the Barber-Surgeons' Group Rediscovered: A Preliminary Report', in *The Tudor and Stuart Monarchy*, I (1995), pp. 55–71; Foister, *Holbein and England*, pp. 65–7.

74 Dobson and Walker, *Barbers and Barber-Surgeons*, p. 121.

75 Both displayed in the Hall of the School where pupils see it every day at mealtimes and on other occasions.

76 The attribution of an original Cabot portrait to Holbein is upheld in the catalogue of the National Maritime Museum, which holds an engraving which it considers to have been based on that work. But no such original portrait is listed in Susan Foister's census of Holbein's known English portraits, nor does there seem firm evidence to support the view that Holbein painted such a portrait or that the Russia Company purchased it in the period at hand. A surviving oil copy of the portrait is eighteenth century in origin. *www. nmm.ac.uk/server/show/conMediaFile.1659/*, accessed November 2006; Foister, *Holbein and England*, Appendix, pp. 299–301; *ODNB*, *vide* Cabot, Sebastian. I am grateful to Prof. Lesley Cormack for bringing this to my attention.

77 Exmewe (c. 1454–1529) served as Lord Mayor in 1517. His portrait, tentatively attributed to John Bettes and dated c. 1550, was only acquired by the Corporation of London in 1919, and must therefore be assumed to be a personal rather than a civic portrait. Guildhall Art Gallery ref. 11068; National Portrait Gallery, Heinz Archive, *vide* Exmewe, Thomas; Knight, ed., *Works of Art of the Corporation of London*, p. 33.

78 Anon., 1568, held in the Guildhall Art Gallery; Knight, ed., *Works of Art of the Corporation of London*, p. 299.

79 Gresham (1519–79), who spent much of his adult life as the crown's financial agent in the Low Countries, was painted several times in the mid-century years by skilled painters including Antonis Mor (Rijksmuseum, Amsterdam). The earliest of the Gresham portraits, done at the age of 25 in 1544, is attributed to William Scots. Now held at the Mercer's Company, the date of its acquisition by the Company remains uncertain. A 1565 portrait, NPG no. 352, has been attributed to Adrian Key.

80 See portraits of London aldermen of the mid-fifteenth century painted in watercolour on paper by Roger Leigh and held in the Guildhall Library (London Guildhall Library, MS nos. 32132–52 and 32170–3), as in fig. 4.

81 See Appendix A.

82 Wardens' Accounts, Grocers' Company, Guildhall Library MS 11571/6, fol. 205v. The Company's celebration of the memory of Lovell, an earlier sixteenth-century master and benefactor, was described in 1612 as including this portrait, along with Lovell's arms and crest, sword and collar (in a frame), all displayed near the 'great bay window' of the hall. Guildhall Library MS 11571/10, fol. 44v.

83 Of William Adams, Thomas Aldersay, Robert Aske, William Jones, and Sir George Whitmore. Haberdashers' Company, Court Minutes, Guildhall Library MS 15842/1, fol. 102r, and also fols 208v, 361 and MS 15842/2, fols, 43 and 52. George Perfect Harding, 'A List of Portraits, Pictures in Various Mansions of the United Kingdom', unpublished manuscript of the Heinz Archive, National Portrait Gallery (3 vols, 1804), II, p. 153. See also Archer, *History of the Haberdashers' Company*, p. 74, where these are dated 1596 instead of 1598.

84 Anthony Gammage of the former and both Sir Thomas White and Robert Dowe of the latter. Elizabeth Glover, *A History of the Ironmongers' Company* (1991), p. 61; Merchant Taylors' Company, Masters' and Wardens' Account Book, vol. 9 (accounts for 1606–7), Guildhall Library MS 34048/9, microfilm frame no. 915.

85 'Mr Buck','Mr Dummer', Sir Thomas Russell, and Sir John Jolles; A.H. Johnson, *The History of the Worshipful Company of Drapers of London* (5 vols, Oxford, 1914–22), III, p. 77 and n. 2.

86 Harding, 'A List of Portraits', II, p. 145; Heinz Archive, *vide* Owen, Dame Alice; *ODNB*, *vide* Owen, Dame Alice; Ordinances of the Brewers' Company, Guildhall Library MS 5458, fols 4v and 12v.

87 Sir Stephen Soame; Wardens' Accounts, Grocers' Company, Guildhall Library MS 11571/10, fol. 410v.

88 John Vernon; Frederick M. Fry, ed., *A Historical Catalogue of the Pictures, Herse-Cloths and Tapestry at Merchant Taylors' Hall* (1907), p. 67 and plate 31.

89 Wardens' Accounts, Grocers' Company, Guildhall Library MS 11588/2, p. 733 (5 February 1612/13).

90 Dr Matthew Gwin, commissioned in 1627/28; now lost. Sidney Young, *The Annals of the Barber-Surgeons of London* (1890), p. 509.

91 A triple portrait of Clement Pargeter, William Peacock and Thomas Babb, Court Minutes, Painter-Stainers' Company, Guildhall Library MS 5667/1 pp. 14–16; Heinz Archive, *vide* Pargeter; Harding, 'A List of Portraits', II, p. 137.

92 William Portington; Memorandum Book, Carpenters' Company, Guildhall Library MS 4329A, fol. A.

93 Hugh Myddleton, by Cornelius Janssen, *ODNB*, *vide* 'Myddelton, Hugh'; Heinz Archive, *vide* 'Myddelton, Hugh'; Sir Walter Shelburne Prideaux, *Memorials of the Goldsmiths' Company* (2 vols, 1896), I, pp. 159 and 136.

94 A second triple portrait, perhaps a speciality of the Painter-Stainers, of John Potkyn, John Taylor and Thomas Carleton; W.A.D. Englefield, *The History of the Painter-Stainers' Company of London* (1923), p. v.

95 James Bunce; Penelope Hunting, *The Leathersellers' Company: A History* (1994), pp. 94–5.

96 Robert Gray; Court Records, Merchant Taylors' Company, Guildhall Library MS 34010/9, fol. 91v (4 December 1639).

97 Bernard Hyde, by 'Mr Cock'; J. Steven Watson, *History of the Salters' Company* (1963), pp. 123–4.

98 Nicholas Leate, by Daniel Mytens, presented by his sons to the Company in the year of his death, 1631. Isabelle Finch, 'Portrait of an Ironmonger' (BA Hons. thesis, University of East Anglia, 2000), p. 76, pl. 18; Freemen's Registers and Inventory, Ironmongers' Company, Guildhall Library MS 16988/5, pp. 7 and 159; *ODNB*, *vide* Leate, Nicholas.

99 William Robson; Watson, *History of the Salters' Company*, pp. 122–3.

100 Sir James Campbell, Sir William Denham, Thomas Hallwood, Rowland Heylin, Thomas Lewen (or Lewin), Thomas Mitchell (or Michell), and Thomas Thorold. Freemen's Registers and Inventories, Ironmongers' Company, Guildhall Library MS 16988/5, p. 159, listing nine portraits in all in July 1640; Quarter Court Minutes, Ironmongers' Company, Guildhall Library MS 16967/2, p. 306; John Nicholl, *Some Account of the Worshipful Company of Ironmongers* (1851), pp. 473–4.

101 B.W.F. Alford and T.C. Barker, *A History of the Carpenters' Company* (1968), pp. 225–7.

102 Finch, 'Portrait of an Ironmonger', p. 76; *ODNB*, *vide* Leate, Nicholas.

103 See Appendix A under name of sitter.

104 See Appendix A under name of sitter.

105 Joseph P. Ward, 'Godliness, Commemoration, and Community: The Management of Provincial Schools by London Trade Guilds', in Muriel McClendon et al., eds, *Protestant Identities, Religion, Society and Self-Fashioning in Post-Reformation England* (Stanford, 1999), pp. 141–57.

106 Brewers' Company Ordinances, Guildhall Library MS 5458, fol. 12v and Heinz Archive, *vide* Platt, Richard.

107 See above, p. 49 and City Audit Book for 1625, Bristol Record Office MS F/AU/1/20, p. 25.

108 Cecil T. Davis, *The Monumental Brasses of Gloucestershire* (Bath, 1899, repr. 1969), pp. 154–8; see Appendix A.2, 'Cooke'.

109 Information provided by Dr Stephen Porter, HM Inspector of Ancient Monuments, ret., to whom I am grateful. See also *ODNB*, *vide* Sutton, Sir Thomas.

110 National Portrait Gallery reference no. 2160; Strong, *Tudor and Jacobean Portraits*,

II, pp. 1–2; Heinz Archive, *vide* Dixie, Sir Wolstan; *ODNB*, *vide* Dixie, Sir Wolstan; Frank Stubbings, *A Catalogue of Portraits at Emmanuel College* (Cambridge, n.d. [1988]), unpaginated, but *vide* Dixie, Sir Wolstan.

111 Nicholas Carlisle, *A Concise Description of the Endowed Grammar Schools of England and Wales* (2 vols, 1818), II, pp. 20–2; Paul Slack, 'Social Policy and the Constraints of Government, 1547–58', in J. Loach and R. Tittler, eds, *The Mid-Tudor Polity, c. 1540–1560* (1980), pp. 108–13.

112 William Bostock's portrait was rejected at that time because of his dubious moral reputation and Thomas Teasdale was painted only in 1684. For the former institution, see Arthur E. Preston, *Christ's Hospital, Abingdon, the Almshouses, the Hall, and the Portraits* (Oxford, 1929 and 2nd edn, 1930) and for the latter, G.P. Harding, *A List of Portraits in Christ's Hospital* (2 vols, 1804) II, p. 123. My thanks for the help extended to me on site to Mr Nigel Hammond of Christ's Hospital, Abingdon, and to Ms. Rhona Mitchell of its namesake in Horsham.

113 Roy Strong, *Tudor and Jacobean Portraits*, I, p. ix.

Chapter 3

Painters

It is already apparent that civic portraiture emerged chiefly out of vernacular traditions which differed sharply from the more formal and 'polite' portraiture being introduced into England by the 1530s. Not until the early decades of the seventeenth century did civic portraits tend to catch up to their personal, and formal, counterparts in point of style and sophistication. In some quarters vernacular traditions lasted much longer. Until that time at least almost all civic portraiture lacked the sophistication or stylistic formality which came with professional training in the portraitist's art, and with extended exposure to continental styles and techniques. Vernacular work flourished outside as well as within London, in the sundry regions, provincial towns and cities of the realm. It reflected strong continuities with older craft traditions, including manuscript illumination, wood and stone carving, stained glass and glass painting, heraldic painting and drawing, religious panel and cloth painting and so forth, which had flourished under ecclesiastical as well as secular patronage in pre-Reformation days, and whose production had always been well dispersed.[1] This wide dispersal had sustained a strong element of regionalism in most such craft traditions, allowing them to exhibit regionally-specific characteristics of craftsmanship, materials and style.

This regionality was perhaps most obvious for crafts relating to the building trades, which were often dependant upon, and shaped by, the occurrence of particular materials in the ambient natural environment: different types of stone, wood, earth, thatch reed and other materials which were difficult to transport and therefore remained largely regional in use. Other factors came into play for different crafts. Major monastic institutions and some cathedrals had been pre-eminent in attracting craftsmen of all sorts, from stone carvers and glaziers to manuscript illuminators and even makers of funerary brasses. The long-standing and very accomplished tradition of gold and silver-smithing in and around the city of Exeter, for example, remained sufficiently vigorous throughout this era to be recognized by the Goldsmiths of London, eventually to be granted an assay office of the royal mint, and to have spawned Nicholas Hilliard, whose father Richard was a prominent member of that Exeter industry.[2] And regional offices of the college of heralds such as that in Chester attracted and employed generations of herald painters, as adept at illumination and related visual techniques as they were at reconstructing genealogies.

Very few of these craftsmen would have had the more sophisticated training in painting portraits on wood or canvas, or in handling the materials, which would have been mastered in myriad workshops of true 'artists' working in continental traditions. For the very large part portraits were carried out by 'painter-stainers', craftsmen to be sure, who would have mastered a wide variety of skills in applying paint and other finishes to surfaces of all types, from ships' prows and myriad religious images to the king's arms, in their time. At least some of them continued to work in the tempera on gesso-prepared panel technique while their more professionally trained counterparts adapted more readily to oil on board or canvas.[3] We must think of them, as they thought of themselves and were thought of by their contemporaries, as craftsmen or artisans rather than artists.[4]

The creation of personal portraits, by contrast, came much sooner to be carried out by academically trained true artists: men who took a professional approach to their craft and who often signed their work as a statement of their own reputation. The best of them were skilled in the latest techniques of naturalistic painting, extending to the illusion of perspective, comprehension of colour theory, use of shading to indicate depth, and similar conventions. Their formal apprenticeships as easel painters had schooled them in the formal stylistic approaches of continental production, and many of them had augmented their initial training through extensive travel. Because most of them, not being native-born, were attracted to England by royal or courtly patronage to begin with, and because the Tudor monarchs made London and Westminster more of a permanent capital than ever before, they concentrated their settlement in that metropolis rather than further afield. Exceptionally, some foreign painters of lesser prominence and skill came with colonies of Dutch and Flemish religious refugees, especially to east coast provincial towns and cities like Norwich, where they plied their crafts locally.[5] We might best think of them as refugees who painted rather than painters who migrated.

Yet most foreign artists, especially the more eminent and skilled, established their workshops and built up both their networks of associated specialized craftsmen (panel and, eventually, canvas makers, frame-makers, apothecaries and others who supplied pigments or even prepared paints) and their fashionable clienteles in London rather than elsewhere. The very status of those clienteles made their work a coveted commodity among ever-wider circles of the better and even, by the mid-sixteenth century in London, some of the middling sort of people. And though most of them had, ironically, been trained in the guild systems of continental cities, they themselves came to enjoy in England (where they were usually barred from guild membership) a more elevated social status than the guildsmen who still predominated among native English practitioners.[6]

These distinctions bring several related issues to the fore. Considering the available sources, art-historical scholarship has provided a fairly comprehensive view of the polite, formal production of portraiture being practised in England at this time, and of those who produced it. Particular studies have investigated most of the prominent portraitists working in England at this time. The accounts of the royal household in particular have yielded up at least the names of scores more who were engaged in painting of some sort or other during the same era. But both sorts of studies have inevitably prejudiced the much better documented court scene and its London setting over activity in other, especially regional, venues.[7]

Understandably, again in view of the sources, the discussion of vernacular painters, especially those working outside the royal household and outside London itself, has remained far less comprehensive. This study of civic portraiture allows us to fill out this picture somewhat further. This chapter responds to questions about authorship: the painters and their occupation. Where were such works created, and by whom? How did their creators learn their craft? How, if at all, were they organized as an occupation? What economic considerations applied to their work? How were they regarded by their contemporaries? Finally, what sort of interaction ensued between this vernacular tradition which predominated outside of London, and that more formal and professional approach which was largely, at least to begin with, London-based?

Though civic portraits were created and dispersed quite widely throughout the realm, they were not all painted in the same locales where they were commissioned or received. The model employed by economic historians, of the demands of the dramatically burgeoning London metropolis as the 'engine of economic growth' for the entire realm, would suggest by analogy that London served as the source or inspiration for much of the nation's portraiture.[8] That model of London as the hub has been applied to other creative endeavours of the same era: dramatic performance and professional theatre, historical writing, English Renaissance architecture, and even the production of polite portraiture in the mainstream traditions established by Hans Holbein and others, with their royal and courtly patronage, in the early going. But how accurately does this assumption apply to the creation of civic portraits, so many of which were completed for display in institutional settings outside the metropolis?

It is certainly the case that the large majority of civic portraits done for London-based livery companies or other institutions were created in London itself. Given the dense concentration of portrait painters in the metropolis, what seems to be the extensive workshops which some of them maintained, and the high quality of much of their work, it made little sense to send elsewhere. In addition, at least some of the civic portraits commissioned and eventually displayed elsewhere were painted in and around London. Then, too, London workshops, which seem to have been established from at least the 1530s, often received portraits from elsewhere for copying or what was called 'refreshing'.

But throughout the period at hand a great many, probably most, of the civic portraits which were commissioned by provincial towns and cities, universities and their colleges, provincial schools and charitable institutions, were also created outside the metropolis, usually but not always in the patronal communities themselves. Even when provincial towns and institutions could not find local hands to do the work, they did not necessarily send to London instead. When in 1594 the corporation of Plymouth wanted a portrait of Sir Francis Drake for their Guildhall, they sent for a copy to be made on site at Buckland Abbey.[9] When the governors of Christ's Hospital, Abingdon, wished to establish a record of its founders and benefactors in the opening years of the next century, they sent for Sampson Strong of Oxford, whose charming but rude vernacular craftsmanship still graces the small hall of that institution. Two decades later Bristol sent for portraits both to Coventry and to Wiltshire.[10] Considering the long-established incidence of local and regional centres of craft and artisanal production in most parts of the realm, most of them ecclesiastical in origin, it should not surprise us that there was no need to rely on London.

Our estimate of how extensive such local and regional activity may have been depends somewhat on how we read the occupational descriptions attached to family surnames in such records as apprenticeship indentures, freemen's admissions, wills and inventories. Clearly one must look sceptically at assumptions that anyone described as a 'painter' might have painted portraits. Without further evidence we cannot attach even tentative attributions of particular work to men or women whose occupations are recorded as 'painters' or 'painter-stainers'.[11]

Nevertheless, there were obviously clusters of those described as 'painters' (to use the contemporary and highly unspecific term) in many of the middling and larger provincial towns and even, by the early seventeenth century, individual 'painters' in virtual villages[12] who turned their hand to portraiture when asked to do so. More often than not, the commission would have yielded precisely the sort of crude vernacular work formerly employed in pre-Reformation depictions of biblical kings and saints – the reredos of

Hexham Abbey come to mind – and now carried over to civic portraits in, e.g., Gloucester, Norwich, Bristol, Bury St Edmunds and elsewhere. And by the very last years of our period there emerged a few provincial painters, men like John Souch of Chester (c. 1594–1645) or the Suffolk gentleman Nathaniel Bacon (1585–1627), who had more (Bacon) or less (Souch) absorbed the styles and techniques of the polite mainstream while continuing to work (or, in Bacon's case, returning from elsewhere to work) in their home regions. Their expertise would have earned the more specific and prestigious tags of 'picture-maker' or 'limner' (both indicating painters of easel paintings rather than painter-stainers' work) in their time.[13]

Norwich had both the largest number of civic portraits of any provincial city by far in our period and a substantial number of 'painters', some of whom must have carried out some of those portraits. Virginia Tillyard's search through the freemen's records of that city turned up fourteen names of 'painters' proposed or approved as freemen between 1554 and 1640, two more identified as 'painters' whose probate inventories remain in the Norfolk Record Office, and a further seven whose wills were proved at the Norwich Consistory Court in that period, making a total of twenty-three men plying that craft in Norwich over approximately three generations. This figure would not have included those itinerant craftsmen from elsewhere in England or refugee 'strangers', especially Dutch and Flemish, who settled in large numbers in that city. A few of those identified by name have confidently been credited with specific works. Two of them, Augustine Isbourne and George True, have been proposed as responsible for at least some of the portraits in Norwich's portrait series, though firm evidence for this likelihood remains elusive.[14]

True, apprenticed to Isbourne and admitted freeman in 1620, is recorded as receiving between 1621 and 1639 specific payments for working at Hellesdon Bridge, at St Anne's staithe, at the Guildhall, for drawing a plan of the choir of an unnamed church, for inscribing the names of benefactors on a table of benefactions (and for making a frame for that table), for painting a wall in the market, for mending tiles, and oiling and staining the cucking-stool.[15] None of these entries refer to portraits, and only one refers to the Guildhall within which such portraits were displayed. Yet True would have been an obvious home-grown candidate for carrying out such work, and he may well have done so.

At least by the early seventeenth century the smaller Norfolk borough of King's Lynn also seems to have had a cluster of painters, some of whom are highly likely to have done portraits. Thomas Snelling, who died aged thirty-nine during his first mayoralty of this thriving port town in 1623, may or may not have relied on painting for his principle livelihood, but he was identified as 'Snelling the Limner' in a posthumous portrait of him done in 1644 by the much more prominent Samuel Cooper. Snelling married Margaret Clarke, a miniaturist, and they seem to have passed on their talents for painting to their son Matthew, also known as a miniaturist. We may conjecture that Snelling painted the earliest extant King's Lynn portrait, of William Atkin, mayor in 1619, and that his circle may have been responsible for one other surviving King's Lynn portrait of that time, of the mayor Joshua Green.[16]

Leicester hosted another cluster of 'painters', probably proportionate in size to that at Norwich in the same years. Here we can more confidently attribute authorship to a few paintings, though the range of recorded artisanal activities is again quite wide. The earliest, whom we have met before, is John Barber or Barbor, who flourished as a 'painter' of many skills in the reigns of Edward and Mary. In view of the many changes in royal policy towards visual objects in these years it is no wonder that such men found ample work even in county towns like Leicester. Between 1549 and 1558 Barber received payment for painting the Guildhall with antique work and adding the King's arms to its walls; painting cloth banners, sepulchre and altar cloths in local churches; and, along with his wife, for gilding the rood-screen figures of Mary and John.[17]

Robert Bradshaw worked in the same sort of capacities. Having apprenticed with the local 'painter-stainer' George Langley and been admitted freeman in 1613, Bradshaw remained in Leicester for most of his life and is recorded as having been paid 15s for 'mending and drawing the two pictures of Mr Heyrickes which hang in the parlour' in 1647–48.[18] (This is also a slightly ambiguous reference: in the loose terminology of the day, 'drawing' could also mean 'painting', as it may well have done here.)[19] Four years later the borough corporation paid Bradshaw for 'blazing' the King's arms on the Guildhall and both east and west gates of the city, and for 'scouring' the chimney piece and pictures in the Guildhall. Such was the varied work of the 'painter'.[20]

Yet some of these local 'painters' certainly did take on portrait work, and in Leicester we know this to have been done by Christopher Carter. It is he who was paid in 1623 to paint a portrait of Henry Hastings, third earl of Huntingdon, a particular friend and patron of the town, for display in the Guildhall.[21] Other Leicester painters include Affabell (or Assabell) Watson (d. 1597), described as a 'picture-maker' from the nearby village of Markfield, who worked briefly in 1597–98;[22] George Langley or Longley, with whom Bradshaw apprenticed and who is recorded as having done a variety of painter-stainer work, though not specifically portraits, between 1590 and 1625;[23] and John Carver, who painted the Queen's arms and did other work at the Guildhall in 1586–87.[24] Any or all of these could have done civic portraits, and are certainly representative of the sorts of men who took on such commissions when they could get them.

Bury St Edmunds employed two men, probably neither of them London-based, to carry out civic portraits and similar work in the early seventeenth century. A 'Mr Fenn, the paynter' received a total of £3 6s 8d in 1616 to produce portraits of Thomas Bright the Elder (d. 1587) and Jankyn Smyth (d. 1481), and

£11 for the much grander portrait of James I produced in the same year to hang alongside the others.[25]

More may be said for the second painter to turn up in Bury St Edmunds at that time: 'Newman, the paynter', of Cambridge, who received £8 for doing the King's arms in the same year of 1616, a sum which presumably covered carving and painting together. Newman was also active in and around Cambridge in the 1610s, and has been credited with painting two of the Peterhouse series, Robert Slade and John Blythe, between 1615 and 1617. Most likely he is also the 'Newman' whom Henry Peacham described in 1606 as one of the two painters engaged in an argument in Huntingdon, and as the one of the two who was a 'stranger' to that town.[26] This tells us that even so small a town as Huntingdon had a resident painter—Newman's antagonist – at least in the year 1606, and also that Newman himself painted widely throughout the neighbouring counties of Cambridgeshire, Huntingdonshire and Suffolk on a more or less itinerant basis.

Newman was far from the last painter to work in and around Bury. Nicholas Hilliard's son Laurence, also a painter, visited and may have stayed for a time around 1631. The Revd John Cradock (d. 1652), his daughter Mary Beale (d. 1699), nephew Nicholas Thach (d. post-1652) and Matthew Snelling, formerly of King's Lynn, have also been identified.[27]

But the most accomplished and illustrious of all was of course Nathaniel Bacon, grandson of the Elizabethan lord keeper Sir Nicholas Bacon and thus a man of quite different social standing, whose seat at Culford Hall was but four miles away. Though Bacon does not seem to have produced civic portraits himself, his presence in the area cannot have been irrelevant to the flourishing of other these other painters who did produce such works.[28] An intriguing suggestion of such ties emerges from the revelation that a John Fenn, quite plausibly the same 'Mr Fenn, the paynter' noted above, served as a witness to Bacon's will of June 1627.[29] This John Fenn served as steward to Nathaniel Bacon and his wife, Jane, at Culford, and acquired painting supplies for his master among his duties.[30] Their mutual interest in painting may have served as part of their association. Though socially separated in rank, Fenn and Bacon may well have been members of an active circle of painters in the Bury area, for which the gentleman Bacon will naturally have served as the dominant member.

At one time or another Bristol no doubt also had its own resident painters, one of them being John Phipps, who was paid for refreshing the crests of Henry VIII in the Guildhall in 1583.[31] But for making copies of the portraits of the brothers Thorne for their grammar school in 1624 the borough corporation employed someone based in Wiltshire (probably Salisbury) for the job.[32] And in 1625 Bristol's chamberlain sent to Coventry for the production of a copy of its portrait of the Thomas White who had been mayor of Bristol. Unfortunately, the chamberlain confused this White with his namesake, Sir Thomas White of London, a benefactor to both Bristol and Coventry, and so received a portrait of the wrong man! He paid for the Coventry copy, and then engaged 'John the Painter', whom we may presume to be a local man, for 'drawing' (which, again, may and probably did mean 'painting' in this case) the intended Thomas White.[33] This suggests that Bristol's own production of paintings may have diminished by 1625, but also that its governors knew and relied upon other provincial centres for portraiture rather than sending to London.

Gloucester served as another centre for civic portraiture in the vernacular idiom in these times, and may well have hosted such work for a very long time before: Edward II is said to have seen portraits of his royal predecessors on a visit to St Peter's Abbey in that city in the early fourteenth century. Judging by the clothing depicted and the few which are dated, the city's twelve surviving portraits of local benefactors and officials (out of an initial eighteen) seem to have been done from the 1590s to about 1620. Their vernacular, even naive quality suggests local hands at work, though a slightly more sophisticated talent may have produced the one of Richard Pate among the rest. There is no indication whose hands these may have been, but they seem to represent two or three different painters in the course of these twenty or twenty-five years. Most likely these were local painter-stainers, quite possibly artisans whose families had been associated with St Peter's Abbey prior to the Reformation and with its successor, St Peter's Cathedral, thereafter.[34]

But outside the universities, perhaps the most intriguing and one of the best documented of all these regional centres is Chester, a city whose role in the production of visual artefacts also extends far back in time.[35] Chester proves particularly interesting for several reasons. While we might perhaps expect affluent areas like Norwich, Bury St Edmunds or Gloucester, with their populous and rich agrarian hinterlands, large and affluent gentry communities and considerable aristocratic presence to provide ample support for local portraiture, Chester was not quite so well favoured in the era at hand. For the most part its hinterland of Flintshire, southern Lancashire and western Cheshire remained sparsely populated pastoral terrain, with mediocre soil and little industry. Save for the Stanley earls of Derby, whose claims of allegiance from Chester itself were variable in their effect,[36] it enjoyed little aristocratic presence. And though many of its gentry families were long-standing, few could stand shoulder to shoulder with their affluent and influential counterparts of, e.g., Norfolk or Suffolk.[37] Though the vibrancy of its pre-Reformation cultural achievements cannot be denied, there seems less reason to anticipate the continuity of that legacy thereafter. And yet Chester continued to shine in that respect, from at least the end of the sixteenth to right into the eighteenth century.

The second of point of interest regarding local portraiture in Chester is to be found in the four generations of a distinguished and very prolific family of heraldic painters, all of them named Randle Holme, and of some of the people associated with them. The best known of these associates is John Souch (1594–1645), who apprenticed with Randle Holme I. At least six of Souch's portraits, albeit none of them of civic figures, have been firmly identified, and he must be considered an accomplished regional portraitist of the second, if not the first, rank.[38] Though no specific portraits may yet be attributed to the first two Holmes themselves, it seems entirely likely that they would have done portraits along with their other activities. Certainly they knew their way round a canvas and a paintbox.

The Holmes and Souch allow us a rare and informative peek at the process by which polite and sophisticated styles could have been absorbed into the traditions of local and regional portraiture without obvious reference to the London hub. The experience of the first two Holmes especially, Randle I (1570/71–1655) and Randle II (1601–59), sheds considerable light on our period.[39]

The first in this dynasty to enter the realm of the visual arts did so through the doorway of heraldic painting. Having apprenticed to Thomas Chaloner, deputy to the Norroy King-of-Arms, Randle Holme I served from 1600 to 1616 as deputy herald for Lancashire, Chester and North Wales, and then as deputy herald for Cheshire and North Wales alone from 1619. This apprenticeship required him to master the arts and techniques of 'hatching, lymminge and staining and seeling' which were part of the formal training of Chester painters admitted to that city's Company of Painters, Glasiers, Embroiderers and Stationers, amalgamated and chartered in 1536.[40] This occupation allowed Holme to move up in status from his start as a blacksmith's son, and to undertake a long and distinguished career in the politics and affairs of both his city and company. It allowed him actively, indeed zealously, to practise his trade and pass it on to sundry apprentices, including his son, Randle Holme II, and John Souch. It also allowed him an extensive and intimate acquaintance with anyone at all of armigerous status in the entire region: those people who formed the natural clientele of a herald also formed the clientele of a portrait painter.

Had the senior Holme not been a curious and ambitious man, and had he not taken a serious and scholarly interest in his work, he may have remained unknown outside the confines of Cheshire. But the enormous energy he expended in collecting heraldic and other manuscripts matched that of his role in local affairs: at his death he was able to hand on to his son the core of what eventually became over 250 volumes of heavily illustrated manuscript material, now mostly in the British Library.[41]

The most critical volume of this collection for our purposes is Harleian 2001: a fascinating collection of chalk and pencil drawings, clippings from printed books and other images, amounting to a visual commonplace book, all in versions of contemporary polite, continental style. While a detailed analysis of this volume remains to be completed, its importance seems abundantly clear. It shows us that even in Chester one could learn of the styles and even techniques current on the continent without much recourse to London or travel to foreign parts. A deputy herald would ordinarily have been required to travel regularly to London. But we know that Randle Holme I suffered from a debilitating hernia from the early 1620s to the end of his life in 1655 which made such journeys dangerous, painful, short and infrequent. It is even less likely that he ever travelled abroad: his modest family circumstances would have precluded anything approaching a 'grand tour' as a youth; his hernia would have ruled it out later on. We also know that he was not receptive to close contact with foreign craftsmen working in Chester. Two by-laws of his company, one in 1591 and another in 1600, prohibited the employment of aliens in the painter-stainers' trade in that city. Holme signed them both, and they seem to have been effective.[42]

While some of these images collected by the second Randle Holme (if not his father) may possibly have been sketched during travels abroad, we must assume that most in this volume must have been garnered from illustrated books or individual engravings in circulation at that time. Among the folios of Harleian 2001 are actual clippings from such books. Another volume in the Holme Collection shows the use of pricking and pouncing as devices for making direct copies.[43] And it is these images which seem to have allowed the first two Holmes to absorb those contemporary styles themselves and introduce them to their apprentices. They and probably others like them present an obvious source of Souch's early exposure to such work. Ironically, though many individual sheets in Harleian 2001 are initialled 'rh i' or 'rh ii', none of the contemporary portraits which can be examined in Chester today bear either signature. In fact, no specific portrait has yet been attributed to either of the first two Randle Holmes. Yet most portraits of that era remained unsigned, many of that time and region remain unattributed, and the archives identify a number which have not survived to our time.[44] Attribution to either one of them remains a distinct possibility.

Turning from Chester and other provincial towns to another sort of patronal institution altogether, we are able to learn at least a little more about those who painted portraits in the universities than elsewhere. Universities and their colleges were more likely to have recorded expenditures in a methodical manner, and to have kept their records safely and securely from that time to the present. Then, too, the many colleges in each university provided a critical concentration of employment opportunities for painter-stainers comparable only to the livery companies of London taken together. Even so, the record for Cambridge is somewhat more elusive than for Oxford. This may well be because Cambridge seems to have relied more on foreign-born and/or court-linked portraitists than Oxford, or simply because it has attracted less methodical research.

The practice of importing people to do their portraits, or of purchasing them from elsewhere, seems evident among Cambridge colleges from that very early time when the executors of the subject's will paid 60s between 1511 and 1513 to 'Maynerde, payntor' for a portrait of Lady Margaret Beaufort, founder of Christ's College, to hang in the College Hall.[45] As noted above, this figure has been identified not as Holbein's painter-friend Harry Maynert as once thought, but as Maynarde Wewycke or Vewicke: a foreign-born painter who resided in All Hallows parish, London, in the 1510s and 1520s while undertaking work of various sorts for the royal household and court.[46]

Any number of men described as 'painters', taking the term in its contemporary artisanal sense, may be found in accounts of the various colleges of both universities.[47] As we have seen with John Newman, a few such men may be identified as painters of the occasional college portrait even if they are unlikely to have been portrait specialists. At Cambridge, a Mr Skinner did a portrait of Queen Elizabeth for the University in 1588–89.[48] The mysterious 'Hand A' has been credited with the bulk of the Peterhouse series done around 1565.[49] Though it is unlikely that this person's identity will yet come to light, he or she produced vernacular portrait work around Cambridge over a considerable time.

The rest of those who have thus far been identified as having painted portraits for Cambridge or its colleges were court-based painters working in the polite tradition: Robert Peake (of Prince Charles in 1612–13 for the University), and both Steven van de Meulen and George Gower (both of whom painted Frances Sidney countess of Sussex in portraits acquired by that College).[50] This may be explained by the extensive and continuing involvement of quite a few Elizabethan privy councillors and other prominent figures in Cambridge colleges, men like William Cecil, Nicholas Bacon, Sir Thomas Smith, Walter Mildmay, and Archbishop Matthew Parker, who would readily have used their court contacts to secure appropriate painters for the colleges with which they retained connection.

Thanks to the long-labouring Mrs Rachel Poole, the Oxford record is much more complete. Here, too, the better-known portraitists working in the polite idiom came in for a fair amount of patronage from individual colleges, both at the start of our era in the person of Jan Rav (Johannes Corvus)[51] and towards the end. But here again the vernacular tradition remained dominant and nearly uninterrupted right into the early seventeenth century.

The most spectacular Oxford effort of all, however, had not yet been discovered when Poole wrote. The Bodley Frieze, which has been described in chapter 2, came to light only in 1949. It appears that the £155 paid to the local painter-stainers John Clarke and Thomas Knight between June 1618 and February 1619 'towards the paynting of the thirde storie over the newe schooles' must, despite the mention of the 'newe schooles', refer instead to at least part of the work of the Frieze, and at about the right time.[52] As painter-stainers we would expect them, and those whom they would have employed to help, to have worked in the vernacular vein, and so they did. These artisans may indeed, as has been suggested,[53] have consulted models for individual images from published engravings which were available to them, but these are not polished works. They are far from exhibiting most of the characteristics of the formal, polite styles of the day.

Oddly enough, in view of the magnitude of their work, Clarke and Knight remain obscure figures. We know much less about them than we know about the intriguing Sampson Strong (also known as 'Sampson the Painter' and 'Sampson the Picturer' and even as 'Starke' or 'Starkey'), to whom quite a few Oxford and Abingdon area portraits done a decade on either side of the century year 1600 have reliably been attributed. If Clarke and Knight may be considered Oxford's answer to Peterhouse's Hand A of the 1560s in producing a large portrait series, Strong certainly serves well as Oxford's counterpart to 'Newman, the paynter' in producing individual portraits over a whole region. Strong is thought to have been born in the Low Countries around 1549 and, unlikely as it may be, is recorded as having matriculated as a forty year-old at Magdalen College in 1589. He soon gave up his studies, settled in St Aldate's parish in that city, married, baptized a daughter in the parish church in 1593, and received a licence to sell ale in 1596: a chequered career to be sure!

We have no idea how or even whether he came by any formal training, but from about that time on Strong began to attract portrait commissions from the city of Oxford and some of the colleges. New College's payment of £6 in 1596 for a portrait of William of Wyckham remains his first documented commission. Before his death in 1611 he produced a copy of one of the numerous portraits of Sir Thomas White for the city of Oxford in 1597, a copy of Rav's portrait of Bishop Richard Fox for Corpus Christi College in 1604, paintings of grotesque figures and monsters for Magdalen in 1605, and a portrait of the College's founder Henry Chichele at All Souls in 1609. Two other portraits of Chichele, at Lambeth Palace, have been attributed to Strong, as have two busts of Cardinal Wolsey, one (as well as a panel portrait of Wolsey) for Christ Church and the other for Magdalen.[54] Strong's activity also extended to the nearby Berkshire market town of Abingdon. Here he is credited with painting at least one and possibly as many as seven of the benefactors' paintings now in the small hall of Christ's Hospital (see fig. 14, 'The Bridge Builders'), as well as the unique paintings still preserved in sheltered positions on the outside of that building.[55]

Given his foreign birth and commercial success, one might be tempted to consider Strong a largely forgotten artist working in the traditions of Holbein

14 'The Bridge Builders', Abingdon; Sampson Strong (?), 1607.

or others of that ilk. Yet one glance at any of his known works will disabuse us of the tendency to think of him as a painter of note in the courtly manner or polite style of either Holbein's time or his own. Mary Edmond writes of them as conveying 'at best … a dignified simplicity'. But that is a polite way of saying that his figures are two-dimensional, crudely worked in detail, and strikingly lacking in subtlety of expression. Mrs Poole emphasized the medieval character of his works, which she attributed to the fact that some of them are copies of earlier drawings in manuscript.[56]

Strong's work may be crude in the context of contemporaries like Peake, Gheeraerts the Younger, or Hilliard, but it remains important in several respects. Preceding even the Bodley Frieze by more than a decade, it sustained what was then but a feeble concern for commissioning founders' portraits for Oxford colleges, and established a tradition of such works which reverberated through the generations. His career demonstrates that, despite the opposition to foreign craftsmen who threatened competition to the native English, foreign-born artists or artisans of even distinctly modest ability could readily find employment, even outside London, and especially in communities lacking well-organized guilds of native English craftsmen. And it shows us that such a painter could establish himself away from London and carry out a successful career without much visible or obvious reference to the London scene or the court and personal patronage associated with that scene.

Such a career as Strong forged in the Oxford/Abingdon area may be even more remarkable in his lifetime, a point at which vernacular painting in his mode was beginning to give way to the works of such mainstream professional portraitists as John de Critz, Cornelius Janssen and Daniel Mytens working in a much more polished manner. A generation later Strong may not have enjoyed the same success. By the mid-1620s Oxford colleges were commissioning the London-based Richard Greenbury (whose patrons included the royal physician Sir Theodore Mayerne; Thomas Howard, second earl of Arundel; and the East India Company), as their portraitist of choice for the sort of work which Strong had so recently commanded from his perch in Oxford itself.[57] Strong's descendants remained in Oxford, but worked as musicians and town waits rather than in the visual arts.[58]

A consideration of what can be learned of Strong's career, added to what we have been able to discover of his lesser-known contemporaries, tells us a lot about the sorts of painters who created civic and other portraiture outside of London at this time, and what sort of civic patronage they attracted. Strong, Newman, Fenn and others like them were obviously able to establish bases of patronage from towns and institutions in provincial England, and to travel within those regions to seek and carry out their commissions.

Other painters who, tantalizingly enough, we often find referred to as, e.g., 'the Dutch painter', will have been trained abroad and perhaps specifically in the art of portraiture. Yet quite a few, like Carter of Leicester and Fenn of Bury St Edmunds, were presumably not so trained, and many or even most will have been trained as mere 'painter-stainers'. Still others, such as the Holmes of Chester, were trained as heraldic painters. Some may well have emerged from the pre-Reformation traditions of manuscript illumination, still residing where monastic employment had rooted them, and adjusting their skills according to changing demands. And a few, like John Souch and perhaps the later Holmes, will have developed their craft well beyond the crude painter-stainer tradition to become fashionable portraitists at least in their regions.

Whatever the specialized or general approach, it seems safe to assume that many of these men and perhaps occasionally women would have been trained through traditional apprenticeship as offered and controlled by the guild system, and that guilds and similar associations will have determined many of the economic circumstances surrounding their occupations. In some of the larger provincial centres at this time there were enough craftsmen working in the visual arts to form painter-stainers' guilds, either as occupationally exclusive entities or, more commonly, by amalgamating with other, smaller trades. In this they followed a pattern established by the amalgamation of the London liveries of the Painters and the Stainers, which joined together to form a single association in 1502, and of other merged London liveries.

Such provincial guilds operated for at least some of the time in our period, and often from an earlier time as well. They did so in towns including York, Coventry, Exeter, Kingston upon Hull, Newcastle upon Tyne and Chester, with the 'Company of Painters, Glasiers, Embroiderers and Stationers' of Chester, formally chartered in 1536, probably being the most active and stable over time.[59] Many of these towns and cities had also served as ecclesiastical centres, with their traditional emphasis on craftsmanship in the visual arts. Numerous guilds operating in the post-Reformation era were carry-overs from pre-Reformation religious fraternities which had sustained occupational affiliations. Occupational continuity also accrued within families. Those employed in a particular craft from one generation to the next by an ecclesiastical institution seem often to have remained in that occupation, and in the same area, following the monastic dissolutions.[60] Such family continuity in monastic-dominated communities, whether in London or elsewhere, and in royal employment as well, certainly extended to the visual arts.[61]

Guilds offered formal apprenticeships with established masters, both apprentices and masters being native-born. Even in London apprenticeships with foreign-born masters, by contrast, and the training in the formal and polite traditions on which such foreigners had a near monopoly, remained very difficult for a native Englishman to obtain. Though aliens were either restricted or altogether banned from taking on alien apprentices,[62] they remained reluctant to take on native-born Englishmen, while Englishmen themselves remained ambiguous about apprenticing with foreigners. Guilds in general, working through London's Court of Common Council as well as through parliament and the Privy Council, opposed any notion which might encourage alien craftsmen in their occupations. And yet these efforts of liveries like the Painter-Stainers' Company proved only partially successful. Neither the crown nor the Privy Council were consistent in their support,[63] the former continuing to employ foreign painters for much of its most prestigious and lucrative work and most of its portraiture right through the century.[64] And despite the support of London City authorities, the Company's writ stopped short of most of London's suburbs, and was easily circumvented. The grating tensions between these rival occupational interests no doubt account for some of the continuing isolation of the native-born from styles and techniques which had become widely disseminated and commonplace over much of Western Europe by this time.

As we have seen with regard to Chester, the role of guild organization in sustaining the painters' craft, and of defending against the incursion of foreign competitors, was as important in at least some provincial centres as it was in London. There seem to be half a dozen to ten masters working in the painter-stainers part of Chester's amalgamated guild at any given time in the late sixteenth and early seventeenth century. Each of them seem to have taken on two or three apprentices per decade on average, a privilege which, as we have seen, was not extended to aliens.[65] It is unlikely that all those who entered such arrangements 'graduated' at the other end of this lengthy process – drop-out rates among apprentices in all trades continued to be substantial throughout this era[66] – or that they remained to practise their craft in and around Chester if they did.[67] But local apprenticeship did manage to perpetuate traditional production of those crafts in Chester and its environs. It did sustain the practice within particular families, the four generations of Randle Holmes being the best example. It did occasionally produce someone like John Souch who went on to better things as a well-supported and considerably sophisticated regional painter of portraits and other works. But no evidence has surfaced in the years under study here to show foreign painters at work in Chester, and none of the names of Chester guildsmen in this craft sound foreign.

At least some of those who had successfully completed an apprenticeship in such guilds as Chester's remained in the trade long enough to establish workshops of their own in the town of their training. Others, like the versatile Newman of Cambridge, may or may not have received such training, but they travelled around as well, often in an area taking in several shires. Save for those like the Holmes, who also relied for some of their income on their role as heralds, or Souch, who broke into the ranks of known and coveted portrait specialists working in the formal idiom, it is doubtful if the run-of-the-mill painter-stainers found their trade particularly lucrative, or succeeded financially to the point of social advancement. That observation brings us to consider other economic circumstances in which portraits were created.

Though these associations in London, Chester and elsewhere remained very active throughout this era, and though their jurisdictions and other powers were considerably strengthened by the Statute of Artificers of 1563 (5 Eliz., c. 4) and other legislation, they faced severe obstacles to their livelihoods. Shoddy work which threatened to demean a guild's honour and reputation remained a constant concern. Guilds and liveries had long developed complicated schemes of self-policing and inspection to deal with it: such efforts constituted one of a guild's most important responsibilities. But the slow and steady erosion of the guild system by enterprising free-lancers, un-apprenticed native-born and well-trained foreign-born competitors among them, proved an even greater threat. Replacement of board with canvas as the painted surface and the advent of ready-made pigments which could be purchased from apothecaries or other painter-stainers allowed all easel painters to cut their relative costs as the era progressed. But we must assume that the general and surprising stagnation in the prices which a painter could command for a portrait over this same era stemmed at least in part from an expansion in unregulated competition.[68]

It must be acknowledged that, in an age where formal, written contracts for portrait work or receipts for payment were almost unheard of, the evidence for pricing still remains sketchy. Aside from market conditions of a particular time and place, prices would have depended on such additional factors as the size of the work, the number and type of colours provided (each one having to be ground or purchased separately), and what sort of surface (either board or the less expensive canvas) was to be covered. Transport, frames and curtains incurred separate and additional costs. Yet whether painted by the skilled, mostly foreign-trained painters in the polite manner or by native-English painter-stainers working in the vernacular, the price of easel portraits does not at all seem to have kept pace with the cost of a market basket of consumer goods throughout the period at hand.[69]

For some standard of comparison from the professional portraitists working in the formal and polite tradition, we might begin with what we know of the fees which Holbein and his leading contemporaries received for their work in the 1520s and 1530s: surely the very top end of the price range at the beginning of our era. Work done for the crown came out of his annual salary of £30, but representative payments for some of Holbein's other works included £14 10s for what must have been a large cloth painting of the Battle of Therouanne in 1527, and £13 6s 8d for two portraits (Anne of Cleves and her sister Amelia) in 1539. Antonio Toto received £20 for four paintings at Hampton Court in 1530, which is considered high even for the time and painter. But Thomas Cromwell paid 30s for making the King's arms on a small 'table' in the same decade, and the accomplished native-born painter John Bettes received only £3 in all for portraits (possibly miniatures) of the King and Queen and six other paintings in 1546/47.[70] In other words, portraits might have cost up to six or seven pounds at the very most, and smaller work as little as seven or eight shillings in the reign of Henry VIII.[71]

Oddly enough, even some of the more prominent professional and London-based portrait painters two and three generations on were not receiving much if anything more than this. This is even more surprising in view of the trend towards larger, and thus more costly, paintings in the second half of the century. George Gower received £6 5s for five paintings in 1573, though it is not clear whether these were portraits or how big they were.[72] The Dutchman Cornelius Ketel, commissioned to do nineteen portraits for the Cathay Company in 1577, received £5 for a full-length and £1 for a head-only image, though again we cannot estimate size for most of them.[73] The value even of Holbein's paintings may not especially have increased by this mid-Elizabethan era, though they began to do so shortly thereafter. An inventory *post mortem* of the estate of the Archbishop Matthew Parker, taken in 1575, valued his Holbein portrait of William Warham at £5, which is just about what Holbein would have received for painting it a generation earlier.[74] Even in 1606–7 the Merchant Taylors paid John de Critz, already a prominent court painter made famous by the extensive patronage of Sir Francis Walsingham, the same £5 'for makinge Sir Thomas Whites picture in a faier large frame'. They gave him another £5 in all for two more pictures, one of Prince Charles and one of Robert Dowe, in the same year.[75]

Only by the mid-1610s, by which time portraits had often become larger still and the fame attached to certain portraitists more pronounced, did the top end of the market for skilled portraiture began to advance. Robert Peake received £13 6s 8d for a large (61" × 34") many-coloured full length of Prince Charles in 1613, Daniel Mytens received £30 for a larger (79" × 49¼"), full-length portrait of James Hamilton, earl of Arran in 1623.[76] Rubens and Van Dyck in turn drove the top of the market to still greater heights thereafter.

But save for the very most affluent of the London liveries like the Goldsmiths or the Merchant Taylors, payments on offer from most civic institutions for portraits of their founders, benefactors, and particular heroes did not and perhaps could not scale these heights. When the London-based painter Edward Cooke or Cocke requested £5 each for two paintings he had done for the Ironmongers Company in 1640, the Company's ruling body, called the 'court', demurred. As they recorded in their minute book, 'the Courte doe not hold them to be soe muche worthe yet they will further inquire what other Companies payes for the like woorke'. That investigation ended in a payment of only £3 5s for each painting. Still, Cooke could not have been too disappointed, because he proceeded to accept that very sum for five more Company portraits plus two of the King and Queen.[77] Cooke's experience with the Ironmongers tells us several things: that Cooke himself was not as well regarded as he thought; that he worked without a contract (which was entirely common); and that there was a fairly standard, and rather modest, rate which the London liveries were willing to pay for canvas portraits by 1640.[78]

The relative stagnation of prices for portraits throughout the period at hand, considered along with the continuing inflow of apprentices into the trade, suggests that those few who rose through the social and economic ranks, like the blacksmith's son Randle Holme, who became a deputy herald, master of his guild and eventually mayor of Chester, had additional means of support. Then, too, by the middle of the senior Holme's career in the 1620s and 1630s, styles had begun to change throughout most of the realm as they had earlier done in London and the universities. It was becoming increasingly possible for civic officials to see, and thus to covet and demand, polite portraits of the sort turned out by some of the court-based foreigners (e.g., Marcus Gheeraerts the Elder and the Younger, Hans Eworth, Cornelius Janssen,

Daniel Mytens) and the occasional well-trained Englishman following on the heels of, e.g., George Gower, Robert Peake, and William Larkin, in country houses and elsewhere.

In consequence, the gap which existed between the two traditions began steadily to close. Adherents of the more formal approach were accepting commissions from civic institutions as well as genteel individuals. As we would expect, the polite and formal styles first found their civic patronage among the London liveries and university colleges, those institutions being in closest touch with London-based cultural productivity and better able to pay for the slightly more expensive work of that sort. Cornelius Ketel stayed in England for only eight years (1573–81) before returning to the Netherlands, but he did manage to obtain the valuable patronage of the Cathay Company noted above.[79] Marcus Gheeraerts the Younger did one of Sir Henry Lee for the Armourers and Brasiers' Company Hall around 1602 and one of William Camden at the request of Degory Whear for the Bodleian Library twenty years later.[80] John de Critz, as we have seen, did portraits for the Merchant Taylors (including Robert Dowe, Prince Charles Stuart, Nowell Southern, and Sir Thomas White), and the Barber-Surgeons in the same decade.[81] Nicholas Lockey (of John King for Christ Church, 1620),[82] and Daniel Mytens (also of John King for Christ Church in 1622),[83] cracked the Oxford college market late in the reign of James I, while the prolific Cornelius Janssen was doing portraits for the Goldsmiths (of Hugh Myddleton, 1628) and (probably) the Merchant Taylors (of Robert Gray, 1633) of London along with his usual clientele among members of the court circle and the landed classes in general, in some cases quite far afield from London.[84]

Around the same time it became increasingly likely that traditional painter-stainers, men like Randle Holme I and II, would learn to work in these more sophisticated styles and begin to adopt their techniques as well. With the broad turn away from earlier vernacular traditions in the visual arts in general, the heyday of vernacular portraiture, both in itself and as the predominant idiom for civic portraits, had begun to wane in most corners of the realm by the 1620s. Even in the provincial towns and grammar schools which comprised the least sophisticated or affluent of the civic patrons, copies of polite and formal portraits done for a benefactor's family or his London livery company, or those done anew directly for the institution, came rapidly to be preferred to a canvas crudely daubed by a local hand. Yet even then local and regional traditions survived. Locally-based or itinerant painters like Newman of Cambridge and Gilbert Jackson in the early seventeenth century, or the Vicar of Wakefield's limner, 'who traveled the country and took likenesses for fifteen shillings a head' continued to paint on the provincial scene for a long time to come.

NOTES

1 Studies devoted to specific industries in specific regional centres are simply too numerous to note, but helpful general lists or surveys include Sally-Beth MacLean, *Chester Art: A Subject List of Extant and Lost Art Including Items Relevant to Early Drama* (Kalamazoo, Michigan, 1982); Peter Lasko and N.J. Morgan, eds, *Medieval Art in East Anglia, 1300–1520* (1974); Gail McMurray Gibson, *The Theater of Devotion: East Anglian Drama and Society in the Late Middle Ages* (Chicago, 1989), especially chapter 3.

2 Anon., *Exeter and West Country Silver*, Exeter Museums Publication no. 86 (Exeter, 1978), pp. 3–4.

3 See especially William A. Shaw, 'The Early English School of Portraiture', *Burlington Magazine*, 61 (Oct., 1934), p. 171 *et passim*.

4 For distinctions between craftsmen and artisans on the one hand and 'artists' on the other, extending to issues of social status as well as skill and training, see, for example, Emma Barker *et al.*, *The Changing Status of the Artist* (London and New Haven, 1999) and Francis Ames-Lewis, *The Intellectual Life of the Early Renaissance Artist* (London and New Haven, 2000), especially chapters 2–4 and 12.

5 Victor Morgan, 'The Dutch and Flemish Presence and the Emergence of an Anglo-Dutch Provincial Artistic Tradition in Norwich, c. 1500–1700', in Juliette Roding, et al., *Dutch and Flemish Artists in Britain, 1550–1800* (Leiden, 2002), pp. 57–72.

6 See for example, Zirka Zaremba Filipczak, *Picturing Art in Antwerp, 1550–1700* (Princeton, 1987), pp. 22–9.

7 This especially true of Erna Auerbach's invaluable and pioneering survey *Tudor Artists: A Study of Painters in the Royal Service and of Portraiture on Illuminated Documents from the Accession of Henry VII to the Death of Elizabeth* (1954); Edward Croft-Murray, *Decorative Painting in England, 1537–1837* (1962); Roy Strong's 'More Tudor Artists', *Burlington Magazine*, 108:755 (Feb., 1966), pp. 83–5, reprinted in Strong, *The Tudor and Stuart Monarchy* (3 vols, Woodbridge, Suffolk, 1995–98), I, pp. 147–52; Susan Foister's 'Foreigners at Court: Holbein, Van Dyck, and the London Painter-Stainers Company', in David Howarth, ed., *Art and Patronage in the Caroline Court: Essays in Honour of Sir Oliver Millar* (Cambridge, 1993), pp. 32–50, and Foister's *Holbein and England* (London and New Haven, 2004). An important exception to this London and court-centred approach is Andrew Moore and Charlotte Crawley, eds, *Family & Friends: A Regional Survey of British Portraiture* (1992).

8 This tradition stems mainly from two seminal essays: F.J. Fisher, 'London as an Engine of Economic Growth', first published in J.S. Bromley and E.H. Kossman, eds, *Britain and the Netherlands, IV, Metropolis, Dominion and Province* (The Hague, 1971), pp. 3–16, and E.A. Wrigley, 'A Simple Model of London's Importance in Changing English Society and Economy, 1650–1750', *Past and Present*, 37 (July, 1967), pp. 44–70.

9 R.L. Poole, ed., *Catalogue of Portraits in the Possession of the University, Colleges, City and County of Oxford* (3 vols, Oxford Historical Society Publications, vols 57, 1912; 81, 1926; and 82, 1926), I, p. 168.

10 Bristol Record Office, Audit Books, 1624 and 1625, MSS. F/Au/1/19, p. 294 and F/Au/1/20, pp. 25, 30 and 44.

11 See, for example, Victor Morgan, 'The Norwich Guildhall Portraits', in Moore and

Crawley, eds, *Family & Friends*, p. 28, and for the contemporary definitions accorded these terms, see above, p. 11.

12 A troll through the wills recorded in early Stuart Suffolk, for example, reveals that in 1625 Peter Stasey, 'Painter' of Kelsale, Suffolk, left his supplies 'that appertain and belong to the trade of painting' to his brother John, also of Kelsale, and that in 1638 Robert Reyce (aka Ryece), author of the well-known 'Breviary' of his county, left his painting supplies to William Milles, 'painter and glazier of Lavenham' so that he could maintain the work Reyce had done in the parish church. Marion E. Allen, ed., *The Wills of the Archdeaconry of Suffolk, 1625–1626* (Suffolk Record Society 37, 1995), p. 106; Nesta Evans, ed., *Wills of the Archdeaconry of Sudbury, 1636–1638* (Suffolk Record Society 35, 1993), p. 223; C.G. Harlow, 'Robert Ryece [sic] of Preston, 1555–1638', *Proceedings of the Suffolk Institute of Archaeology*, 32 (1973), pp. 43–70.

13 Julian Treuherz, 'New Light on John Souch of Chester', *Burlington Magazine* 139:1130 (May, 1977) pp. 299–307; Karen Hearn, *Nathaniel Bacon: Artist, Gentleman and Gardener* (2005).

14 Virginia Tillyard, 'Civic Portraits Painted for, or Donated to, the Council Chamber of Norwich Guildhall before 1687 with Documentary Evidence relating to the Artistic Background of the City' (MA thesis, Courtauld Institute, 1978), pp. 3–11; Tillyard, 'Painters in Sixteenth and Seventeenth Century Norwich', *Norfolk Archaeology*, 37 (1980), pp. 315–19; Morgan, 'Norwich Guildhall Portraits', pp. 21–30, and Morgan, 'The Dutch and Flemish Presence', pp. 62–6.

15 Tillyard, 'Painters in Norwich', pp. 315–19.

16 Mary Edmond, 'Bury St Edmunds, a Seventeenth Century Art Centre', *Walpole Society*, 43 for 1987 (1989), pp. 111–12. Also based on a site visit to the King's Lynn's Trinity Guildhall, which houses these paintings, and on information kindly provided by David Pitcher on that occasion.

17 Mary Bateson, ed., *Records of the Borough of Leicester*, III (1905), p. 64; Thomas North, ed., *The Accounts of the Churchwardens of St Martin's Leicester* (Leicester, 1884), pp. 67, 70, 72, 78, 79.

18 Helen Stocks and W.H. Stevenson, eds, *Records of the Borough of Leicester* (Cambridge, 1923), p. 377. The reference is slightly ambiguous, as there were two portraits of a Mr Heyricke: one of William, painted in 1594, and one of Robert, done by 1618. Bradshaw may be 'mending and drawing' them both, as the Heyricke names are rendered (in the uncertain orthography of the day) in what may either be a plural or singular form.

19 Lucy Gent, *Picture and Poetry, 1560–1620: Relations between Literature and the Visual Arts in the English Renaissance* (Leamington Spa, 1981), p. 10.

20 Stocks and Stevenson, eds, *Records of Leicester*, p. 412 for 1651–52.

21 Leicester Museum, *Catalogue of Local Portraits* (Leicester, 1956), pp. 12–13; Stocks and Stevenson, eds, *Records of Leicester*, p. 217.

22 Bateson, ed., *Records of Leicester*, III, p. 263; Henry Hartopp, *Register of the Freemen of Leicester, 1196–1770* (Leicester, 1927), p. 89.

23 Hartopp, *Register of the Freemen of Leicester*, p. 108; Stocks and Stevenson, eds, *Records of Leicester*, pp. 12, 109, 126, 157; North, ed., *Accounts of St Martin's Leicester*, pp. 136, 142–3, 149 and 163.

24 Bateson, ed., *Records of Leicester*, III, p. 241.

25 Margaret Statham, ed., *Accounts of the Feoffees of the Town Lands of Bury St Edmunds, 1569–1622* (Suffolk Record Society 46, 2003), pp. lii and 239.

26 *Ibid.*, pp. lii and 239; Henry Peacham, *The Art of Drawing* (1606), pp. 26–7; T.A. Walker, *A Biographical Register of Peterhouse Men* (2 vols, Cambridge, 1927 and 1930), II, p. 294.

27 Edmond, 'Bury St Edmunds', pp. 106–18.

28 In general, see Hearn, *Nathaniel Bacon*.

29 *Ibid.*, p. 30, n. 4, citing PROB 11/152. I am grateful to Karen Hearn for pointing this out.

30 Joanna Moody, ed., *The Private Correspondence of Jane Lady Cornwallis Bacon, 1613–1644* (Madison and Teaneck, New Jersey, 2003), pp. 43, 112, and 292. I am grateful to Karen Hearn for this reference.

31 Bristol Audit Book, 1583, Bristol Record Office MS F/Au/1/12, p. 159.

32 Bristol Audit Book, 1624, Bristol Record Office MS F/AU/1/19, p. 294.

33 Bristol Audit Book, 1625, Bristol Record Office MS F/AU/1/20, p. 44.

34 Brian Frith, *Twelve Portraits of Gloucester Benefactors* (Gloucester, 1972), pp. 5–6 *et passim*.

35 MacLean, *Chester Art*; Maurice H. Ridgway, 'Chester Goldsmiths from Earliest Times to 1726', *Journal of the Chester and North Wales Architectural, Archeological and Historic [sic] Society*, 53 (1966), pp. 1–198.

36 Barry Coward, *The Stanleys: Lords Stanley and Earls of Derby, 1385–1672; The Origins, Wealth and Power of a Landowning Family* (Chetham Society, 3rd series, 30, 1983), pp. 136–8.

37 *Ibid.*, chapter 8; J.S. Morrill, *Cheshire 1630–1660: County Government and Society during the English Revolution* (Oxford, 1974), chapter 1; Joan Thirsk, ed., *The Agrarian History of England and Wales, IV, 1500–1640* (Cambridge, 1967), pp. 80–4.

38 C.H. Collins Baker, 'John Souch of Chester', *Connoisseur*, 130 (1928), pp. 131–3; Treuherz, 'John Souch of Chester', pp. 299–307; Ellis Waterhouse, *Painting in Britain, 1530 to 1790* (4th edn, 1978), pp. 63–4.

39 This and the following are largely based on *ODNB*, *vide* Holme, Randle.

40 Copy of the Company charter, granted in 1536; BL Harleian MS 2054, fol., 88r–89v.

41 BL Harleian MSS 1920–2177, 5955, and 7568–9. Some of this material he inherited from Chaloner; some came into the collection through his sons and grandson, but a great deal of it seems to have been the work of Randle Holme I. See also Lawrence M. Clopper, ed., *Records of Early English Drama, Chester* (Toronto, 1979), pp. xxiv–xxv.

42 Chester Record Office MS ZG 17/1, unpaginated.

43 The latter reference is to British Library, Harleian MS 2093, fols 128–9 and 131. This technique consisted of placing a sheet of paper under the original, pricking holes at critical spots in the outline of the latter, and connecting the dots made by those holes to form the outline of the copy. Sometimes charcoal dust was shaken through the holes to make more visible the dots in the bottom sheet: a technique known as 'pouncing'. See Susan Foister, 'The Production and Reproduction of Holbein's Portraits', in Karen Hearn, ed., *Dynasties: Painting in Tudor and Jacobean England, 1530–1630* (1995), p. 22.

44 E.g., a letter from earl of Derby to Randle Holme I, 16 September 1624, refers to portraits of the barons of the Exchequer at Chester, Chester Record Office MS ML/6/166; an order

of the Painter-Stainers' (etc.) Company refers to 'Sertaine pictures of ancient brethren of the company given to the house for the ornament thereof', Chester Record Office MS ZG 17/1, unpaginated. Surviving Chester civic portraits from this era include those of William Offley and John Vernon, both anonymously done. Others, of Sir Thomas White and Richard Harrison, seem mislabelled. Though a portrait of White painting is listed as being in the possession of the Chester city corporation by 1593, the portrait so-labelled currently in the Town Hall does not resemble the numerous other extant portraits of White. The Harrison painting in the same venue has obviously been done at a later time. A contemporary portrait of William Aldersley, attributed to Robert Peake, did not come into the city's hands until recent times. My thanks to Peter Boughton for showing me these works and discussing them with me.

45 J.W. Goodison, ed., *Catalogue of the Portraits in Christ's, Clare and Sidney Sussex Colleges* (Cambridge, 1985), pp. 35–6.

46 See above, p. 60 and n. 6. The latter provided the drawings for Lady Margaret's tomb in 1513, and so knew her from life. Roy Strong, *Tudor and Jacobean Portraits* (2 vols, 1969), I, p. 20; Foister, *Holbein and England*, pp. 37, 16, 19–20.

47 See, for example, Alan H. Nelson, ed., *Records of Early English Drama, Cambridge* (2 vols, Toronto, 1989), I, pp. 202, 226, 246, 500; II, p. 719; John R. Elliott, et al., eds, *Records of Early English Drama, Oxford* (2 vols, Toronto, 2004), I, pp. 423, 460.

48 Henry Bradshaw, 'On the Collection of Portraits Belonging to the University before the Civil War' [1872], *The Collected Papers of Henry Bradshaw* (Cambridge, 1889) p. 292.

49 See Appendix A.

50 Bradshaw, 'On the Collection of Portraits', p. 292, and Goodison, ed., *Catalogue of the Portraits in Christi, Clare and Sidney Sussex Colleges*, pp. 86–7.

51 Of Bishop Richard Fox, as above, p. 41. See also *ODNB*, *vide* Fox, Richard, and Heinz Archive, National Portrait Gallery, *vide* Fox, Richard.

52 J.N.L. Myers and E. Clive Rouse, 'Further Notes on the Painted Frieze and Other Discoveries in the Upper Reading Room and the Tower Room', *Bodleian Library Record*, 5 (Oct., 1956), pp. 290–308.

53 M.R.A. Bullard, 'Talking Heads: The Bodleian Frieze, its Inspiration, Sources, Design and Significance', *Bodleian Library Record*, 14:6 (Apr., 1994), pp. 465–7.

54 This and the previous paragraph are based on Mary Edmond, 'Sampson Strong', in Jane Turner, ed., *The Dictionary of Art* (34 vols, 1996), 29, p. 781; Poole, ed., *Catalogue of Portraits*, II, pp. xi–xiv; Andrew Clark, ed., *Historical Register of the University of Oxford* (2 vols, Oxford, 1887), II, Part 1, p. 326, and 2:1, p. 175; Ellis Waterhouse, *Dictionary of Sixteenth and Seventeenth Century British Painters* (1988), pp. 257–8.

55 The firmest Strong attribution seems to be for the painting of Sir John Mason, with those of Lionel Bostock, both Geoffrey Barbour and John Howchion (the double portrait known as 'The Bridge Builders'), Peter Bessils and William Bostock (not initially accepted by the institution) possibly Strong's work as well. Arthur E. Preston, *Christ's Hospital Abingdon: The Almshouses, the Hall and the Portraits* (Oxford, 2nd edn, 1930), pp. 30, 45–6, 51; Heinz Archive, 'Abingdon' file.

56 Edmond, 'Sampson Strong', p. 781; Poole, ed., *Catalogue of Portraits*, II, p. xii.

57 Poole, ed., *Catalogue of Portraits*, I, pp. xvi–xxi, and II, pp. xiv–xxiii, 107, 141, 149, 153, 172, 209, 217–19 and plate 27. *ODNB*, *vide* Greenbury, Richard.

58 Sampson Strong the Younger was sworn a member of the city waits in 1629 and *his* son William followed him in 1637/38. Elliott, et al., eds, *REED, Oxford*, I, pp. 481 and 568.

59 Foister, *Holbein and England*, p. 119; Wallace T. MacCaffrey, *Exeter, 1540–1640: The Growth of an English County Town* (2nd edn, Cambridge, Mass., and London, 1975), p. 87; J.J. Anderson, ed., *Records of Early English Drama, Newcastle upon Tyne* (Toronto and Buffalo, 1982), p. x; Alexandra F. Johnston and Margaret Rogerson, eds, *Records of Early English Drama, York* (2 vols, Toronto, Buffalo and London, 1979), *passim*; Records of the Chester 'Company of Painters, Glasiers, Embroiderers and Stationers', Chester Record Office, MS ZG 17/1–2, and Minute Book of the same, Chester Record Office MS CR63/2/131 (1624–51). The charter of the Chester Company recognized that these trades had been operating as a single brotherhood for some time, and that the painters among them were henceforth to be licensed to carry out the work of 'hatching, lymminge, staining and seeling'; BL Harleian MS 2054, fols, 88r–89r.

60 A clear pattern of occupational and familial continuity has been observed for three major monastic communities in Janis C. Housez, 'The Impact of the Dissolutiion of the Monasteries on Patronage Structures in Yorkshire and East Anglia' (Ph.D thesis, McGill University, 1997), *passim*.

61 Susan Foister, 'Foreigners at Court: Holbein, Van Dyck, and the London Painter-Stainers' Company', in David Howarth, ed., *Art and Patronage in the Caroline Court: Essays in Honour of Sir Oliver Millar* (Cambridge, 1993), pp. 37–8; David R. Ransome, 'Artisan Dynasties in London and Westminster in the Sixteenth Century', *Guildhall Miscellany*, 6 (1964), pp. 236–47.

62 See especially 14/15 Henry VIII, c. 2.

63 Laura Hunt Yungblut, '*Strangers Here Among Us': Policies, Perceptions, and the Presence of Aliens in Elizabethan England* (1996), p. 105; Jacob Selwood, '"English-born Reputed Strangers": Birth and Descent in Seventeenth Century London', *Journal of British Studies*, 44:4 (Oct. 2005), pp. 730–41.

64 For the rivalry between London painter-stainers and foreign painters, see especially Foister, 'Foreigners at Court', pp. 32–50.

65 On average, the amalgamated Company consisted of roughly twenty masters at any given time, of which six to eight were 'painters', but they seem to have been the most prominent and dominant occupation within the brotherhood, and to have contributed aldermen to the city government in almost every year. The election of the senior Randle Holme as mayor in 1630 suggests his, and the occupation's, considerable prominence in local affairs. Based on an examination of the Company accounts to 1624, Chester Record Office MS ZG 17/1 (to 1624) and ZG/17/2 (after 1625).

66 Keith Wrightson, *Earthly Necessities: Economic Lives in Early Modern Britain* (London and New Haven, 2000), p. 59.

67 Though the Statute of Artificers of 1563 reinforced the traditional seven-year apprentice-ship, this was sometimes construed as a minimum term. The first of the Randle Holmes apprenticed to the herald-painter Thomas Chaloner of Chester for ten years beginning in January 1588. He served the entire course of that arrangement before being admitted a Brother of the Company in June 1598, paying 40s for his admission, and hosting the traditional dinner for his brethren and their wives in November of that year. Chester Record Office, MS ZG/17/1, unpaginated, *vide* entries for 1587 and for 3 June 1598.

68 See Appendix B. A lucid introduction to the economic and technical aspects of the

painter's craft at this time may be found in Jo Kirby, 'The Painters' Trade in the Seventeenth Century', *National Gallery Technical Bulletin*, 20 (1999) pp. 5–49.

69 The cost of a basket of consumables in southern England is reckoned to have increased fivefold over the course of the sixteenth century and sixfold from the beginning of the sixteenth to the middle of the seventeenth. D.M. Palliser, *The Age of Elizabeth: England Under the Later Tudors, 1547–1603* (2nd edn, London and New York, 1992), fig. 6, p. 153 and table 5.2, p. 164.

70 Hearn, *Dynasties*, pp. 46–7; Foister, *Holbein and England*, p. 99; *ODNB*, *vide* Bettes, John. The word 'table', frequently cited as a surface for painting or writing, had several meanings in this era. When Hamlet says 'Yea, from the Table of my Memory, Ile wipe away all triuiall fond Records' he seems to mean a writing tablet (Shakespeare, *Hamlet*, First Folio [1623] I.5.858–9); and when the accounts of the Grocers' Company of London refer to 'A hangyng table with Sir Thomas Lovells will' in the jewel house of the Company Hall, they may mean a tablet or small board with writing on it, another common usage and replicated in other livery company accounts (Grocers' Company, Wardens' Accounts, Guildhall Library MS 11571/6, fol. 80v). The 'table' could obviously be made of wood as well as paper, for the borough accounts of Leicester record that a carpenter was paid to make a 'table' for a picture, while someone else was paid to paint upon it; Stocks and Stevenson, eds, *Records of Leicester*, p. 217. And when the Royal Household painter Toto del Nunziata was paid in 1530 for painting on the 'olde paynted tablis in the King's prevy closet', he seems to have been re-using already painted wooden panels, thereby saving the cost of priming new panelling; Auerbach, *Tudor Artists*, pp. 17 and 145, as cited in S.J. Gunn and P.G. Lindley, eds, *Cardinal Wolsey: Church, State and Art* (Cambridge, 1991), p. 47. But when Francis Little, one of the governors of Christ's Hospital, Abingdon, had inscribed on the frame of a portrait ('The Bridge Builders', Geoffrey Barbour and John Howchion) which he donated to that institution in 1607, that he 'gave this table', he could only have meant the painting framed therein: one still sees it mounted in the Hospital hall.

71 Foister, *Holbein and England*, pp. 97, 99.

72 Hearn, *Dynasties*, p. 102.

73 *Ibid.*, *Dynasties*, p. 108.

74 As cited in Roy Strong, 'Holbein in England I and II', *Burlington Magazine*, 109 (Dec., 1967), pp. 276–81. Susan Foister expresses some doubt (albeit without explanation or documentation) about this attribution, but also acknowledges that £5 would have been an 'unusually large sum' in 1575. Foister, *Holbein and England*, p. 266.

75 Merchant Taylors' Company, Masters' and Wardens' Account Book, vol. 9, Guildhall Library MS 34048/9, microfilm frame no. 915, for 1606–7.

76 Hearn, *Dynasties*, pp. 188 and 218–19.

77 Ironmongers' Company, Quarter Court Minutes, 29 April 1640, Guildhall Library MS 16967/2, pp. 306 and 318.

78 Further evidence for the stability of civic portrait prices over time may be seen in Appendix B.

79 Hearn, *Dynasties*, pp. 104–5, 108. Only a few have survived.

80 *ODNB*, *vide* Lee, Sir Henry; Poole, ed., *Catalogue of Portraits*, I, pp. 322–3.

81 Courtauld Institute, Witt Library file, 'de Critz, John; National Portrait Gallery, Heinz

Archive, *vide* de Critz; Sidney Young, *The Annals of the Barber-Surgeons of London* (1890), p. 508; and Tittler, 'Three Portraits by John de Critz for the Merchant Taylors' Company', *Burlington Magazine*, 147:1228 (July, 2005), pp. 491–3.

82 Poole, ed., *Catalogue of Portraits*, III, pp. 19–20.

83 *Ibid.*, III, p. 20.

84 *ODNB, vide* Myddelton, Hugh; Heinz Archive, *vide* Myddelton, Hugh; Merchant Taylors' Company, Court Records, Guildhall Library MS 34010/9, fol. 91v; Frederick M. Fry, ed., *A Historical Catalogue of the Pictures, Herse-cloths and Tapestry at Merchant Taylors' Hall* (1907), p. 89 and plate 36; Turner, ed., *Dictionary of Art*, 17, pp. 644–6; The National Galley, *The British School* (1998), p. 432.

Chapter 4

Timing and circumstances

One of the ways in which civic portraiture differed from its personal or courtly counterpart was in the chronology of its appearance. Very few civic portraits in the sense of easel paintings can be identified before the mid-sixteenth-century mark, and we cannot consider civic portraiture a widely established phenomenon until the very last years of the century. This time lag is unlikely to be random; it begs an explanation. It suggests that, just as civic portraiture emanated from different sorts of patrons and occupied different venues than its personal counterpart, it also arose in very different circumstances.

As noted in chapter 1, personal, courtly and especially royal portraits, on panel if not yet on canvas, did appear in England prior to the sixteenth century, but they blossomed especially in the latter half of the reign of Henry VIII. His consolidation of royal authority at Westminster, its effective dissemination over most of his dominions, and its projection in the highly symbolic forms of contemporary visual culture, marked the emphatic arrival not only of a more centralized and forceful royal authority, but also of a highly polemical royal portraiture. With Holbein's considerable help, Henry VIII became an iconic image as well as a powerful monarch.[1]

These years also saw a substantial turnover in the ranks of aristocratic families. Some families died out in the male line, a few nobles were attainted for disloyalty. Henry VII had not systematically replenished vacant peerages, so that there were substantially fewer noble families at his death than at his accession. In order to fill and expand these ranks, reward his followers, and strengthen his support both in the diverse regions of the realm and in the House of Lords, Henry VIII created numerous new titles and offices.[2] The possession and resale of monasteries, religious guilds and fraternities, chantries and similar ecclesiastical endowments provided an ideal means of doing this, creating a larger and more dependent landed elite in the process.

Royal patronage thus came first to challenge and then to overcome traditional regional and local networks of authority based on kinship, retaining and tenancy as the chief source of aristocratic power. By and large, and save for the far northern parts of the realm, Tudor monarchy succeeded in redirecting aristocratic attention from the localities to Westminster.

These circumstances changed the political landscape of the nation in ways which created keen competition for status, recognition and favour among the English landed classes. It created precisely the preconditions for personal self-fashioning through portraiture – 'the frenzied status-seeking ancestor worship of the age' and the attestation to 'the sitter's position and wealth by opulence of dress, ornament, and background' – which the late Lawrence Stone so eloquently described.[3] The fashion for courtly, personal portraits among the landed classes, many of them also striving for iconic status, readily responded to this quest.

The salient conditions which produced a civic portraiture were substantially different. They derived only indirectly from the consolidation of monarchy in the 1530s and 1540s, and more directly from other forces of change characteristic of that era. Humanist-derived visions of the right ordered society, the awareness of continental models of governance, and even the social aspirations of contemporary merchant elites, no doubt played their part, but other factors loomed even larger. One was the religious and the secular aftermath of the Henrician Reformation, in which many of the beliefs and values of the traditional Church were proscribed or revised according to secular and civic requirements. From this followed a second factor: the consequent and only partially successful effort to refound or replace dissolved institutions, including schools and colleges, charitable institutions and religious fraternities, so that their secular functions might be sustained and the common weal continue to be served. Yet another lay in the increasing sense of economic and social malaise, evident by the 1540s and climaxing in the late-Elizabethan years. That malaise seems largely to have been rooted in population growth and other economic factors. But it must also be explained by the surging challenge of early free enterprise capitalism, the threat to guild monopolies and the traditional economic morality which that entailed, and the void in institutional responses which had traditionally been undertaken by the Church.

These myriad circumstances also created a widespread disruption of traditional identities, one which applied to groups of people and to civic institutions as well as to individuals and families. Conventions of belief, status and loyalty, of authority and obedience, of making a living and behaving responsibly, all came up for grabs. The consequent search for refashioned identities and redefined roles, whether on the part of the crown or the cobbler, the individual or the institution, emerged as one of the underlying cultural and social dynamics of the age.

Among their other effects, these underlying circumstances also imparted a sense of urgency to ideas about intervention and reform, and placed increased pressure on governing bodies at every level. English government in these years was indeed, as Norman Jones has noted, essentially local government.[4] The crown had no choice but to depend on 'small knots of reliable men', each in their particular civic institution, to enforce the royal fiat, keep the peace, and maintain stability among those over whom they exercised authority.[5] Particularly by the 1540s, and in some cases sooner than that, crown and parliament began to act on this recognition. They did so by supporting more vigorously than ever before, by charter or statute, the powers of local authority, and by encouraging the foundation and/or fortification of all sorts of intermediate and local governing bodies. That 'multitude of little common weals', as Paul Slack has termed them,[6] included the borough governments, university colleges, grammar schools, charitable institutions, guilds and livery companies. For their part, mayors and aldermen, livery company and college masters, and institutional benefactors strove as best and as innovatively as they could to carry out their responsibilities as the accustomed firmament shifted beneath them, redefining their roles and eliciting loyalty and engendering compliance along the way. The stability of commonweal depended on no less.[7]

Seen in this light the patronage of civic portraiture by these ruling elites cannot be coincidental. Portraits of benefactors and officials both past and present became icons of civic identity and models for civic behaviour. The aldermanic portrait did indeed become the face of the city. This chapter offers a succinct survey of these several contextual factors as they appeared to the civic institutions at hand.

Perhaps the most direct effect on English cultural life in and after the 1540s came about through the extraordinary and substantial destruction of a thousand years of popular belief, institutional foundation, and visual culture fostered by and for the medieval Church. In just a few years' time the very doctrines which had lain at the heart of this culture, including salvation by the performance of good works and pious bequests, the intercessionary powers of the Virgin Mary and the saints, and the very existence of purgatory itself, were ruled erroneous and irrelevant. With them, albeit gradually and incompletely, went many of the attitudes, assumptions, behavioural norms and conventions, civic values and collective memories which had been part and parcel of the old faith. Through the institutional fabric of lay religious bodies like the chantries, religious guilds and fraternities, and ecclesiastical institutions like abbeys, monasteries, and the parishes themselves, these elements had supplied the very foundations of traditional civil behaviour and civic integrity: for philanthropic acts, harmonious social relations, education, social integration, and recognized conventions of civic behaviour.

In addition, by such practices as the periodic reading of the names of deceased parishioners in the bede-roll or of deceased liverymen by the performance of obits, and by the visual depiction of local parish saints and patrons in religious imagery and church fabric, traditional religion had also provided a specific collective memory for both the parish and the local secular community which it embraced. Memories of this sort, along with sundry other mnemonic devices characteristic of European culture prior to the development of printing,[8] became critically important in defining a sense of communal identity. In these and other ways faith did indeed, as Susan Brigden has stated, 'bind the community as nothing else could'.[9] When these mnemonic images and devices were largely obliterated in the course of the Reformation[10] a substantial part of the communal identity went with them, leaving a considerable void to be filled in some more politically acceptable fashion.

In addition to its destructive and disruptive consequences, this complex process created the largest turnover in land-holding since at least the Norman Conquest. It opened the door for myriad new families to join the ranks of the gentry and aristocracy; it allowed institutional bodies (both surviving and refounded or new) and their ruling elites to make strategically important purchases of local properties and other resources.[11] The implications of this round of acquisitions will be noted below, but the social and economic context in which these events took place must first be observed.

The same mid-century era which saw the unfolding of these seismic changes also ushered in a number of severe economic and social pressures of virtually equal consequence. Triggered by the effects of resumed and sustained population growth, with its inflationary pressures on the supply of both food and housing, and by fluctuations in the export market for English wool and woollen cloth, the mid-century years especially witnessed substantial economic and social dislocation. Demographic pressures pushed up food prices, created housing shortages in some, especially urban, areas, and generally depressed wages. Population grew not only in numbers but in mobility, as people now moved with greater frequency from place to place, often searching for employment.[12] These changes coincided almost exactly with the sudden disruption of the traditional imperatives, resources and institutions which had long helped communities and individuals to cope with such circumstances. By throwing many monastic employees out of work, suddenly decreasing the role of monastic communities as consumers, and effectively wreaking substantial changes in land use under new owners, the Dissolutions may even be seen as a further cause of economic upheaval, especially in the short-term. To say the least, this was a challenging time for governing authorities at every level.

The authority of craft and trade guilds and especially the livery companies of London also came under sustained pressure as the burgeoning force of capitalist free enterprise subverted traditional controls on production and trade in order to maximize profit. Given the dramatic and ever-widening differences in population levels and economic complexity between London and provincial towns and cities, in which London's population grew from about 55,000 in 1500 to about 220,000 in 1600,[13] London's livery companies experienced these and additional pressures on a much larger scale and with ever greater intensity than their provincial counterparts.

In consequence of all these factors, English men and women found themselves bedevilled by fears of economic change and dislocation, and of the crime, rootlessness and unrest which seemed to follow: concerns which the popular rebellions of 1536, 1549 and 1569 did little to allay. Crown and parliament were deluged by requests for various forms of support. Some such petitions came from individual towns like Hereford, Warwick and Exeter seeking corporate status, which would allow them to hold newly purchased lands in that more secure form of tenure known as 'mortmain' and to govern them with increased revenues and greater authority.[14] Some came from groups of townsmen and women in places like St Albans, Stafford, Saffron Walden, Higham Ferrars, Wisbech and Louth who sought to refound, or to establish anew, grammar schools and other local social institutions which had been victimized by dissolution.[15] They also came from groups of craftsmen and merchants seeking to formalize or otherwise augment the authority of their livery companies or trade guilds, thus to protect their traditional monopolies of trade or manufacture against unlicensed free-lancers. And influential benefactors of particular religious persuasions, men like Sir Walter Mildmay, sought to found new colleges at the universities, especially, in the sixteenth century, at Cambridge.

The crown readily honoured most of these requests, undertaking from the 1540s onwards what amounted to a large-scale, orderly, and legally sound delegation of governing authority to the ruling elites of local institutions. After but 13 boroughs gained incorporation between 1485 and 1540, no fewer than 44 received such charters between 1540 and 1558, while the total between 1540 and 1640 rose to 149 borough incorporations and 72 re-incorporations in all. Most of these charters in the mid-century decades incorporated towns which had never enjoyed that status before. But the crown later engaged in a second round of incorporating charters so as to strengthen the terms of corporate entitlement already on the books. No fewer than 65 boroughs successfully petitioned in the period 1590–1640 for re-incorporation so as to fortify and expand existing authority.[16] One effect was substantially to expand the number of English towns which enjoyed the kind of autonomous authority long enjoyed by hundreds of towns and cities across the English Channel.[17] Another was to endorse virtually oligarchic powers which, in light of the crown's obsession with order and stability, seemed a highly desirable objective.

As for grammar schools, not quite as many were disrupted by the

Dissolutions as once thought, nor as many refounded thereafter as contemporaries had hoped for. Yet a substantial number *were* refounded, or had their previous endowments confirmed and augmented, in Edward VI's reign especially. Further endowments, foundations and refoundations, all of them entailing a considerable degree of laicization in authority, curriculum and personnel, continued in ensuing decades.[18] Some foundations and refoundations came by letters patent; some by the more formal and extensive authority of a royal charter; some by warrant through the Court of Augmentations.[19] Some such refoundations, like St Albans School in Hertfordshire and Marlborough School in Wiltshire, resulted from the petitions of local townspeople or of the mayors and aldermen who spoke for them.[20] Others came through the efforts of powerful patrons with personal ties to a particular community: men like Richard Platt on behalf of Aldenham School in Hertfordshire, Sir Andrew Judd on behalf of Tunbridge School in Kent, Sir Wolston Dixie on behalf of Market Bosworth in Leicestershire, and Archbishop Robert Holgate on behalf of East Retford in Nottinghamshire and other schools.[21] For the mid-century years of 1540–70 alone Paul Slack has identified the incorporation of forty-one grammar schools just by letters patent, and the similar establishment of seventy-five new or restored almshouses and hospitals.[22]

Livery companies saw a similar empowerment, albeit at a time when their traditional function threatened to disappear under the strong tide of early capitalist free enterprise. To the seventy-eight London companies listed at the beginning of the sixteenth century at least fourteen more were added during the course of that century. At the same time several of the older and better-established companies redefined themselves by merging with others: the Painters and Stainers; Pouchmakers and Leathersellers; Armourers, Bladesmiths and Brasiers; Spurriers and Blacksmiths; Hatters, Cappers and Haberdashers; Fullers and Shearmen (making the Clothworkers); Barbers and Surgeons; and Grocers and Apothecaries.[23]

Though they must be considered a very particular type of civic institution, universities also expanded during this era. Six new colleges were established with royal charters at Oxford (Christ Church, Trinity, St John's, Jesus, Wadham, and Pembroke); and five at Cambridge (Magdalene, Trinity, Gonville and Caius, Emmanuel, and Sidney Sussex).

For its part, parliament responded with similar sensitivity to the requirements of local interests. Social and economic concerns dominated mid- and later Tudor sessions as never before, and as they would not again do for some time to come.[24] In such landmark statues as the Statue of Artificers of 1563 (5 Eliz., c. 4) and the culminating Poor Laws of 1597 (39 Eliz., c. 4) and 1601 (43 Eliz., c. 2) the Tudor regime tried to roll the clock back to defend traditional regulatory measures in the former case and to augment the traditional charitable role of town and parish in the latter. More often than not, statutes such as these invested local officials with additional regulatory powers, thus attending responsively to social and economic issues while inadvertently creating additional burdens of enforcement at the local level.

Local authorities used these new powers in all sorts of ways, presumably the better to govern those over whom they ruled, but also, in practical terms, to fortify their grip as ruling oligarchies. In this vein they encouraged such practices as co-option rather than election of office holders and otherwise restricted full participation in the exercise of authority.[25] This augmentation of authority and responsibility may have seemed necessary under the circumstances, but it created an even more emphatic need to legitimize these ruling elites in the minds of those over whom they held sway. In the event, they had to work earnestly at this goal: their practical ability to govern depended on it.

Legitimacy came from at least two sources. That legal, *de jure*, legitimation conveyed from above by charter or letters patent spoke for itself, but that more practical, *de facto*, legitimation which came from the respect and deference of the governed had constantly to be earned. Mayors of provincial towns and cities, rarely elected by a broad franchise, often found themselves in an especially tight corner. On the one hand they were obligated to enforce royal fiat, parliamentary statute and Privy Council orders in their communities. Yet they also had to retain good personal relations with their families, neighbours and fellow citizens into whose ranks – following conventional terms in office of but a single year – they would all too shortly return. And they had to perform this balancing act while maintaining the dignity of their office.

External relations also weighed heavily for most civic bodies. Corporate borough officials had to defend their authority against manorial lords; county, hundred and royal officials; and even the crown itself. When not contesting turf with rival crafts, provincial trade guilds as well as London livery companies had to fight off economic competition from free-lancers who flouted regulations, set up shop outside the boundaries of guild and company jurisdictions, circumvented the apprentice system, and/or sold their wares or skills below established rates. School and college authorities were sometimes challenged by ecclesiastical officials, as were, on occasion, those who ran the almshouses and hospitals.

These circumstances required a civic culture of deference and loyalty on the part of the governed, a high standard of civic decorum on the part of the governors, and an overall image of political authority, civic virtue and institutional identity for the community itself. Throughout the post-Reformation years urban corporations and other civic bodies developed a variety of strategies to meet these needs Some were adaptations of traditional activities. Others were new in kind. Several examples of such cultural devices will illustrate the point. Taken together they describe much of the ambient political culture of post-Reformation civic bodies. Although the emphasis here remains on the experience of provincial town governing bodies and London livery companies, much the same sort of things could be said of the school, charity or university college, at least the larger provincial guild, and even the crown. All felt similar pressures, and responded in similar ways according to available means.

The first point to be considered here is that broad and deep shift in the very nature of public morality itself, whereby, as Norman Jones has put it, 'a new economy and the new, paternalistic style of government, blessed by an emerging Anglican theology' arose from the ruins of traditional certainties.[26] Where the traditional emphasis on the Seven Deadly Sins, and their attendant visions of purgatory and hell, had formed the basis of Christian social obligation, the new, post-Reformation, scripture-centred order left the individual with a great many more choices and fewer eternal consequences. No longer enforced by quite the same threat of eternal damnation, socially harmonious behaviour had now to be encouraged by persuasion, by the recognition and operation of self-interest, and by both the secular law and those who administered it.

Acceptance of this responsibility motivated local governing authorities to support activities like the public sermon and the endowed lectureship. Both became widespread in the latter years of the sixteenth century, especially in urban environments where progressive Protestantism had established the deepest roots. Myriad more radical communities like Gloucester, Ipswich, Bury St Edmunds and Colchester employed such devices to bring about the moral and political ideal of 'godly rule'.[27] It is surely what the ruling elite of Jacobean Dorchester had in mind when they supported their preacher John White's exhortations to aspire to a higher moral standard, and to a greater respect for their magistracy. White did so in terms of which Calvin himself would heartily have approved.[28]

For those who endorsed this new way of looking at things, the civic body in general and the town and city in particular became the vehicles for moral and social reform among the public at large. Recognizing their responsibilities in that regard, mayors and aldermen came to understand the imperative of inculcating civic behaviour on their fellows, while they themselves strove to become models for civic virtue and guardians of public morality.[29] Town and city gained in moral stature in the process. This new role began to dispel the black cloud under which urban life had long lingered in the wider public view, and it did so at a critically important time. The deep-seated image of the city as a morally suspect environment – avaricious, licentious, disorderly and dangerous[30] – had combined in recent decades with general concerns in English society at large for the decline of traditional charity, hospitality, and other such values.[31] The contrasts in the social perception of the rapacious and unprincipled townsman on the one hand and the virtues of the honest ploughman or country gentleman on the other had grown ever more pronounced, becoming a stock theme of Jacobean city comedy.

Both views can be seen in John Stow's classic *Survey of London*, first published in 1598 and then in a second edition in 1603. Stow's general defence of London as a place of considerable moral accomplishment and potential was also tempered by his sense of a contemporary moral decline, and by his nostalgia for the simpler and more hospitable city of his youth.[32] His observations of a decline in charity and hospitality echoed a long list of other writings to the same effect: part of the 'literature of complaint' which marked the era.[33]

Yet in addition to preachers and religious writers, playwrights and publicists of a younger generation, men like Thomas Dekker, Thomas Deloney and Richard Johnson,[34] also broke with some of their contemporaries in rejecting the negative moral image of the city. They recognized the opportunities implicit in the new order, and the potential for individual advancement and success in realizing them. In so doing they worked at creating a viable legitimation of private enterprise, based on individual virtuosity and unbridled competition. They extolled the achievements of heroic Londoners like Dick Whittington and Sir Thomas White, who rose above their birth-rank, rejected temptation, and employed their individual prowess and courage to make their fame and fortune. These stories presented a more positive view of the city itself as a vehicle for social advancement, but not necessarily at the expense of social harmony or stability.

This literary reconstruction of the moral reputation of the city and its governors also extended in this era to the writing of civic histories. The efforts of the Tudor monarchs to employ polemicists, including historians, in their service almost from the inception of the dynasty have long been recognized.[35] By the end of the century we find provincial townsmen following suit, either on their own initiative or with the encouragement of civic governments, by writing civic histories meant to honour, explain and legitimize particular towns, and by extolling the authority of their ruling elites. These came in a variety of forms. Town chronicles extended well back to an earlier time, but while chronicles of the *nation's* history gave way more rapidly to other forms of historical writing, the frequency and sophistication of *local* chronicles, written for local consumption and often circulated in manuscript rather than published form, may even have accelerated in the sixteenth century and thereafter.[36] Annotated lists of mayors and similar officials became more common at the same time, emerging partly as well both out of the greater concern for local record keeping, and the contemporary humanist emphasis on the deeds of famous men.[37]

By the latter years of the sixteenth and early years of the seventeenth century we find more recognizable prose narratives, set in at least rudimentary interpretive frameworks, and often guided by a close and obvious reading of primary sources. Stow's *Survey*,[38] though not strictly speaking a 'history' at all, again comes readily to mind. His listing of London mayors, and his concern to emphasize the accomplishments of particular Londoners, exemplifies the search for civic heroes who could serve as models for virtuous leadership. William Jaggard's *A View of all the Right Honourable the Lord Mayors of this Honourable City of London* (1601), with its stereotyped woodcut 'portraits' reminiscent of the royal woodcut portraits in John Rastell's *The Pastyme of People* of two generations earlier,[39] works to the same effect. So does the playwright John Webster, in his choice of the Merchant Taylor/philanthropist Sir Thomas White as the centrepiece of his pageant entitled the 'Monument of Charity and Learning'.[40] It is this era which sees enduring legends emerging around figures like Jack Straw, Sir Thomas More, Dick Whittington, and Sir Thomas Gresham. And it is in Thomas Heywood's contemporary play, *If You Know Not Me, You Know Nobody* (1605) where we find the oft-cited example of Alexander Nowell, dean of St Paul's, showing his guests through his own portrait gallery of London civic worthies, much as if he were the lord of the manor displaying images of ancestors in the long gallery of his country home.[41]

Numerous provincial efforts, some of them much more clearly recognizable as histories, must be considered as well. These include, for example, a handwritten and unpublished Elizabethan era history of Wallingford;[42] Dr Taylor's history of Shrewsbury, c. 1570s and 1580s;[43] David Rogers' history of Chester;[44] Thomas Damet's and Henry Manship's of Great Yarmouth;[45] William Sommer's of Canterbury;[46] and the best known of all such works emanating from outside London, John Vowell, alias Hooker's *The Description of the Citie of Excester ...* (c. 1575).[47] Early histories of colleges, schools, and some charitable institutions emerged at about the same time.[48]

These writers went at their tasks with a variety of motives, but virtually all of them offered a highly polemical apologia for the history of their particular institution or town and for the moral rectitude and political legitimacy of its governing powers. Virtually all conveyed gentle or even pointed exhortations to appropriate civic behaviour: to civic harmony and cooperation in the case of towns, to philanthropic initiatives in the case of endowed schools and similar institutions, and to the honour of the institution in all of these particular communities. In celebrating particularly distinguished civic worthies, past as well as present, they created a virtual genealogy of the civic body, enhancing the identity and legitimizing the current leadership and the institution itself as they did so. In these ways they tapped a wellspring of humanist concern which was as ancient as Plutarch's *Lives* and as recent as More's *Utopia*, the latter urging his Utopians to set up statues of virtuous forebears in the market-place so as to glorify their achievements.[49]

Of course not all such efforts were literary in form. Material objects and even defined spaces counted heavily as well. As particular forms of clothing have often served as communicative devices, civic virtues could also, for example, be projected by appropriate attire, especially on the part of the civic elite. Virtually every corporate town and many livery companies seem almost obsessed with the civic raiment of their officers. Though a fuller discussion of this issue has been saved for chapter 5 below, suffice it to say here that school and livery company masters and similar officials were expected to wear whatever gowns were appropriate to their particular institutions, while mayors and aldermen all wore the same style of gown which universally applied to theirs. These were knee-length, fur-trimmed gowns of scarlet or sometimes black velvet, usually with sleeves but sometimes without, and with lace or ruff collars according to contemporary fashions. In schools, colleges, and many charitable institutions the concern for appropriate dress extended from the masters to the pupils or residents as well. In many cases they still do. Mayors and aldermen of particular towns were repeatedly enjoined to wear their appropriate gowns and tippets on public occasions when attending the civic hall and, in some cases, even in their everyday appearance in the very streets.

Particular forms of civic building, and the deliberate creation of a built environment appropriate to political objectives, offer another example of post-Reformation civic culture. Though much work remains to be done on the design, construction and furnishing of livery company and guild halls, on market halls and prisons, on school and college halls, hospitals and many other types of civic edifice, evidence for town halls themselves provides strong indications of how such buildings might be designed and operated to further the civic agenda.[50] Known by various synonyms and hosting a variety of activities having to do with the governance of particular towns, such buildings may be traced as far back as the twelfth century.[51] Yet no earlier period seems to have matched the intensity of town hall construction or reconstruction attained in the period 1540 to 1640. Close to 200 towns in England seem to have undertaken such a project in those years.[52]

Undoubtedly any period of sustained population growth will require an equivalent expansion of its built environment, and so it was in the era at hand. Yet the need for natural expansion or even replacement of derelict buildings, even with the greater availability of former ecclesiastical or guild premises, does not by itself account for the intensity of this activity in these years. We can best explain this striking departure from normal patterns of such building by the augmented need, in those same years, to accommodate the growing authority acquired by local government. Close correlations appear, for example, between hall building and the acquisition of charters of incorporation.[53] In addition, a more complex but equally close correlation may be observed between the acquisition of new halls on the one hand and the development of their decoration, furnishing and other material features intended to proclaim and enhance the governing authority in such towns on the other.

In short, the newly puissant governments of myriad towns and boroughs required a civic hall which would symbolize, in its choice of layout, design, furnishing, iconography and even location, the authority of those who ruled from within. Such buildings thus served as more than augmented office space. They represented the seat and symbol of local authority, and they projected that authority to the community. They served to legitimize both the community and its governing authority by so doing. The ruling elites of these towns designed and operated their halls to meet these ends in various ways. Some strategies were meant to create deferential behaviour: standards of appropriate dress and speech within the hall were strictly enforced. Some were meant to intimidate: many halls came to have their gaol cells built within, or gibbets built near them in times of civic unrest.[54] And several strategies were contrived simply to symbolize the authority of the offices held within and the dignity of the town and its government as a whole.

One way of accomplishing these goals was to pay particular attention to how such halls were furnished. Some specialized furnishings had already appeared in English civic halls before the Reformation, many of them adaptations of ecclesiastical use. But that development accelerated after c. 1540 in pace with the expansion of hall building and civic authority. Of the numerous adaptations of the basic types of furniture, tables, chairs, wall hangings and the like, the most vivid illustration of how this came to be done lies with the evolution in these years of the mayor's chair in the town or guildhall. In earlier times there is but faint indication of any markedly elaborate development of specialized seating for the mayor or analogous presiding officer in the civic meeting place. This may be due in part to a paucity of surviving evidence, but it does seem clear that at the opening of the sixteenth century chairs, and especially arm-chairs, as opposed to benches, stools, pews, and so forth, were reserved for figures of authority. Here they served as 'seats of honour', they were associated with dignity, with formal occasions, with power, much as the bishop's throne would have served in a cathedral.[55] By the latter decades of the sixteenth century mayors and similar officials came regularly to be provided with special seating of their own, and the design and designation of that seat took on characteristic forms appropriate to that role.

Along with the creation of such 'seats of power' within the civic halls of the day were the items of civic regalia displayed within the same buildings. Such objects, including maces, swords and chains of office, hats of maintenance, and arms both of the town and the crown, were by no means new to the post-Reformation era. Yet substantial evidence suggests that such objects proliferated in number, and that they were often linked to the enhancement of particular offices or powers of command, during this same era.[56]

Maces, for example continued to evolve from their initial purpose, as actual weapons of war, to their ceremonial function as symbols of mayoral or other such authority. The smaller, sergeant's mace yielded in many towns to the larger, 'mayor's mace' in the sixteenth century, and thence to the even larger 'great mace' in the seventeenth. By the end of the Elizabethan era some towns had the names or arms of an actual mayor engraved on their maces.[57] Most towns required their mayors to have their maces carried before them by the mace-bearer, not only on official occasions, as is often still done in English corporate boroughs, but also on all occasions when they went forth from their houses.[58] When not being carried forth to convey the symbol of mayoral authority elsewhere, such objects were prominently displayed in the hall, much as the maces of, e.g., Exeter and other corporate towns and cities are today, so that they could be visible to all who entered the hall on civic business. The design and employment of maces in some London livery companies and even in some schools and colleges followed along similar lines and seem to have undergone similarly augmented importance in the civic ceremonial of their institutions. The striking manuscript image of a generic lord mayor of London preceded by his sword-bearer, depicted in 'A Caveat for the City of London', shows us that ceremonial swords worked, and were designed to work, in the same manner as maces.[59]

Finally, the design and layout of town halls, livery company halls and other such 'chambers of authority' came even more often than before to provide dedicated spaces to enhance the authority and dignity of those who governed from within their walls. Over the long run of time, single and undifferentiated halls, such as one may still see in such smaller boroughs as, e.g., Aldeburgh or Banbury, became divided into discrete council chambers and court halls. Mayoral dignity came to be enhanced with the addition of mayors' parlours, as in Leicester, Coventry, Exeter, King's Lynn and Totnes.[60] These rooms probably began as places where the mayor or similar official could have private conversations and carry on official business in a more private setting, but they also became places in which mayoral dignity, and thus the dignity of the corporation, could be displayed to those admitted to the mayoral presence.

All these dedicated spaces became natural areas of display for civic imagery, whether the imposing 1637 mantelpiece in the Mayor's Parlour of Leicester, with its elaborate carved strap-work encircling the borough's arms; the courtroom of the Totnes Guildhall with the arms of Edward VI, who had granted the borough its charter of incorporation, over the mayor's chair; or the small, wainscoted council chamber of Christ's Hospital in Abingdon, where the governors met and still meet, under the watchful gaze of the portraits of founders and early benefactors of that 1555 refoundation. In sum, all the material objects noted above, including halls and their distinctive spaces, presented what Clifford Geertz has termed the 'tangible formulations of the notion of civic authority'.[61]

Though provincial trade and crafts guilds and London livery companies shared many of these elements of institutional celebration, they also had their own devices and emphases. Conviviality within the livery had long served to negotiate the tensions between the ideal of harmony and the reality of hierarchy among its members. These frequent occasions, gradually secularized over the decades after the Dissolutions,[62] were typically marked by feasting and commensality; 'hanging the hall' with banners, lights and greenery; and even some lingering religious observances. A general tendency towards social polarization may have detracted from sociability across the full span of companies' ranks as was once the case. Yet in post-Reformation years such occasions did allow livery company elders to rub shoulders with the great men of the day, both from within the ruling elite of London and also from court and aristocratic circles, and to enhance the honour of their craft by so doing.[63]

The vocabulary by which livery companies' masters were celebrated may not have been quite the same as that which provincial towns employed to celebrate their mayors, there being somewhat less concern with their dress outside formal occasions and with such wands of office as the mayoral mace represented in towns. Yet they were regaled in other ways, and with every bit as much concern for their role in upholding the honour of the institution. Names, and memories, of individual company masters were sometimes commemorated in plate which they donated, or in small temporary 'table' portraits or inscribed lists which were, in some cases, later replaced with the portraits of successors to the same office.[64] By the early 1570s companies like the Mercers commissioned terracotta busts of famous brethren and other Londoners for their halls.[65] Particular pride ensued when a company master became Lord Mayor of London, in which case, as is well known, his company spared no expense in ceremonial observations of the occasion, even extending in time to ceremonial barges and grand processions to trumpet the fact.

The celebratory and commemorative appearance of company halls themselves perhaps drew more often and directly upon roots which were religious and fraternal as opposed to secular and feudal (though many a corporate town also derived its organization from a religious guild and most 'guildhalls' were indeed the halls of former religious guilds or fraternities). In addition, they often drew upon greater material resources to carry out the desired effect. This meant a greater incidence of, e.g., stained glass imagery, painted cloth banners, tapestry, wood carving, napery and plate, than one would have found in the conventional town hall culture of the day.

Taken together, these events and cultural responses in provincial town governments, London liveries and other 'little common weals' gradually negotiated the requirements of reformed belief and the realities of economic and social developments. In so doing, they came to articulate in the civic institutions of the day a revised political culture which was secular, hegemonic, material, mnemonic, and highly visual. Given the perhaps inevitable dissemination of cultural forms from one part of Europe to another, civic portraiture would undoubtedly have come to England in some form, and at some time, whatever the ambient conditions had been. But in reality it is this complex amalgam of events and responses at this particular time which brought the depiction of civic figures to board and canvas, thence to civic display, on to the English scene. It remains now to examine that portraiture itself: to see how the civic portraits of the day served their patrons' needs, and what, as texts of their time and place, they had to say.

NOTES

1 See especially Roy Strong, *Holbein and Henry VIII* (1967); Christopher Lloyd and Simon Thurley, *Henry VIII: Images of a Tudor King* (1990), and Susan Foister, *Holbein and England* (London and New Haven, 2004).

2 Helen Miller, *Henry VIII and the English Nobility* (Oxford, 1986), chapters 1 and 2.

3 Lawrence Stone, *The Crisis of the Aristocracy, 1558–1641* (Oxford, 1965), p. 718, and as above, p. 30.

4 Norman Jones, *The English Reformation: Religion and Cultural Adaptation* (Oxford, 2002), p. 135.

5 The phrase, and the context for it, is Peter Clark and Paul Slack's in *Crisis and Order in English Towns, 1500–1700* (1972), p. 22.

6 Paul Slack, *From Reformation to Improvement: Public Welfare in Early Modern England* (Oxford, 1999), p. 26.

7 For varied and fuller explications of this thesis, see Clark and Slack, eds, *Crisis and Order*, Introduction; Slack, *Reformation to Improvement* (in which these events and responses are seen as well under way before 1540), chapter 1, and Robert Tittler, *The Reformation and the Towns in England: Politics and Political Culture, c. 1540–1640* (Oxford, 1998).

8 See, for example, Frances Yates, *The Art of Memory* (1966); Karol Berger, 'The Hand and Art of Memory', *Musica Disciplina*, 35 (1981), pp. 87–120; Mary Carruthers, *The Craft of Thought: Meditation, Rhetoric and the Making of Images, 400–1200* (Cambridge, 1998); Carruthers, *The Book of Memory: A Study of Memory in Medieval Culture* (Cambridge, 2000); Mary Carruthers and Jan M. Kiokowski, eds, *The Medieval Craft of Memory: An Anthology of Texts and Pictures* (Philadelphia, 2002).

9 Susan Brigden, 'Religion and Social Obligation in Early Sixteenth Century London', *Past and Present*, 103 (May, 1984), p. 71. See also Mervyn James, 'Ritual, Drama and Social Body in the Late Medieval English Town', *Past and Present*, 98 (Feb., 1983), pp. 3–29; Charles Phythian-Adams, 'Ceremony and the Citizen', in Clark and Slack, eds, *Crisis and Order*, pp. 57–85; John Bossy, 'The Mass as a Social Institution, 1200–1700', *Past and Present*, 100 (Aug., 1983), pp. 29–61; Ben McRee, 'Religious Guilds and the Regulation of Behaviour in Late Medieval Towns', in Joel Rosenthal and Colin Richmond, eds, *People, Politics and Community in the Late Middle Ages* (Gloucester, 1987), pp. 108–22 and McRee, 'Charity and Gild Solidarity in Late Medieval England', *Journal of British Studies*, 32:3 (July, 1993), pp. 195–225; and Tittler, *The Reformation and the Towns*, chapter 2, 'The Ethos of Community'.

10 The literature on this is vast, but essential readings include John Phillips, *The Reformation of Images: Destruction of Art in England, 1535–1660* (Berkeley, Los Angeles and

London, 1973); David Knowles, *Bare Ruined Choirs: The Dissolution of the English Monasteries* (Cambridge, 1976); J.J. Scarisbrick, *The Reformation and the English People* (1984); Margaret Aston, 'English Ruins and English History: The Dissolutions and the Sense of the Past', *Journal of the Warburg and Courtauld Institutes*, 36 (1973), pp. 231–55; Aston, *England's Iconoclasts, I, Laws Against Images* (Oxford, 1988); Eamon Duffy, *The Stripping of the Altars: Traditional Religion in England, c. 1400–1580* (London and New Haven, 1992), especially Part II.

11 This and the succeeding paragraph has been summarized from my *Reformation and the Towns*, chapters 4 and 5.

12 This is extensively, if sometimes too enthusiastically, summarized in W.G. Hoskins, *The Age of Plunder: The England of Henry VIII, 1500–1547* (1976), but for a more tempered and balanced view, see also Keith Wrightson, *Earthly Necessities: Economic Lives in Early Modern Britain* (London and New Haven, 2000), especially chapters 5–6.

13 Vanessa Harding, 'The Population of London, 1550–1700: A Review of the Published Evidence', *London Journal*, 15 (1990) pp. 111–28 and Jeremy Boulton, 'London, 1540–1700', in Peter Clark, ed., *The Cambridge Urban History of Britain*, II (Cambridge, 2000), p. 316.

14 Tittler, *The Reformation and the Towns*, pp. 78–9.

15 Tittler, 'The Incorporation of Boroughs, 1540–1558', *History*, 62:204 (Feb., 1977), pp. 35–6.

16 Tittler, *The Reformation and the Towns*, pp. 188–93.

17 Summarized in *ibid.*, especially p. 88.

18 Salient contributions to this discussion begin with A.F. Leach, *English Schools at the Reformation* (1896) and *Schools of Medieval England* (1915), followed by the critique of his views by Joan Simon in *Education and Society in Tudor England* (Cambridge, 1967), and additional contributions by Nicholas Orme, *English Schools in the Middle Ages* (1973), and *Education in the West of England, 1066–1548* (Exeter, 1976); A.R. Morris, 'The Effect upon Schooling in Sussex of the Legislation Dissolving the Religious Houses and Chantries', *Sussex Archeological Collections*, 199 (1981), pp. 149–56; JoAnn Hoeppner Moran, *Education and Learning in the Diocese of York, 1300–1500* (York, 1979), and *The Growth of English Schooling, 1340–1548* (Princeton, 1985); and Tittler, *The Reformation and the Towns*, pp. 131–4 and table V, pp. 352–3.

19 Foundations by both letters patent and charter, as recorded in the Patent Rolls, are more familiar than awards granted through the Court of Augmentations. The latter, applying to the reigns of Edward VI and Mary, may be found in the 'Particulars for Grants', National Archives, Exchequer MS 319, files 1–26 and rolls 1–14; see also W.C. Richardson, *A History of the Court of Augmentations* (Baton Rouge, Louisiana, 1961), pp. 175–7 and the patent creating the commission to investigate the state of schools following the Dissolutions, *Calendar of Patent Rolls, Edward VI*, (6 vols, 1924–29), III, p. 215.

20 *Calendar of Patent Rolls, Edward VI*, V, pp. 33–4; *Victoria History of the Counties of England, Wiltshire*, V (1957), p. 359; and Nicholas Carlisle, *A Concise Description of the Endowed Grammar Schools of England and Wales* (2 vols, 1818), II, p. 744.

21 Carlisle, *Endowed Grammar Schools*, I, pp. 528, 626, 752–3, and II, 280–1.

22 Slack, *Reformation to Improvement*, p. 26 and, more generally, chapter 1.

23 Steve Rappaport, *Worlds within Worlds: Structures of Life in Sixteenth-Century London*

(Cambridge, 1989), p. 25, n. 7; and W. Carew Hazlitt, *The Livery Companies of the City of London* (2 vols, London 1892, repr. 1969), I, *passim*; George Unwin, *The Gilds and Companies of London* (4th edn, New York, 1963), p. 168.

24 The best guides to this aspect of Tudor legislation remain G.R. Elton, *The Parliament of England, 1559–1581* (Cambridge, 1986), and David Dean, *Law-Making and Society in Late Elizabethan England: The Parliament of England, 1584–1601* (Cambridge, 1996).

25 Tittler, *The Reformation and the Towns*, especially chapter 10.

26 Jones, *English Reformation*, chapter 6 and especially p. 137.

27 This large subject is well introduced by works including Patrick Collinson, *The Elizabethan Puritan Movement* (1967); Paul S. Seaver, *The Puritan Lectureships: The Politics of Religious Dissent, 1560–1662* (Stanford, 1970); Patrick Collinson, *The Religion of Protestants: The Church in English Society, 1559–1625* (Oxford, 1982), and *The Birthpangs of Protestant England: Religious and Cultural Change in the Sixteenth and Seventeenth Centuries* (1988), especially chapter 2; David Underdown, *Fire From Heaven: Life in an English Town in the Seventeenth Century* (London and New Haven, 1992); Patrick Collinson and John Craig, eds, *The Reformation in English Towns, 1500–1640* (1998); Tittler, *The Reformation and the Towns*; and Jones, *English Reformation*, especially chapters 5–6.

28 See Underdown, *Fire from Heaven*, especially chapters 2 and 4.

29 Converging approaches to this theme may be found in, e.g., James Knowles, 'The Spectacle of the Realm: Civic Consciousness, Rhetoric and Ritual in Early Modern England', in J.R. Mulryne and Margaret Shewing, eds, *Theatre and Government under the Early Stuarts* (Cambridge, 1993), pp. 157–89; Anna Bryson, *From Courtesy to Civility: Changing Codes of Conduct in Early Modern England* (Oxford and New York, 1998), pp. 24–35 *et passim*; Slack, *Reformation to Improvement*, chapters 1–2.

30 Among a wide literature on this subject, see especially Lawrence Manley, *Literature and Culture in Early Modern London* (Cambridge, 1995), especially chapter 2; John McVeagh, *Tradeful Merchants: The Portrayal of the Capitalist in Literature* (1981); Alexander Leggat, *Citizen Comedy in the Age of Shakespeare* (Toronto, 1973); Laura Stevenson O'Connell, 'Anti-Entrepreneurial Attitudes in Elizabethan Sermons and Popular Literature', *Journal of British Studies*, 15 (1976), pp. 2–20.

31 In her definitive work on the subject, Felicity Heal notes the continuity of some forms of hospitality over the span of the early modern period, along with the institutionalization of alms-giving and other forms, but also documents the widespread perception of a decline among many contemporaries. Heal, *Hospitality in Early Modern England* (Oxford, 1990).

32 Charles Lethbridge Kingsford, ed., *A Survey of London by John Stow, Reprinted from the Text of 1603* (2 vols, Oxford, 1908), I, pp. 89–91, 148, 154, 198 (hereafter Kingsford, ed., *John Stow's Survey*); Ian Archer, 'The Nostalgia of John Stow', in D. Smith et al., eds, *The Theatrical City* (Cambridge, 1995), pp. 17–34; Patrick Collinson, 'John Stow and Nostalgic Antiquarianism in Early Modern London', in J.F. Merritt, ed., *Imagining Early Modern London: Perceptions and Portrayals of the City from Stow to Strype, 1598–1720* (Cambridge, 2001), pp. 27–51.

33 Summarized in Manley, *Literature and Culture*, especially pp. 91–8.

34 Stow was born in 1525, Deloney in 1543 – only eighteen years later but *after* the break from Rome and the dissolution of the monasteries – Dekker in 1570, and Johnson c. 1573.

35 Foundational explorations of this issue include W. Gordon Zeeveld, *Foundations of Tudor Policy* (Cambridge, Mass., 1948); F. Smith Fussner, *The Historical Revolution: English Historical Writing and Thought, 1580–1640* (1962); Arthur B. Ferguson, *The Articulate Citizen and the English Renaissance* (Durham, North Carolina, 1965), pp. 192–4; F.J. Levy, *Tudor Historical Thought* (San Marino, California, 1967); Antonia Gransden, *Historical Writing in England* (2 vols, 1982), II, chapter 14.

36 Ralph Flenley, ed., *Six Town Chronicles of England* (Oxford, 1911); Alan Dyer, 'English Town Chronicles', *Local Historian*, 12:6 (May, 1977), pp. 285–91; D.R. Woolf, 'Genre into Artefact: The Decline of the English Chronicle in the Sixteenth Century', *Sixteenth Century Journal*, 19:3 (Fall, 1988), pp. 321–54, and Woolf's sweeping and definitive study *The Social Circulation of the Past: English Historical Culture, 1500–1700* (Oxford, 2003).

37 See, for example, 'Escutcheons of the Bailiffs and Mayors of Shrewsbury', uncatalogued manuscript in the Library of Shrewsbury School, for access to which I am grateful to Mr James Lawson and Dr Michael MacCarthy-Morrogh of Shrewsbury School. Other examples include Henry Hartopp, ed., *Roll of the Mayors of the Borough and Lord Mayors of the City of Leicester, 1209–1935* (Leicester [1935]); 'A List or Catalogue of all the Mayors of the City of York', BL Harleian MS 6115; 'Majores Villae et Burgi de Grimesby Magna in Com Lincoln', BL Lansdowne MS 207(a), fols, 272–5; 'A Biographical List of the Mayors ... of Southampton from 1498', BL Egerton MS 868; Salisbury Borough Archives, Wiltshire County Record Office MS G23/1/235; King's Lynn Mayoral List, untitled, BL Add. MS 8937; J.W.F. Hill, 'Three Lists of the Mayors, Bailiffs and Sheriffs of the City of Lincoln', *Associated Architectural Societies' Reports and Papers*, 39 (1928–29), pp. 217 ff., as cited in Peter Clark, 'Visions of the Urban Community: Antiquarians and the English City before 1800', in D. Fraser and A. Sutcliffe, eds, *The Pursuit of Urban History* (1983), p. 107, n. 7; and the remarkably large number produced in the City of Chester, as described in Lawrence Clopper, ed., *Records of Early English Drama, Chester* (Toronto, 1979), pp. xxxvi–xliii.

38 Kingsford, ed., *John Stow's Survey*.

39 *Ibid.*, I, pp. 104–17 and II, pp. 147–86; William Jaggard, *A View of all the Right Honourable the Lord Mayors of this Honourable City of London* (STC 14343, 1601); John Rastell, *The Pastyme of People: The Cronycles of Dyvers realmys and most specyally of the realme of Englond brevely co[m]pylyd* (STC 20724 [1529]). My thanks to Susan Foister for bringing Rastell to my attention.

40 John Webster, *Monuments of Honour* (1624), in F.C. Lucas, ed., *The Complete Works of John Webster* (6 vols, 1927), III, pp. 333–4. I am grateful to Lawrence Manley for bringing this to my attention.

41 *The Dramatic Works of Thomas Heywood* (6 vols, 1874, repr. New York, 1964), I, p. 276. As cited in Manley, *Literature and Culture*, p. 129 and elsewhere. We cannot consider these fictitious portraits 'civic', as they were displayed in Nowell's own residence. Yet both 'guests' and 'sitters' were certainly civic figures, and some of them were the subjects of civic portraits in the full sense of the term. 'Guests' were Sir Thomas Gresham, Sir Thomas Ramsey and Lady Mary Ramsey, and 'Hobson the Merrie Londoner', of whom contemporary portraits exist of all but Hobson. Those 'depicted' included the former lord mayors Sir John Filpot, Sir Richard ('Dick') Whittington, and Sir John Allen, plus the benefactresses Agnes Foster and Anne Gibson. Contemporary portraits certainly existed for Gresham, both Sir Thomas and Lady Mary Ramsay (at Christ's Hospital, Horsham) and possibly John Allen (whose undated portrait was recorded in the Haberdashers' Hall in 1802). See George Perfect Harding, 'A List of Portraits, Pictures in

Various Mansions of the United Kingdom', unpublished manuscript, Heinz Archive, National Portrait Gallery (3 vols, 1804), II, p. 133.

42 Wallingford Borough Archives, Berkshire County Record Office MS W/AC1/1.

43 Uncatalogued manuscript in the Library of Shrewsbury School. My thanks again to James Lawson and Michael MacCarthy-Morrogh for access to this document.

44 Rogers compiled five successive editions of this work between c. 1609 and 1637, none of which have been published in their entirety. See Clopper, ed., *REED, Chester*, pp. 232–54.

45 Thomas Damet, 'Greate Yermouthe: A Book of the Foundacion and Antiquitye of the Saide Towne … ', written c. 1594–97 but not published until 1847; Henry Manship, *The History of Great Yarmouth*, written c. 1619 and first published in Great Yarmouth, 1854, both edited by Charles James Palmer. See Paul Rutledge, 'Thomas Damet and the Historiography of Great Yarmouth', *Norfolk Archaeology*, 33 (1965), pp. 119–30 and Rutledge, '"Thomas Damet and the Historiography of Great Yarmouth"', *Norfolk Archaeology*, 34 (1969), pp. 332–4; Robert Tittler, 'Henry Manship: Constructing the Civic Memory in Great Yarmouth', in *Townspeople and Nation, English Urban Experiences, 1540–1640* (Stanford, 2001), pp. 121–39.

46 William Sommer, *Antiquities of Canterbury* (1640).

47 Hooker, alias John Vowell, *The Description of the Citie of Excester* … [c. 1575], eds, W.J. Harte, et al. (Devon and Cornwall Record Society, 3 vols, 1919–47).

48 See, for example, Francis Little, *A Monument of Christian Munificence, or An Account of the Brotherhood of the Holy Cross, and of the Hospital of Christ in Abingdon* [1627], ed., Claude Delaval Cobham (Oxford and London, 1871); John Caius, *De Antiquitate Cantabrigiensis Academiae* (1568) and J. Josselin, *Historiola Collegii Corporis Christi*, ed., J.W. Clark (Cambridge Antiquarian Society, 17, 1880).

49 Phil Withington, *The Politics of Commonwealth: Citizens and Freemen in Early Modern England* (Cambridge, 2005), p. 54, citing Thomas More, *Utopia*, eds, George M. Logan and Robert N. Adams (Cambridge, 1998), p. 84.

50 The following summary is largely based on my *Architecture and Power: The Town Hall and the English Urban Community, c. 1500–1640* (Oxford, 1991).

51 *Ibid.*, p. 12.

52 The current tabulation, subject to further findings, is that 178 of the approximately 650 to 700 towns extant in England at that time may be certified as having built a total of 202 town halls in the period 1500–1640. In addition, there is at least some evidence that an equal number *may* have done so, but for which documentation remains incomplete. *Ibid.*, pp. 10–17, 160–8.

53 *Ibid.*, table V and pp. 89–91.

54 *Ibid.*, pp. 122–8.

55 John Gloag, *The Englishman's Chair: Origins, Design and Social History of Seat Furniture in England* (1964), p. 41; S.W. Wolsey and R.W.P. Luff, *Furniture in the Age of the Joiner* (1968), p. 69; R. Tittler, '"Seats of Honour, Seats of Power": The Symbolism of Public Seating in the English Urban Community, c. 1560–1620', *Albion*, 242 (Summer, 1992) pp. 205–23.

56 Tittler, *The Reformation and the Towns*, pp. 272–5.

57 Tittler, *Architecture and Power*, pp. 108–9; G.W Eustace, *Arundel: Borough and Castle* (1922), p. 255; J.H. Matthews, *A History of the Parishes of St Ives, Lelant, Towednack and Zennor in the County of Cornwall* (1892), p. 194.

58 Tittler, *Architecture and Power*, pp. 108–9.

59 Anon., 'A Caveatt for the City of London', Folger Shakespeare Library MS VA 318, as reproduced in Ian W. Archer, *The Pursuit of Stability: Social Relations in Elizabethan London* (Cambridge, 1991), dust jacket and R. Tittler, 'Freeman's Gloves and Civic Authority: The Evidence from Post-Reformation Portraiture', in *Costume* 40 (2006), p. 18.

60 Tittler, *Architecture and Power*, pp. 35–7, 42, 45, 112–14, 117–18.

61 Clifford Geertz, *The Interpretation of Cultures* (New York, 1973), p. 91.

62 The gradual secularization within the liveries is best described in Jones, *English Reformation*, pp. 111–15.

63 One of the best and most succinct summaries of the ceremonial activities of the liveries in general may still be found in Unwin, *Gilds and Companies*, especially chapters 11, 13 and 18. See also Archer, *The Pursuit of Stability*, pp. 116–20, which emphasizes both the lavish scale of such feasting, and the growing tendency to exclude the lesser ranks from it.

64 Sidney Young, ed., *The Annals of the Barber-Surgeons of London* (London, 1890), pp. 508–10. These seem to have been the Tudor equivalent of small photographs, which were placed forty or so in a 'table'. For the varieties of meaning held by this term, see chapter 3, n. 70.

65 Jean Imray, *The Mercers' Hall* (London Topographical Society Publication no. 143, 1991) p. 20.

Chapter 5

Content and meaning

It should already be clear that personal and civic portraits emanate from different motives, different ambient circumstances, and different sorts of patrons. If we consider the portrait as a text, it is therefore not surprising that civic portraits had different things to say than personal portraits. The visual repertoire which Joanna Woodall has described as 'the courtly console tables, wooden chairs, curtains, columns, helmets and handkerchiefs', and including such subordinate figures as 'dogs, dwarfs, servants, jesters and black attendants', may have become the common vocabulary of personal portraits, but its components were rarely employed in the civic idiom.[1]

Portraits commissioned directly by the civic institution would have had no particular need to illuminate characteristics of birth, marriage, personal wealth, residence, family, feudal or chivalric service, or military prowess, the qualities represented by the symbolic devices in Woodall's list. Considering how pervasive such images became in mainstream portraiture by the end of the era at hand, one might well wonder what there might be left to show in portraits intended for civic purposes. The answer lies in a symbolic vocabulary which was certainly narrower and often less visually engaging, but which was nevertheless especially constructed to serve the aims of civic patronage. And as there were several types of civic institution commissioning portraits, so were there different emphases in the use of that vocabulary to suit particular needs. Portraits of provincial mayors and aldermen, for example, might have conveyed slightly different messages than those of London livery company masters; portraits of college founders and benefactors often bore still other messages.

Whatever the message, and however much it differed from the conventional personal portrait type, it had still to be accessible to its intended viewers. And, in part because of the frequent lack of skill among civic portrait painters, such practitioners developed a textual vocabulary of symbolic devices and inscriptions which conveyed the civic virtues of the sitter when those virtues could not be communicated by any more subtle means.

This chapter investigates the content and meaning of civic portraits, once again in implicit contrast to their personal counterparts. It will consider the question of verisimilitude, explore their most common symbolic devices (especially regarding dress, gloves, books, scrolls and skulls), and discuss the use of inscriptions before concluding with observations about the mnemonic content of these sundry devices. Once again, if we think of these portraits as texts, this chapter explores their content and vocabulary.

VERISIMILITUDE

We tend to assume that one of the prime tasks of any portrait is to show what the sitter looked like. This was certainly central to Thomas Whythorne's concerns: he who wanted a record not only of his appearance of the moment but also of how his appearance had changed through the years.[2] It remains more or less true to our own concerns. Yet this is not an assumption we can always bank on when it comes to civic portraits, especially in their earlier, vernacular form.

As noted in the Introduction, and notwithstanding more formal models introduced into the social and cultural mainstream by Holbein and others, most civic portraits done outside the London area, and many done within, remained largely artisanal and vernacular, sometimes altogether naive, at least to the end of the sixteenth century. Most lack any consistent engagement with what we would consider naturalistic portrayal: their creators simply lacked the skills which would have allowed them to do so. Very good examples of this vernacular quality may be found in the twelve civic portraits done of Gloucester founders and benefactors, all of them anonymously produced, and all probably completed – judging by elements of costume and by local attribution – somewhere between the 1590s and c. 1620. These include portraits of Sir Thomas Bell, John Falkner (fig. 2), Joan Goldston, William Goldston, John Haydon, Richard Pate, Thomas Poulton, John Thorne, Isabel Wetherstone, Sir Thomas White, Gregory Willsheire, and the double portrait of John and Joan Cooke (fig. 3). Save for this last, all hang today – appropriately enough – in the Gloucester Folk Museum rather than the Gloucester City Museum and Art Gallery.

By the time the tide began to turn towards more formal, sophisticated and aesthetically accomplished work at the opening of the seventeenth century, networks of extended artisanal families and workshops of foreign-born or trained craftsmen had become well established in London, and could readily be drawn upon for work of this sort. Regional craftsmen continued to pursue their artisanal traditions in several provincial centres thereafter, but civic portraits produced outside London began by the early decades of the seventeenth century to catch up to the emerging stylistic sophistication of their London counterparts. This transmission of the more sophisticated styles, and the greater concern for verisimilitude which they exhibited, came in part as foreign-trained painters became more widely employed outside the metropolis, and as the more stylistically sophisticated personal portraits of London liverymen came to be copied for display in the schools and other institutions which a number of them founded elsewhere in the country.[3]

By the last years of our period vernacular painting could certainly still be found outside London and the larger provincial centres. It would survive for a long time to come. But the stylistic format and technical expertise of both civic and personal portraits undeniably came much closer together. While different levels of skill continued to apply, some degree of verisimilitude, and the techniques which permitted it, became common features of both types by the 1630s. Concurrent with developments in scientific activities and mensuration in the same era, some portraits now even took care faithfully to portray blemishes and deformities. The portrait of Sir Richard Dobbs, benefactor of Christ's Hospital, now in Horsham, clearly shows the wart on the bridge of the sitter's nose despite the clearly vernacular character of the whole. That of the puritan preacher William Perkins held by Sidney Sussex College, Cambridge, done shortly before 1639, accurately depicts his deformed right hand.[4]

Yet despite this tendency for civic portraits to come gradually closer to the stylistic mainstream of their time, precise verisimilitude, especially in the early decades and in provincial settings, simply remained less important for a longer time in the civic portrait than in the personal. This distinction had little to do with the sitter's social status, nor was it meant to suggest that sitters outside the ranks of courtly or landed society would not personally have cared what their portraits looked like as much as those within those ranks. Whythorne's testimony suggests just the opposite.[5] Men and women well down into the middling ranks of society were having their portraits painted for personal reasons, and demanded accurate likenesses, even by the mid-sixteenth century. Then, too, it is entirely conceivable that some people will have sat for both civic and personal portraits. Yet unless one portrait had been copied from the other, it remains unlikely that they would have been painted in quite the same manner or with the same objectives in their civic guise as in their personal.

In addition to factors of skill, the lesser attention to verisimilitude in civic portraiture stems from this distinction in form and intent. Particularly in the early years of the genre some civic figures served more or less as dressmakers' dummies on which the appropriate symbols of office or mnemonic icons could be displayed. In this casual regard for precise representation early civic portraits resembled some of the written civic histories of the same early era. As Daniel Woolf has aptly put it, 'When the historian spoke of the "truth" of histories, he meant their moral as much as their factual veracity.'[6] This was especially so in those quite numerous civic portraits done of figures long deceased, but whose examples of civic service or benefaction had become important in this era to recall and to celebrate. It would simply have been impossible to recapture the actual appearance of such figures. Who could really know if Lady Godiva had blond hair or brown, dimpled knees or rounded, when she was painted in 1586? And what did it matter?

DRESS: ROBES OF OFFICE

What *did* matter was whether the subject looked the part. 'Looking the part' meant wearing the clothing, chains and badges of office, and holding the objects, which identified the sitter's civic standing and contribution, and thus conveyed the intended meaning of the whole. And although mere lay benefactors, as opposed to office holders, may not have been dressed in any distinctive livery – or, in Godiva's case, not dressed at all – it is the gown or robe which is the most obvious feature of the civic official.

Masters of schools and livery companies, and officials of colleges, often wore gowns of one sort or another. From at least the mid-fifteenth century on mayors and aldermen of both London and provincial towns wore the 'standard issue' ankle-length gown. Mayors' gowns were most often of scarlet, though gowns of London lord mayors underwent several colour changes, by official decree, during the course of the fifteenth century, with black, violet or green being common alternatives.[7]

Aldermanic gowns were very similar to mayoral gowns in cut and style. They were also often red of either scarlet or crimson hue, but as numerous ordinances confirm, and as Lucas de Heere shows in his mid-Elizabethan manuscript depiction of the generic type of both gowns, they could also be of a different colour.[8] The intriguing series of ink and watercolour depictions of London aldermen produced by Roger Leigh in the mid-fifteenth century shows his subjects wearing gowns similar in most respects to the mayoral version of the following century (fig. 4).[9] A red over-gown, clasped at the shoulder, lies swept back over the left arm in all the figures to reveal a lighter-coloured (usually red), ankle-length robe below. This is cinched by a long belt at the waist, hanging quite far down from the buckle. There are no ruffs or lace collars, the ruff especially having come into common use only in the second half of the sixteenth century. Each figure in Leigh's series save for Thomas Pomeroy, the tonsured prior of Holy Trinity, wears a hat. These hats varied widely in style and colour, were much larger and more elaborate than their successors of the next century and, in any event, probably should not be counted as part of the official dress. None of the aldermanic gowns were trimmed with fur down the front, a distinction probably still reserved for lord mayors and sheriffs, though the pattern drawn on the inner lining of the outer-robe may be meant to indicate fur.

We do have one late fifteenth-century painting of the mayor and aldermen of a provincial town to show that the sixteenth-century dress style of those officials had begun to appear at least by the 1480s. This is not an easel portrait, but rather the illumination-style painting on a page of the Bristolian Robert Ricart's late fifteenth-century book on civic government in that politically precocious centre, 'The Maire of Bristowe is Kalendar' (fig. 5).[10] Ricart's representation of the swearing-in of the mayor of Bristol before the out-going mayor, aldermen, and other officials shows both the familiar mayoral robe and its distinctive crimson or scarlet colour with fur trim which we see elsewhere by that time and which, indeed, is still (or perhaps once again) widely in use today. Oddly, Ricart's figures wear no hats, though this may have been a local anomaly, and, unlike some other examples, Bristol's lesser officials wore red as well.

We may take most of these characteristics to represent prototypes of the mayoral and aldermanic robes shown in our civic portraits of the following century, though the colour coding of lesser officials' dress was often more complex. Tudor mayors of Exeter, for example, wore both gowns and cloaks of scarlet, the cloaks being lined with sarcenet, and so did that city's recorders and sheriffs. But the stewards wore violet-coloured gowns and the aldermen sported gowns of violet or a deeper, mulberry shade known as murrey.[11] In Oxford's Accession Day celebrations of 1530, and presumably in more secular civic occasions thereafter, the mayor, ex-bailiffs and ex-chamberlains wore scarlet robes, but the common councillors wore gowns of murrey. In Great Yarmouth what was referred to as the 'ancient and honourable custom of the town' in 1542 had the bailiffs (equivalent, in Yarmouth, to mayors) and ex-bailiffs wearing scarlet gowns trimmed with fur. Orders affirming similar dress appeared in Wells (1547), Leicester (1585) and other towns as well.[12] In Kendal, aldermen wore black gowns for ordinary occasions but violet ones for special occasions. The jurats of Faversham – the local term for the executive officers of that Kentish town – wore black, while the mayor and aldermen of Newbury and Preston wore gowns of blue.[13] Whatever the colour of the day, mayoral gowns were usually trimmed with fur, with a lace or ruff collar according to contemporary fashion. They were often topped off with conspicuous chains of office. Chains worn by the lord mayors of London were distinguished by the device of a double 's' at intervals in the length of the chain.

Mayors and aldermen thus dressed would have been a common sight for any townsman or woman of the time. It seems hard to find a borough assembly book of the sixteenth or early seventeenth century which does not regularly remind all mayors and aldermen to don their civic dress when 'going abroad', at least to civic functions, and in some towns they were expected to do so at all times. By 1560 the aldermen of Elizabethan Chester, for example, were constantly reminded 'to come in decent and orderly sort' in their gowns and tippets to church every Sunday, and to every meeting of the city council. Sheriffs were enjoined to wear their official dress when going anywhere at all outside their own homes during the entire term of their office. As obedience to this expectation began to wane, the Chester city council extended this injunction to election days and other red-letter moments on the civic calendar, adding that aldermen were to wear murrey gowns, and all freemen were to come in their best attire.[14]

As Ricart records in his illustration, Bristol mayors and other officials obviously wore their civic raiment at mayor-making ceremonies in the late fifteenth century and probably long before. But by stages during the course of the sixteenth century Bristol officials were also enjoined to wear their civic dress on holidays and fair days (1563), when on business in the Tolzey, Guildhall or Council House, and when accompanying the mayor to burials, sermons, weddings, and other special occasions (1570). Even the wives of Bristol's former mayors and sheriffs were required to wear scarlet gowns when their husbands did (also 1570), and by 1598 councillors had to wear caps and not hats when attending the mayor unless specifically exempted from so doing.[15]

The expectation that the wives of mayors, both past and sitting, would also wear scarlet or crimson dress, extended to numerous other towns as well, and seems to have been common even in the fifteenth century.[16] Though Bristol's constant concern for dress regulations remains better documented than that of most towns and cities, the concern itself seems virtually universal at this time.

As indicated by the fines which were incurred by negligent officials, this etiquette of official dress was no empty gesture. It reflected gravely on the honour of the community itself. The civic livery bore the symbolic power to transform the layman into the civic official, and thus to invoke the mystery and memory of the institution. It also represented the civic authority, not only of the individual wearer, but of the town or city. As the London writer John Earle remarked about a London alderman in 1622,

> He is Venerable in his gowne ... wherewith he setts not forth so much his owne, as the face of a City ... His Scarlet gowne is a Monument, and lasts from generation to generation.[17]

The concept of the mayoral or aldermanic gown being a monument and lasting from generation to generation must also be considered carefully. As Ann Rosalind Jones and Peter Stallybrass have shown, clothing, like the portrait itself, does have the power to remind.[18] The continuity of gown-wearing by mayors and other officials over the long haul did certainly emphasize the continuity, and thus the stability, of the civic community and its governing authority. In places like Totnes, King's Lynn and Exeter, it still does so.

Contemporaries clearly considered it important to uphold this etiquette throughout this era, and there are some indications that the frequent injunctions for mayors and aldermen not to go 'abroad' without their official dress corresponded with times of particular stress in specific places. Certainly this is the case with London,[19] and also for provincial towns and cities like Boston and Chester, whose regulations to that effect have been noted above. Boston officials, anxious to establish the legitimacy of their newly won corporate status after lingering for centuries under the tight control of the local monastery, actively sought to adopt devices working to that effect. After their borough incorporation in 1545, Boston borough officials rapidly sought to adopt the forms and customs appropriate to their new status. One of their earlier ordinances was for the members of both borough councils, the Twelve and the Twenty-four, to come 'in a decent order in their gownes like Townes men of such a corporation at all tyme and tymes when ther dewties is to be at the Guildhall'.[20]

For Chester, as for many other, especially western, towns, the mid–1590s were years of severe crisis. It experienced sharply elevated food prices even to the threat of famine, the rigours of serving as a prime staging point for English troops being sent to fight in the Irish War, and the civic unrest associated with several thousand troops embarking for or returning from the war. The extraordinary steps which the city took to combat those perils, and both to restate and restore civic authority, have been treated in detail elsewhere.[21] But one cannot help but note that the injunctions to wear proper official raiment, in effect to flaunt something tantamount to the civic flag, came emphatically at this same time.

As for setting 'not forth so much his owne, as the face of a City', there would be little point in a portrait commissioned by a civic body showing the sitter in his own clothes or with objects reflecting his personal as opposed to his civic career. Civic portraits like John Vernon's, initially commissioned by the sitter and then given to the institution, present exceptions to this practice. Their civic nature depended largely on their acquisition by the institution and their display in the civic surroundings of that body. Yet that purer form of civic portrait commissioned by the institution itself would almost always display the official raiment.

In fact, given the deep-seated contemporary English ambiguity about the moral and social standing of the merchant, and the reality that most English civic portraits of this age depicted members of the merchant elites,[22] it might well even have been counter-productive and irrelevant for civic-commissioned portraits to show the sitter in the context of his personal life or occupation. Northern European merchants, who enjoyed a much more secure position in their ambient societies, had no such concerns. Holbein's depiction of Hanseatic merchants typifies the general Northern European tendency to display the full range of occupational artefacts. Thus he shows us George Gisze in his counting house with all sorts of objects connecting him to the mercantile life.[23] But civic portraits of individual English people, by contrast (of which there are none which can be confidently attributed to Holbein), strove to indicate what a man or woman might have done with their money while remaining coy about how they had earned it.

Excluding the almost invariable depiction of books in the hands of university scholars, who were not merchants, there remain but few exceptions to this convention. The 1603 St John's College, Oxford, portrait of its early benefactor George Benson, a London Merchant Taylor, does depict merchant ships over the sitter's right shoulder.[24] A merchant ship also appears under the identifying inscription of the 1625 posthumous portrait of Robert Thorne, merchant and eventually mayor of Bristol and co-founder of the Bristol Grammar School.[25] William Portington, Master Carpenter in the King's Works and Master of the Carpenters' Company, is portrayed at age 81 in 1626 with his rule and calipers.[26] But in general, the convention of camouflaging mercantile or artisanal identities held firm. Violations risked the sort of censorious remark of John Weever who, as late as 1630, rued the apparent fact that '[in] some of our epitaphs more honour is attributed to a rich quondam Tradesman, or griping usurer, then [sic] is given to the greatest potentate entombed in Westminster'.[27] Despite the admiration for mercantile enterprise expressed by such playwrights as Dekker or Heywood, it would be a long while before overt references to commercial and maritime activities became a widely accepted feature of English civic portraiture.

As it happens, an outpouring of social and economic legislation and letters patent in the mid-sixteenth century considerably boosted the authority of civic officials in governing their communities. As most such officials were merchants, this also enhanced the social standing and reputation of that status group. It is worth noting in this regard that the sumptuary legislation passed throughout this period allowed mayors, aldermen, heads of colleges and charitable institutions, and often their wives as well, to wear materials and forms of dress otherwise reserved for the aristocracy and upper gentry: privileges which would not ordinarily have applied to merchants in their own right.[28] Towards the same end, it became customary during the sixteenth century for the crown to recognize the social standing of London Lord Mayors by knighting them upon accession to their office. Though his term of office lasted but a year, a mayor or Lord Mayor's social elevation, and the sartorial distinctions marking that status, remained with him ever after. The tendency of some such civic officials to have themselves depicted in official dress on their funeral monuments emanates from the same objective: they wished to be remembered as having attained the status to which office-holding, if not occupation alone, had entitled them.

A final consideration regarding dress must be given to the thought that in one exceptional case, the importance of appropriate dress in civic portraits also extended to its complete and literal absence. The 1586 portrait of Lady Godiva, famously riding undressed through the streets of Coventry, provides an interesting twist to the conventional theme while still effectively representing the spirit of civic beneficence in the history of that particular borough (fig. 11).[29] According to her legend, she had made a bargain with her husband, the oppressive earl Leofric of Coventry, to ride naked through the town if he would agree to rescind a harsh tax which he had imposed on the townspeople. The story had obviously been well preserved from some very much earlier time in Coventry itself. Leofric and Godiva actually lived in the eleventh century but several chroniclers, including Roger of Wendover, Matthew Paris and Ranulphus Higden, kept the story alive up to and through the Reformation.

By the mid-Elizabethan era (and, perhaps not incidentally, after the disappearance of the Virgin Mary as a much celebrated local protectress) the legend of Godiva (or, as it has sometimes suggestively been constructed, 'Good-Eve')[30] had come to the fore as a heroic personification of due process and fairness in governing the city, and of the rights of the townspeople against oppressive rule.[31] Katherine French has recognized in Godiva's dramatic transformation from a subservient wife to a defiant champion of the community a vivid symbol of the transition in Coventry's own post-Reformation identity. A city which had once been entirely subservient to its abbatial lord became in the mid-sixteenth century an autonomous, chartered, borough corporation, chiefly responsible for its own administration and well-being.[32]

PROPS: BOOKS, GLOVES, SCROLLS AND SKULLS

Numerous other elements appear in both personal and civic portraits, though they may be read differently in each. This is especially true of those devices or 'props' which are portrayed as being held in the subject's hand or hands. Civic portraits had little need to display those elements suggesting personal fecundity, strength, prowess, grace, beauty or other conventional masculine or feminine attributes. Even in the three-quarter or full-length portraits, especially on canvas, which became more common after c. 1600, the basic shape of the body lay largely camouflaged by the voluminous robes in which most figures were cloaked. Partly by process of elimination, hands and heads tended to be more visible in civic than in personal portraits. Heads allowed the focus to fall on the attributes of mind which characterized civic virtues, and there is certainly an emphasis on the appearance of gravity and sagacity.

Hands, and what they held or did, are often the most important feature in a civic portrait. But the demands of depicting them bore their own challenges. Their size, position, flesh tones, and potential for gesture and expression could easily distract the viewer from the subject's face. Then, too, the realistic depiction of hands remained well beyond the ability of most who painted civic portraits in this era. All of these factors contributed to the desirability of having the painter either conceal them entirely or give them something useful to do, the latter alternative considerably enhancing their potential to convey the meaning of the whole. Quarter-length portraits showing the subject only from the chest up, which were more common in the earlier years of English portraiture than later, effected concealment readily enough. But as the patrons of civic portraiture recognized the symbolic opportunities offered by the images of hands and the objects which could be held in them, painters more often incorporated them into the scene.

The greater value placed on symbolic display in both personal and civic portraits, often concentrating on the hands, and the growing complexity of symbolic programmes themselves, may help explain the general movement towards the half-, three-quarter or even full-length figure in the latter years of the sixteenth and the opening years of the seventeenth century. The larger the picture, the more it could contain.

The most common objects to be seen in, on, or under the hand of our civic subjects include books, skulls, scrolls, and especially gloves. The inclusion of books had no doubt developed in pre-Reformation images in which living donors and deceased patrons of pious bequests wished to be depicted with them as a sign of piety. This is well exemplified in the extant portrait of Bishop Alcock at Jesus College, Cambridge (fig. 7).[33] Alcock has what we are to assume is his prayer book spread out before him, next to his mitre, resting on his priedieu. The books in those cases would have been service books: books of hours, missals, breviaries, and so forth.

With the Reformation and the advent in England both of Humanism and Protestantism, books in portraits of all types came to represent learning as much as piety. We see this in Holbein's 1523 portrait of Erasmus[34] and his first (1527) portrait of Archbishop William Warham';[35] in Gerlach Flicke's 1545 or 1546 portrait of Thomas Cranmer;[36] the anonymous portrait of Archbishop Matthew Parker done in Norwich;[37] and the 1620 portrait of Samuel Ward, the town preacher of Ipswich.[38] Rowland Lockey's familiar group portrait of 'The More Family, Household and Descendants' (c. 1593–94) shows no fewer than seven members of this learned dynasty, three of them women, holding books.[39]

Books appear in the clear majority of university and college portraits, as we would expect, and in portraits of school officials and benefactors like Sir Richard Dobbs, founder of Christ's Hospital (now in Horsham), Lady Mary Ramsay, benefactress to the same,[40] and Richard Platt, founder of Aldenham School in 1599 (fig. 13).[41] Sometimes sitters are shown holding books which they have written themselves. Worcester College, Oxford's portrait of William Camden shows him with two books, one of which is a copy of his *Britannia*.[42]

15 'Thomas Layer, Sheriff of Norwich'; anon., 1606.

Brasenose College, Oxford's portrait of its fellow and benefactor Alexander Nowell, better known as dean of St Paul's and, as we have seen, putative host in his picture gallery, engages in a rare and playful recognition of both his vocation and his avocation in displaying both books and fish-hooks, with a

16 'Francis Wyndham, Steward and Recorder of Norwich'; anon., 1592.

flyrod on the wall behind him.[43] And St John's, Oxford's portrait of Sir William Paddy, BA and fellow of the College and also President of the Royal College of Physicians, shows him with an opened book of anatomical drawings to celebrate his erudition in that field.[44] Those few portraits depicting lawyers and judges also tend to include books as testaments to the sitter's learning in the law. The Gloucester portrait of Richard Pate, who was both a barrister and a school-founder and perhaps the most important Gloucester citizen of his time, touches several of these bases at once.[45]

On the other hand, we find fewer depictions of books in portraits of courtly or aristocratic subjects – especially the men of those groups – for whom book learning in general took longer to become the virtue which it represented for others. Nor do they frequently appear in mayoral or livery company portraits save when a prominent liveryman also founded a school or college.

As symbols of personal mortality, most often employed in *memento mori* portraits, skulls appear less often in civic than in personal portraits. Tarnya Cooper's definitive study of the subject sees this device as linked to particular changes in popular belief about salvation, and to have been most common from the early Reformation to about the 1630s.[46] We should not expect to find such personal testaments in civic portraits. Yet we do see them in several of the Norwich series of civic portraits (e.g., Robert Jannys, Sir John Pettus, John Marsham, Robert Yarham, Thomas Anguish, Francis Wyndham, Augustine Steward and Thomas Layer (fig. 15)) if not widely elsewhere. It may well be that these and perhaps others in that Norfolk portrait series, were commissioned by the city government as copies of personal portraits held by the sitters or their families. Rather than recast the entire symbolic programme of the original, the copyist may simply have gone about his task by completing a 'verbatim' quotation, and thus have incorporated in the civic work an imagery initially intended for quite a different purpose and patron.

Then, too, the reminder of man's mortality, even in a post-Reformation world where good works were thought to be to no avail in gaining salvation, might still be taken as encouragement to manifest divine grace by charitable benefaction while time permitted. Something of this suggestion may be read into the Norwich portrait of its Recorder, Francis Wyndham, scion of a prominent Norfolk gentry family, who took an interest in the city which later honoured him (fig. 16). Wyndham's hand not only lies on a skull but next to an hourglass: that other, and even more laconic symbol of time's passage.[47]

Other reminders of mortality appear as well, if less frequently. The several extant portraits of Joyce Frankland, benefactress to Brasenose and Lincoln Colleges, Oxford, Gonville and Caius College Cambridge, and Newport (I.o.W.) Grammar School, show an open pocket watch marking the time (fig. 17).[48] St John's' 'Sir William Paddy' shows a similar watch.[49]

Except for university colleges, where the proportion is lower, well over half of the male civic portraits which have been examined from this period show either a scroll or a pair of gloves. Many show both, and both play similar compositional roles in civic portraits though scrolls bear a more precise meaning than gloves. Many civic portraits, especially those done for schools and charitable institutions, were produced to commemorate the founder and

17 'Joyce Frankland', Emmanuel College, Cambridge; anon., c. 1586/87.

the foundation of an institution or the acquisition of a charter. The actual charters or letters patent by which such foundations were granted were often large and unwieldy affairs, not readily rolled up tightly in one handful. The leather thongs by which they were often tied and the thick wax seals with which they were certified would have dangled loosely; the stiffness of freshly made parchment will have made them cumbersome to roll.

The few extant 'charter presentation' group portraits do show charters in their literal form, as in the painting of uncertain date and provenance, showing Edward VI presenting the charter to Christ's Hospital (now in Horsham) and to Bridewell Hospital. As documentation for the act of foundation, and also as very large paintings, these representations were important to render in their full and complete form. But in individual portraits of founders themselves, there was neither room nor need to be quite so literal in displaying the document. The tightly rolled and fairly small bundle of paper or parchment we so frequently see in such portraits thus served as a schematic representation of such documents, but their meaning can hardly have been lost on the viewer.

We see just this implication of a held scroll in the portrait of Sir John Mason commissioned for and still displayed at Christ's Hospital, Abingdon (fig. 1). A national figure as a member of Mary Tudor's Privy Council in any event, Mason was also a loyal native son of Abingdon. He was educated in its grammar school, which then sent him to Oxford; he helped secure its charter of incorporation during Mary's reign; he was one of two petitioners for the refounding of Christ's Hospital in 1553 after it had been dissolved. When the petition succeeded, Mason served as the Hospital's first lay governor.[50]

The portrait was commissioned by the governors, and especially by one of their number named William Bostock, to be copied from a personal portrait of Mason which had been done for his family. Mason wears clothing which probably has no association with the office, but the meaning of the scroll in his right hand, often seen and understood as the hand of power and authority, seems clear. The same may be said for the scroll-bearing figure of Robert Thorne of Bristol, founder of its Grammar School,[51] while the scroll held by John Vowell, alias Hooker, probably marks the new charter for the Merchant Adventurers of Exeter which Hooker helped to secure as one of many civic acts in a long and illustrious career.[52]

Gloves are such a common portrait feature in this era that they have sometimes been considered symbolically neutral devices. Lorne Campbell relates the story, told first in J.G. Nichols's edition of the anonymous *Chronicle of Queen Jane and Two Years of Queen Mary*, that when Mary Tudor entered London with her newly wed consort Philip of Spain in 1554, their route took them past Grace Street Conduit, where they saw images of Mary's predecessors on the English throne. The picture of Henry VIII, showing him holding a book bearing the words *Verbum Dei*, suggested to Stephen Gardiner, the conservative bishop of Winchester, an inappropriate proclamation of Protestant faith. Gardiner objected, and later called the painter to account. 'And so he paynted him shortly after', the *Chronicle* continues, 'in the sted of the booke of *Verbum Dei*, to have in his handes a newe payre of gloves.' Campbell quite reasonably interpreted this as replacing an offensive object with a neutral one.[53]

As Campbell also points out, gloves had long been taken as a sign of gentility.[54] They were expensive items, often delicately laced or embroidered, and they were difficult both to clean and to repair. Only the reasonably well-off could easily afford them, and they protected the hands from manual labour, which the landed classes did not perform. Gloves figure very frequently and prominently in the courtly portraits of both men and women throughout the period at hand, becoming more elaborately designed and decorated up to about the 1620s and 1630s.[55]

And yet, despite their frequent significance of gentility, we find gloves as well on civic portraits of sitters who were not only below the status of the landed elites, but urban people (merchants, traders, and some professionals), and especially in livery company and provincial town portraits. This begs a question. How would contemporaries have interpreted the appearance of gloves in that geographic and social context? Would townspeople viewing such portraits have seen them as pretensions to gentility, or would they have read alternative or additional meanings? One answer is surely that different sorts of people would have seen them in different ways. While a nobleman might see gloves in a merchant's hands as a pretentious claim to higher status, perhaps invoking Weever's 'rich quondam tradesman', a townsperson would have read that image quite differently, while milking its symbolic ambiguity for all its worth.

The first meaning which gloves would have held for the townsperson and citizen would have been a signification of the subject's full membership in the civic body, the freemanry. In many towns throughout the realm a newly elected freeman signified his election, and his new status as one of the brethren of that inner circle, by giving pairs of gloves to his fellow freemen. The practice signified gratitude for admission to their ranks, submission to the collective will of the corporate body, willingness to share in its burdens and costs, and perhaps the extension of a sign of friendship: a figurative or symbolic shaking of the hands with his new peers. In the Somerset town of Wells the very recording of a new freeman's admissions in the town book, the Great Assembly Book, included a glove – clearly not a hand – drawn in the margin of the page at that point to signify that entry.[56] Though the number of civic portraits which can be discovered of women remains quite limited, it is extremely unusual for women to be shown with gloves in such paintings, just as it remained very unusual for a woman to enter the freemanry, save by inheritance, to begin with.

An interesting exception to this notion proves the rule: the intriguing double portrait of John and Joan Cooke, Mayor and Mayoress of Gloucester, probably dating to the period c. 1590s to c. 1620 (fig. 3). John Cooke (d. 1528) left in his will monies for the founding of a school in St Bartholomew's church and for expanding a local causeway. His wife Joan (d. 1544) outlived him by sixteen years and saw his bequest to fruition. The portrait shows Joan, looking much more alive than her spouse (she looks bright-eyed and directly at the viewer while he stares blankly into space), leading his apparently moribund form forward with her right hand while holding his freeman's gloves in her left. This can only be meant to show that a transfer of John's freeman's status to Joan has taken place with his death, and that she has inherited, at the end of their childless marriage, the obligation to carry his bequests to fruition along with that status. The lengthy inscription written along the bottom of the painting makes this even clearer.[57]

A second connotation borne by glove-holding in civic and urban portraits is also at least indirectly connected to the notion of the freemanry, and bears links as well with the symbolism of gloves among the landed classes. This usage concerns the traditional and perhaps most essential role of the freemanry, which was to regulate the market and, by extension, virtually all economic activities in the town. Most markets began as perquisites of feudal lordship, in which the lord of the town, either as the king's representative or in his own right, served as the immediate authority. He either ran the market himself, through his bailiff or steward, or permitted selected townsmen to do it on his behalf. Directly or, in most cases, indirectly, he exercised the judicial authority over its activities.

To reflect this responsibility, the custom arose whereby the erection of a leather glove or carved wooden hand on a long pole signalled the opening of the market day, and the lowering of the gloved pole signalled its close. The hand or glove represented the hand of that lord under whose protection the market proceeded, and under which buyers and sellers could be assured of that jurisdiction. When the hand came down, that protection, and the market itself, came to an end for the day. (When associated with royalty the glove continued to represent authority, and the frequent giving of gloves to monarchs like Elizabeth and James I by their subjects continued to suggest a recognition of that authority by the giver.)[58]

Like many such customs, this is difficult to document archivally and impossible to trace in its inception. But the folkloric tradition of such use of gloves and carved hands, reported as still active in the late nineteenth century, is supported by the actual survival into the twentieth century of a carved wooden glove (again, as the drooping position of the fingers shows, specifically a glove and not a hand) in Chester,[59] (fig. 18) and the record of such practice in, e.g., Portsmouth, Southampton, Newport (I.o.W.), Macclesfield, Exeter, Liverpool, and Barnstaple.[60] A print which was photographed and published in 1914 and probably dating to no later than the mid-nineteenth century shows the erection of the Chester market glove on a pole at the head of the market on market day (fig. 19).[61]

The traditions of the market glove and the freeman's glove nicely tie together the symbolic meaning of the gloves as a sign of gentility and feudal lordship, both in gentle society, and in urban and civic society, especially where, as was very common, the rights over the market had devolved over the course of time upon the freemanry. The freemen or their predecessors would have laboured hard and long to obtain this perquisite, and would have understood this full

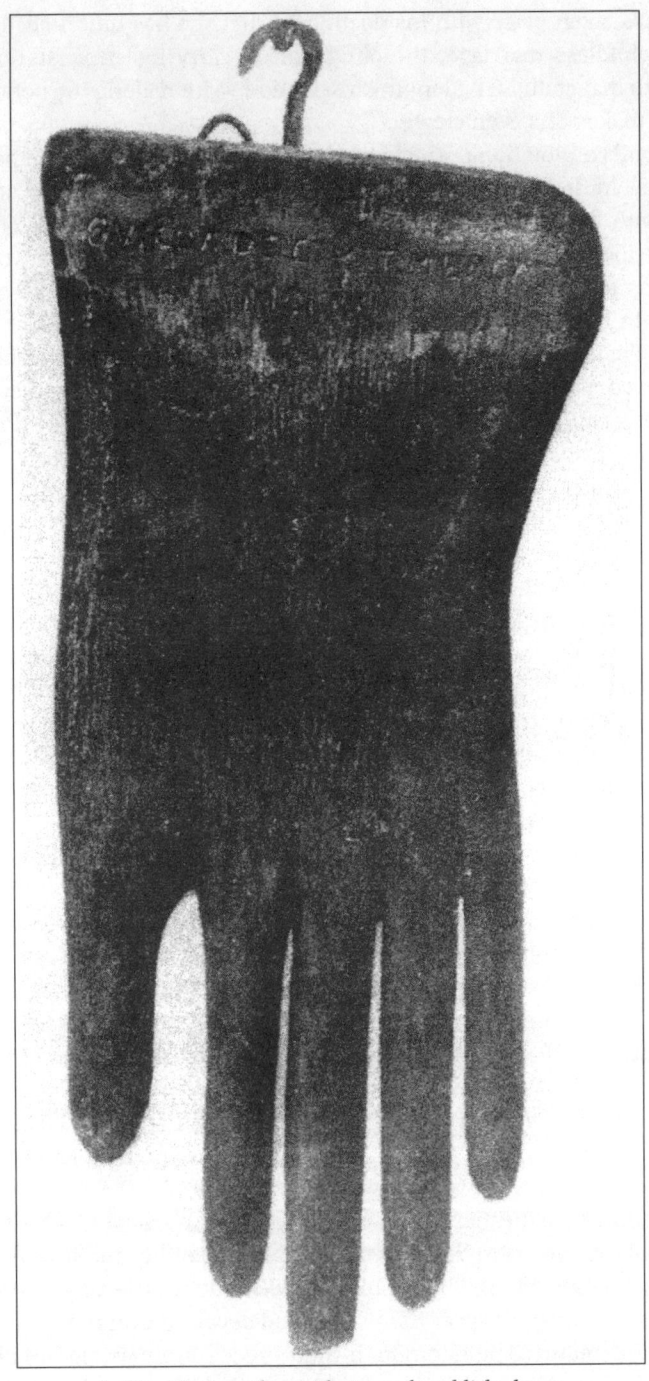

18 'The Chester Glove'. Photograph published 1914.

19 'Raising the Chester Glove'.

well. But in addition, and taken in the context of social aspirations among the civic elite, it may indeed have been seen as a symbolic assertion of gentle status.

As one might imagine, this was a very long-term transition. The significance of gloves as an indication of a superior status among merchants and craftsmen certainly extends back to pre-Reformation days, not only in, e.g., Wells, where Gary Shaw has found signs of this practice as early as the 1380s,[62] but undoubtedly elsewhere and probably in other contexts as well.

Though Netherlandish portraits of this era, for example, exhibit a much wider range of objects, gloves were also common elements in portraits of townspeople, and may have held some of the same connotations there when associated with marketing. On the south-east corner of the Square outside Gravensteen castle in Ghent, the site of the Kleine Vismarkt, an ancient building may be seen on which a sculpted hand has been carved into the facade and gilded with gold leaf.[63] One is powerfully tempted to see this as a surviving symbol of the lord's authority over that market.

The frequency with which the image of gloves will have come to denote freeman's status can only have increased in the sixteenth century, when so many towns effectively gained so much local administrative authority from their current or former lords. This sort of devolution, especially common

after about 1540, served as part of the general trend towards stronger corporate liberties which characterized that era.[64] It is not surprising under these
circumstances that gloves should have become such a common element when
English civic portraiture began to flourish a few decades later. This is perhaps
especially so outside of London where corporate liberties were rarely as well
established, or uncontested, as in the metropolis itself. But gloves appear less
frequently and less conspicuously in other civic portrait types, where none of
these mercantile associations applied.

However awkward it may have been to find room for them in the picture,
especially when one wanted to show other appropriate objects as well, gloves
were very frequently included. As noted above, the portrait of Thomas Layer
(1528–1614) (fig. 15), three-time mayor and long-time member of the civic elite
of Norwich, shows the sitter holding a skull in one hand and a prayer book in
the other, leaving no obvious place to display the gloves. But lest the announce-
ment of his standing in the city be lost in this more complex symbolic
programme, he has his gloves artfully but conspicuously protruding from his
waistband.[65] This image may strike us as amusing, but for those sharing John
Weever's perspective it would only have confirmed a festering prejudice. Some
other such examples would have done so even more vividly. The contemporary
drawing of a generic Lord Mayor of London, preceded by his sword-bearer and
brazenly striding forth with gloves brandished stiffly upright and weapon-like
before him, speaks for itself.[66]

INSCRIPTIONS

These devices of dress, books, skulls, scrolls and gloves obviously held clear
symbolic meanings for their anticipated audience. One additional and even
more literal device may be found in the inscriptions which many such portraits
bore, either on the frame or on the painting itself. Because inscriptions may
have been contemporary with the painting or added on at a later time they can
be misleading sources. Yet examination of the handwriting, brush-strokes,
language, or other elements can often distinguish the original from the addition.

In the case of personal portraits contemporary inscriptions were usually
composed by the sitter, or by the sitter's family: it is they who are speaking
through the medium of the portrait. In addition to conveying the age of the
sitter and year in which the painting may have been done – the most common
forms of inscription – they often record personal mottoes, statements of
service and loyalty, faith and moral rectitude. They may be seen as claims
to fame or immortality, self-justification, social legitimation, and other such
personal motives.

Contemporary inscriptions on civic portraits, especially when commissioned by the institution rather than presented to it, represent the voice of the institution and not the person. But even those presented portraits, done of sitters for whose life the civic affiliation was often central, tended to express themes which in some manner address the civic context. Some, too, were privately commissioned with the clear intent of donating them to the civic body, so that they convey something even closer to the civic voice.

The most common inscriptions in virtually all portraits of this era merely convey the sitter's name, age and a date. Most of the time this date marks the sitter's age at the point of portrayal and therefore helps us date the work. But not always! As have seen in the case of Shrewsbury's portrait of Degory Wartur, this can be misleading.[67] It might well mean the date of coming into a certain office, as in Wartur's case, or the date of the sitter's death. In an institutionally commissioned portrait displayed in a civic space the subject's specific deeds were sometimes deemed to be so familiar in the collective memory of the community as not to need spelling out. This seems to be the case with the portrait of Robert Heyricke of Leicester, mayor, MP, and co-founder of Trinity Hospital in that borough, who died in 1618. The portrait was meant to hang on one side of and over the mayor's chair in the main council chamber of the Guildhall. Here, despite what is to us its humorous rather than admonitory inscription, it appeared to one observer to be 'looking down ... in solemn composure'; 'he may be imagined to be still exercising a kind of tutelary influence over the affairs of that body'.[68]

Some inscriptions even in civic portraits still addressed religious themes, paralleling in tone the addition of the skull as *memento mori* in some civic portraits. They celebrate the sitter's piety but also emphasize the charitable acts or civic attainments which it inspired. Given its context and placement, the rather conservative religious sentiment inscribed on the 1606 portrait of the Merchant Taylor Robert Dowe, 'A vertuous lyfe is the fairest passage to a blessed death', hung prominently in the main hall of the Merchant Taylors' Hall, clearly equated civic benefaction with virtue.[69]

Other inscriptions leave the implication of piety to the viewer and concentrate instead on the specific bequest or service rendered to the institution. This is obviously the case with the Cooke portrait inscription, in which John Cooke's role in founding the local school in the crypt of the parish church, and in extending the local causeway, were rehearsed as generous benefactions to the city of Gloucester.[70] Robert Orpwood's portrait at Christ's Hospital, Abingdon, presented in 1615 by his brother to mark Robert's benefactions, offers a more prosaic explanation of a comparable endowment:

Effigies Robert: Orpwood Quondam Civis et
Auri Fabri London qui Natus in Hac villa de Abingdon
legavit elemzina[m] pauperibus huius Hospitalis perpetuo
duratur[am] anno Domini 1615.[71]

Though virtually all civic portraits served by their very nature, and even without inscription, as invitations to imitate worthy deeds, inscriptions added more laconic or specific reminders. The 1638 portrait of Philip Crew, school-master and benefactor of Salisbury, urges his successors to exhibit particular virtues in their work: '*Haeredes isti quoties succeditis aulae fraternis vestris mentibus adsit amor*'.[72] That on the undated portrait of Richard Dobbs, now in Horsham, is even more detailed.[73]

Portraits in university colleges tended, as we would expect, to have more elaborate inscriptions, ones in which the contributions to learning and schol-arship took pride of place, and ones expressed more often in Latin than in English. Those in the long Peterhouse series at Cambridge provide the best examples of this. Each portrait bears a brief inscription on the panel itself, usually in one of the upper corners, fully identifying the subject: e.g., '*Johannes Holbroke M[agiste]r Collegii A[nn]o Dom[ini] 1430*' (fig. 9). But in addition to this each has a separate panel fixed below with a lengthier inscription typically describing such things as the piety, benefactions and wisdom of the sitter. In the case of John Holbroke, Master of the College in 1430, this has been done in impressively imaginative terms: '*Partus dant similes Usura, et Vipera, foeta, Qui jurat afflictos, foenerat ille Deo*'.[74]

Statements by civic patrons, sometimes found in civic accounts explaining the reason for commissioning a portrait or in corporate minute books docu-menting the decision to do so, further affirm these themes. The most exten-sive evidence for this is probably the full discussion in Francis Little's 1627 account of the portraits in Christ's Hospital, Abingdon.[75] Writing within two decades of the portraits' probable creation, he was able to comment both at first hand and at length. In commissioning a portrait of Philip Bisse, founder of the Wadham College Library, Dorothy Wadham, wife of the College founder, took a more direct approach. She had a long explanation of her commission inscribed with the painting itself.[76]

But it is worth noting that the Drapers' Company of London chose in 1605 to display portraits of four of their members and benefactors specifically so that their charitable acts could be remembered.[77] In 1604 the Ironmongers, a particularly portrait-conscious company, ordered their portraits of alderman (Anthony) Gammage, Mrs Margaret Dane, 'and such others as are not all reddie sett upp there' to be hung 'at the como[n] hall of this mysterie'.[78] They would soon be joined by a portrait of the Company's three-time Master Nich-olas Leate (d. 1631) by no less a painter than Daniel Mytens, given by Leate's sons in the year of the sitter's death as a remembrance of their deceased father.[79] The painting seems to have been hung in the Court Parlour of the Company Hall, presumably the room in which members of the ruling body or 'Court' held their meetings, and where its display is noted in subsequent inventories. Though it is not clear if the sons had the idea of commissioning it for the Company to begin with, it was readily accepted and displayed as a civic portrait thereafter.[80] The decision to commission a portrait to commemorate Margaret Craythorne, widow of the London cutler John Craythorne, for her benefactions to the Cutlers' Company, falls into the same category.[81]

MEMORY

The last thoughts in this chapter must be devoted to the concept of memory, and to the mnemonic significance of civic portraits. All of these inscriptions and affirmations, like the portraits for or about which they speak, invoke memory of one sort or another. Though they were produced in the post-Reformation years, couched in secular terms, and viewed in secular spaces, they perpetuated a culture of memory which was both intrinsic to local communities and institutions and deeply rooted in pre-Reformation times. Portraits served to remind living members of the civic body of the lives and benefactions, service and leadership, of their forebears and fellows. Their constant presence in portrait form perpetuated such acts in the collective consciousness of the institution.

As Suzanne Kuchler and Walter Melion have recently observed, memory must not be thought of as a sequence of objective recollections drawn randomly from some mental storehouse of past events and impressions.[82] It must be construed as a process as well as a faculty, one which is triggered by a conscious need to remember the past as a means of making sense of the present. Individuals tend to draw upon a particular memory in a deliberate and subjective manner rather than randomly or objectively. These memories are almost always purposeful recollections, driven by a common need, and are both consciously and subjectively constructed.

The mnemonic quality of the portrait and its schematic programme, including symbolic devices of dress and ornament as well as accompanying inscriptions, must be seen in this light as 'sites of memory'.[83] Its composition must be understood as having a particular desired effect on those who would see it over the centuries. This had certainly been the case before the Reformation, where the predominantly religious culture of the medieval world took on highly complex mnemonic forms, and when contemporaries found a rich and equally complex visual imagery to articulate them. Preserving the memory of the dead, for example, came to form a central preoccupation of medieval popular belief. Souls would have to be remembered, and prayed for, to save them from the prolonged rigours of purgatory. Acts of remembrance and prayer counted heavily in the expectation of salvation among the living.[84] Visual images of charitable benefactors certainly played their part in this, providing constant reminders of that beneficence on the one hand while identifying the soul to be prayed for on the other.

All of this, beginning with the belief in purgatory itself, became proscribed during the Reformation. Within a generation or two it faded from the belief system of most English men and women. But the need to remember particular sorts of attainments, and the people associated with those attainments, commonly survived this transition. The perpetuation and encouragement of civic benefaction required that this be so. Where traditional commemorations in the form of, e.g., patrons' images in wood or stone, or funeral brasses or parchment, were principally designed to invoke prayer for the souls of the benefactors, post-Reformation commemoration invoked the civic virtue of benefaction itself, quite apart from any implications for salvation. The forms of this commemoration might include company or college plate, the endowed sermon or other benefactions, but they certainly included portraiture as well.

An exemplary representation of the transition from pre- to post-Reformation commemorative practice may be found in the curious 1599 panel painting-cum-memorial of William Smarte, benefactor of the borough of Ipswich, in the Church of St Mary-le-Tower in that borough. Smarte and his wife are depicted in the lower-right and left corners of the composition respectively, each in a traditional pose of prayer. They kneel with hands clasped before them as if venerating a saint or the Virgin, and an angel sits on each of the top corners of the same panel. But instead of a religious scene dominating the whole, we have a unique view of the borough of Ipswich itself across the bottom plane. This is partly obscured by a large cartouche, replete with Flemish-style strap-work of a sort which was often carried over to East Anglian vernacular design. On this is written a lengthy invocation to the donors' charitable impulses as they pertained, not to a patron saint or the parish, but to the borough itself.[85] Though this is not in a strict sense a civic portrait – it hangs in the parish church rather than a civic hall and it seems to have been commissioned by the sitters – it demonstrates a transitional stage between the pious benefactions of the old faith and the secular beneficence which replaced it.

To carry this line of thought a step further, civic portraits served to invoke memories to fit a civic agenda: to remember the past in order to negotiate the challenges of the present and future. We cannot deny that, as in the case of Smarte, or of the ironmonger Nicholas Leate, there may have been a personal element in the donation of a portrait of a living member of a particular community, or of one recently deceased, commissioned by the sitter or his family. But the decision to display such images in civic spaces, and to do so in order to recall past benefactions to the common weal, cannot be construed as anything but the effort to exemplify the critical importance of continuing benefaction to the civic institution.

This could be accomplished through imagery or inscriptions, and of course by the choice of the subject in such mnemonic works to begin with. Sometimes institutional memory could be invoked, and thereby sustained over time, even by the placement of the portrait in a particular proximity to other works in a specific civic space. Though the importance of proximity in displaying civic portraits will be pursued in a different context in chapter 6, it is worth pointing out here how this came to be done to sustain an institutional memory over time in the small hall of Christ's Hospital, Abingdon.

This foundation traced its origins to the project undertaken in the 1410s to build a new bridge over the River Thames at Abingdon, and to the establishment of the Brotherhood of the Holy Cross, c. 1430, partly to aid in that endeavour. Three local men were prominently engaged in the building of the bridge and the foundation of the brotherhood: the 'Bridge Builders' Geoffrey Barbour (d. 1417) and John Howchion or Hutchin (d. 1436) (fig. 14) and the patron, Sir Peter Bessils (d. 1424). As a religious fraternity, the brotherhood was dissolved under Edward VI, shortly to be refounded as Christ's Hospital, a charitable trust, in 1553. In order to emphasize its origins, thus to enhance its legitimacy as a civic institution, the governors of the Hospital in the early years of the seventeenth century turned to portraiture as we have seen. But in addition to commemorating post-Reformation benefactors and patrons (including the refounding monarch Edward VI), they also acquired a double portrait of Barbour and Howchion, one of Bessils, and an engraving of the initial founding monarch, Henry VI. The resulting display, all hung in the same smallish room, provides a seamless portrait record of the institution as if the hiatus occasioned by the Reformation had never occurred.[86]

There can be no mistaking this intent. Francis Little, a governor of the Hospital himself and probably responsible at least in part for obtaining some of these portraits, wrote eloquently to the point in his 1627 history of the institution:

> And that their memories may yet more lively remain and longer continue, the Master and Governours have caused their pictures to be made ... and have placed them in the Hospital Hall, ... which precedent posterity shall do well to imitate and follow ... For when all commonweals, cities and towns do end and perish, yet the histories thereof do remain and live.[87]

As specific memories are triggered by specific circumstances, it should not surprise us that the timing by which civic portraits tended to appear is often more than coincidental. In broad terms, as we have seen, they emerged especially following the vast mid- and late sixteenth-century shift in the political culture of English institutions away from religious vehicles for the expression of political ideas and towards secular surrogates for some of the same ideas. But more specifically, and just as personal portraits were often commissioned to mark an occasion or milestone in the sitter's personal life – marriage, inheritance, parenthood or career advancement – so do some civic portraits appear at particularly dramatic times in the life of a civic body.

The most obvious example of this is the group portrait marking the convey-
ance of a charter to a civic body, especially when some such bodies were being
refounded in the reigns of Henry VIII and Edward VI. Thus we have Holbein's
'Great Painting' of Henry conveying the charter which merged the companies
of the Barbers and the Surgeons to form the Barber-Surgeons in 1541 (fig. 12).
The theme is repeated to mark Edward VI's giving the charter to the founders
of Christ's Hospital, now in Horsham, and in his refounding of the Bridewell
in 1553.

As we have seen, these events are recorded in great detail, made even more
specific as documents by the care taken to depict a number of those who were
actually present on the occasion. The Barber-Surgeons' mural depicts, with
considerable verisimilitude, a number of members of both founding bodies,
as well as members of the King's immediate circle to add dignity to the occasion. Bridewell's 'Charter Picture' shows what amounts to actual portraits of
those on hand, who thus became recorded as witnesses to the event just as if
they had signed their names to it.

The Christ's Hospital painting, on the other hand, by far the largest of the
three, shows three sorts of people aside from the King. Double ranks of pupils
line the foreground, boys on the viewers' left and girls on the right, thirty in
all, and no effort has been made to construe them as individual portraits.
In the top rank and centre of the scene we do have four figures (obviously
eminent men of state) flanking the enthroned boy-King. And below these
on either side of the throne we have some thirty mostly anonymous figures
forming the Greek chorus in the play before them. This massive tableau will
have been displayed, as we have noted above, for all members of those bodies
to see on a daily basis, and thus they served as particularly vivid reminders of
the royal foundation which lay behind the institution and its officials of the
day.

In one sense, we may take these charter paintings as tantamount to
legal documents, equal in effect to the charters themselves, and as part of
the contemporary trend towards the more methodical keeping of written
records.[88] In fact, at a time when the crown sometimes treated charters with
disdain, the recording and, indeed, witnessing, of such a grant in the form of
a group portrait of this type may have taken on particular importance. The very
few examples of 'charter group portraits' come in the tumultuous last years of
Henry's reign and in Edward's, contemporary with the dissolutions of chantries, religious guilds and fraternities.

In addition to recording the event itself, these works also record the images
of those present on the occasion, and thus they call to mind for succeeding
generations those founding fathers of the institution: those whose energy
and fortitude in approaching the King, through his Attorney-General, secured
the event being celebrated. This, too, becomes part of the historical lore and

collective memory of the institution. It, too, serves to legitimize and strengthen the civic body.

University portraits usually invoke memory in much the same manner, but there are some special cases. The Bodley Frieze, for example, invokes mnemonic association in a very particular way, and one which is not quite replicated in any of the other civic portraits under consideration here (fig. 10). Instead of commemorating founders or benefactors, it presents a virtual pantheon of the European intellectual and spiritual heritage, tailor-made for its display in the Bodleian Library, and created very shortly after the foundation of the Library itself. It was obviously meant both to herald the intellectual commitment of the University and its new Library to pursue classical and post-classical traditions of learning, and to inspire scholars at all levels with the achievements of their intellectual forebears. It follows that the iconography represented those aims as well. Many subjects hold books as we might expect from such a cast of characters, but it is also important to note the devices painted in between the successive portraits: books again, quills, inkpots, and scrolls represent learning and scholarship; hour-glasses, skulls and urns represent the mortality of the scholars themselves and, by contrast, the immortality of their works. In both its possible inspirations and its influences the Bodley Frieze serves as a signal achievement in the record of English civic portraiture, but also a unique one. Very few civic portraits or portrait series display such a clear assertion of intellectual determination and inspiration, and with such complete disregard to elements of direct material benefaction.

Other examples of using portraiture to mark noteworthy events in the history of particular civic communities may be found. We see this in Coventry's decision to commission a portrait of its heroine Godiva, who had stood up for the interest of local townspeople, when that City was recovering from hard times in the 1580s.[89] We see it in the tendency of at least some of the twenty-four communities (twenty-three corporate towns plus the Merchant Taylors' Company) which received the rotating benefaction of Sir Thomas White to display his picture around the time each recipient's turn came to pass. We probably see it in the sudden determination of the Ironmongers' Company, amidst the intrigues, rumours and uncertainties foreshadowing civil war by 1640, to record in portrait form a number of their former worthies. Metaphorically speaking, portraits do remember, and civic portraits bore an even wider responsibility than personal for so doing.

This discussion of the common elements of the civic portrait further distinguishes it from the more familiar, personal portrait, and helps establish its role in the political and social discourse of the day. To respond to the question, 'what were these portraits saying?', it speaks directly to the requirements of these institutions in the time at hand. It remains to be seen to whom these messages were being beamed.

NOTES

1 Joanna Woodall, ed., *Portraiture: Facing the Subject* (Manchester and New York, 1997), p. 2.

2 See above, pp. 27–8.

3 For the extensive role of London liverymen as benefactors of provincial schools, see above, p. 57, and also Joseph P. Ward, 'Godliness, Commemoration, and Community: The Management of Provincial Schools by London Trade Guilds', in Muriel McClendon, et al., eds, *Protestant Identities: Religion, Society, and Self-Fashioning in Post-Reformation England* (Stanford, 1999), pp. 141–57.

4 J.W. Goodison, ed., *Catalogue of the Portraits in Christ's, Clare and Sidney Sussex Colleges* (Cambridge, 1985), p. 84.

5 See above, p. 28.

6 D.R. Woolf, *The Idea of History in Early Stuart England* (Toronto, 1990), p. 12.

7 Llewellyn Jewitt and W.H. St John Hope, *The Corporation Plate and Insignia of Office of the Cities and Corporate Towns of England and Wales* (2 vols, 1895), II, pp. 138–45.

8 *Ibid.*, I, pp. lxxxvii–lxxxviii, and II, pp. 140–5; BL Add. MS 28,330, fol. 30. An estimate of the dating may be made on the basis of de Heere's sojourn in England in the years 1567–76, during which he made several observations of English customs and costume. My thanks to Jenny Tiramani for explaining the distinctions between scarlet and crimson.

9 London, Guildhall Library, record numbers 32132–52, and 32170–3, covering aldermen from 1427/28 (John Gedney) with several gaps to 1458/59 (Thomas Scott). Though most of these figures became mayors or sheriffs thereafter, Leigh has shown and labelled them as aldermen.

10 Robert Ricart, 'The Maire of Bristowe is Kalendar', Bristol Record Office MS 04270(1) fol. 152, published under that title by Lucy Toulmin Smith, ed. (Camden Society, NS, 5 1872). Ricart became town clerk in 18 Edward IV (1478–79) and is thought to have completed the work a few years thereafter.

11 Hugh Lloyd Parry, *The History of the Exeter Guildhall and the Life Within* (Exeter, 1936), p. 66.

12 Jewitt and St John Hope, *Corporation Plate and Insignia*, I, pp. lxxxvii–lxxxviii.

13 George Clinch, *English Costume from Prehistoric Times to the end of the Eighteenth Century* (1909, repr. Wakefield, 1975), pp. 284–7.

14 Chester Record Office MS AB/1 unpaginated, references for 19 November, 2 Elizabeth and May, 36 Elizabeth.

15 Maureen Stanford, ed., *The Ordinances of Bristol, 1506–1598* (Bristol Record Society 41, 1990), pp. 32–2, 44–5, 97, 105–6. See also, for example, similar requirements in Beverley, Salisbury, Hedon, Hereford and Coventry. Beverley Borough Archives, Humberside Record Office MS BCII/4 ('Small Order Book', 1575–83), fol. 3v; Salisbury Borough Archives, Wiltshire County Record Office MS G23/1/3, fol. 63v; Hedon Borough Archives, Humberside Record Office MS DDHE/26, fol. 131v; 'The Great Black Book of Hereford', Hereford County Record Office, fol. 183r; R. Ingram, ed., *Records of Early English Drama, Coventry* (Toronto, 1981), p. 201.

16 Jewitt and St John Hope, *Corporation Plate and Insignia*, I, pp. lxxxv–lxxxvi. Salisbury and

Southampton are among those towns which required this as of the mid-Elizabethan era, though the practice may well have been much older. Salisbury Borough Ledger Book, Wiltshire County Record Office MS G/23/1/3, fol. 63r.; Alan Mansfield, *Ceremonial Costume: Court, Civil and Civic Costume from 1660 to the Present Day* (1980), p. 251.

17 John Earle, *Microcosmographie, or a Peece of the World Discovered* (STC 7439, 1622) (unpaginated), part 5.

18 Ann Rosalind Jones and Peter Stallybrass, *Renaissance Clothing and the Materials of Memory* (Cambridge, 2000), p. 3.

19 As acknowledged, for example, in the London Court of Aldermen in November 1560; Corporation of London Record Office, Rep. Book 14, fol. 417r.

20 Order of 11 October 1555, John F. Bailey, ed., *Transcription of the Minutes of the Corporation of Boston* (3 vols, Boston, 1980–83), I, p. 24.

21 See Robert Tittler, 'Henry Hardware and the Face of Puritan Reform in Chester', in *Townspeople and Nation: English Urban Experiences, 1540–1640* (Stanford, 2001), pp. 140–55.

22 On the negative or ambiguous image of the English merchant of this era see, for example, Alexander Leggatt, *Citizen Comedy in the Age of Shakespeare* (Toronto, 1973); Laura Stevenson O'Connell, 'Anti-Entrepreneurial Attitudes in Elizabethan Sermons and Popular Literature', *Journal of British Studies*, 15 (1976), pp. 2–20; John McVeagh, *Tradeful Merchants: The Portrayal of the Capitalist in Literature* (1981), *passim*; Keith Wrightson, *English Society, 1580–1680* (1982), pp. 27–31; Richard Grassby, *The Business Community of Seventeenth Century England* (Cambridge, 1995), pp. 29–36; and Lawrence Manley, *Literature and Culture in Early Modern London* (Cambridge, 1995), chapter 2.

23 Staatliche Museem Preussischer Kulterbestiz, Berlin, no. 586, reproduced in Susan Foister, *Holbein and England* (London and New Haven, 2004), p. 212.

24 R.L. Poole, ed., *Catalogue of Portraits in the Possession of the University, Colleges, City and County of Oxford* (3 vols, Oxford Historical Society Publications, vols 57, 1912; 81, 1926; and 82, 1926), III, p. 26.

25 Jean Vanes, *Education and Apprenticeship in Sixteenth Century Bristol* (Bristol, 1982), plate 1; Richard Quick, ed., *Catalogue of the Second Loan Collection of Pictures held in the Bristol Art Gallery, 1905* (Bristol, 1905), no. 202, p. 61.

26 This is one of those hybrid portrait types done – as the inscription tells us – at the bequest of the sitter's friend, Matthew Bankes, also a Master of the Carpenters' Company, who presented it to the Company in 1637.

27 John Weever, *Ancient Funeral Monuments* (1631), pp. 10–11.

28 See, for example, 3 Edward IV, c. 5; 1 Henry VIII, c. 14; 6 Henry VIII, c. 1; 7 Henry VIII, c. 6; 24 Henry VIII, c. 13; and 1 and 2 Philip and Mary, c. 2.

29 Attributed to Adam van Noort and currently displayed in the Herbert Art Museum and Gallery of Coventry. Payment of 3s 6d is recorded in Coventry City Record Office, MS A7, Account Book, p. 142, for 1586. Ronald Aquila Clarke and P.A.E. Day, *Lady Godiva: Images of a Legend in Art and Society* (Coventry, 1982). My thanks to Ron Clarke, Keeper of Visual Arts at the Herbert Gallery, for his interpretation of this and for suggesting its attribution.

30 The feminine imagery implicit in the legend cannot be overlooked. 'Good-Eve' served as a common variant of 'Godiva' in the city's traditions, with the celebration of 'Goodyves

Day' eventually becoming an annual event. Other versions of the Godiva legend readily associated her with the Virgin Mary, and it is in the former St Mary's Abbey, in its secular guise as a town hall after the Reformation, where her portrait hung from 1586 to 1976. *ODNB, vide* Godiva; Katherine L. French, 'The Legend of Lady Godiva and the Image of the Female Body', *Journal of Medieval History*, 18 (1992), pp. 7, 12–13.

31 *ODNB, vide* Godiva; French, 'The Legend of Lady Godiva', pp. 3–19; F. Bliss Burbage, *Old Coventry and Lady Godiva* (Birmingham, n.d.); Clarke and Day, *Lady Godiva, passim*; and Daniel Woolf, *The Social Circulation of the Past: English Historical Cultures, 1500–1730* (Oxford, 2003) pp. 317–18.

32 French, 'The Legend of Lady Godiva', p. 11. Despite its rudimentary 1345 charter of incorporation, Coventry remained largely dominated virtually until the Dissolutions by the earl; by the presence, influence and wealth of the Benedictine Priory; and also by the proximity of the bishops of Coventry and Lichfield whose palace stood near to it. Charles Phythian-Adams, *Desolation of a City: Coventry and the Urban Crisis of the Late Middle Ages* (Cambridge, 1979), p. 21.

33 See above, p. 39. My thanks to Professor Keith Wrightson, formerly of Jesus College, who brought this illustration to my attention.

34 Paul Ganz, *The Paintings of Hans Holbein* (1950), plate 64, catalogue no. 34 (Longford Castle, Salisbury).

35 *Ibid.*, plate 81, cat. 46 (Lambeth Palace, London).

36 Karen Hearn, ed., *Dynasties: Painting in Tudor and Jacobean England, 1530–1630* (1995), plate 12 (National Gallery, London).

37 Now located in the Castle Museum of that city, but presumably done for the Guildhall as one of the Norwich civic series.

38 Reproduced in John Blatchley, *The Town Library of Ipswich, Provided for the Use of the Town Preachers in 1599: A History and Catalogue* (Woodbridge, Suffolk, 1989), opposite p. 9.

39 National Portrait Gallery, no. 2765.

40 Both portraits are still in the possession of the Hospital, are displayed on the walls of its buildings, and are fully identified in their inscriptions. My thanks to Ms Rhona Mitchell for guiding me through this collection.

41 Nicholas Carlisle, *A Concise Description of the Endowed Grammar Schools of England and Wales* (2 vols, 1818), I, p. 528–30.

42 Poole, ed., *Catalogue of Portraits*, III, p. 256.

43 *Ibid.*, II, p. 249.

44 *Ibid.*, III, pp. 163–4.

45 Brian Frith, *Twelve Portraits of Gloucester Benefactors* (Gloucester, 1972), pp. 12–13; S.T. Bindoff, ed., *The House of Commons, 1509–1558* (History of Parliament Trust, 3 vols, 1982), III, pp. 69–70, and P.W. Hasler, ed., *The House of Commons, 1558–1603* (History of Parliament Trust, 3 vols, 1981), III, pp. 185–6.

46 See Tarnya Cooper, '*Memento Mori* Portraiture: Painting, Protestant Culture and the Patronage of Middle Elites in England and Wales' (Ph.D thesis, University of Sussex, 2001). I am grateful to Dr Cooper for allowing me to read and cite from her thesis.

47 Hasler, ed., *House of Commons, 1558–1603*, II, pp. 668–70.

48 Poole, ed., *Catalogue of Portraits*, II, pp. 247–9; Heinz Archive, *vide* Frankland, Joyce. F. Thompson, *Newport Free Grammar School: A Brief History* (Newport, 1987), p. xx.

49 Poole, ed., *Catalogue of Portraits*, III, pp. 163–4.

50 Bindoff, ed., *House of Commons, 1509–1558*, II, pp. 582–84; Hasler, ed., *House of Commons, 1558–1603*, III, pp. 29–31; Arthur E. Preston, *Christ's Hospital, Abingdon: The Almshouses, the Hall and the Portraits* (Oxford, 1929), pp. 40–5; *ODNB, vide* Mason, Sir John. I am grateful to Mr Nigel Hammond, Hon. Archivist of Christ's Hospital, for his hospitality and expertise on my visit of 24 June 2002.

51 Carlisle, *Endowed Grammar Schools*, II, p. 404; Vanes, *Education and Apprenticeship*; C.P. Hill, *A History of the Bristol Grammar School* (Gloucester, 1951), frontispiece. My thanks to Ms Sheena Stoddart, Curator of the Bristol Museum, for guiding me through the relevant holdings in her care.

52 Hasler, ed., *House of Commons, 1558–1603*, II, pp. 333–5. The painting hangs in the Exeter Guildhall.

53 Lorne Campbell, *Renaissance Portraits: European Portrait-Painting in the 14th, 15th and 16th Centuries* (London and New Haven, 1990), p. 134, from J.G. Nichols, ed., *The Chronicle of Queen Jane and Two Years of Queen Mary,*(Camden Society 48, 1850), p. 79.

54 Campbell, *Renaissance Portraits*, p. 99.

55 Valerie Cumming, *Gloves* (1982), pp. 21–7.

56 This tradition has even been traced back to pre-Reformation times. Newly elected freemen would give a pair of gloves to be distributed to all members of the guild merchant. David Gary Shaw, *The Creation of a Community: The City of Wells in the Middle Ages* (Oxford, 1993), pp. 157, 198–9. I am grateful to Dr Shaw for offering his perceptions on this issue with me.

57 For a fuller explanation, see Robert Tittler, 'John and Joan Cooke: Civic Portraiture and Urban Identity in Gloucester', in *Townspeople and Nation*, pp. 81–99. The inscription reads: *Though death hath rested these life mates / Their memory survives / Esteemed myrrors may they be / For Majestrats and wives / The School of Crist ye Bartholomews / The Cawseway in ye West / May wittnes wch ye pious minde / This Worthy man possest. This vertuous dame perform'd ye taske / Her husband did intend And after him in single life / Lived famous to her end. Their bountye & benificence / On earth remaines allways / Let present past a[nd] future time/Still Celebrate yr praise.*

58 Cumming, *Gloves*, p. 21; W.S. Beck, *Gloves: Their Annals and Associations, a Chapter of Trade and Social History* (1883, repr., Detroit, 1969), pp. 227–31; J.W. Norton-Kyshe, *The Law and Custom Relating to Gloves* (1901), *passim*.

59 R. Stewart-Brown, 'Notes on the Chester Hand or Glove', *Journal of the Architectural, Archeological and Historic [sic] Society for Chester and North Wales*, NS, 20 (1914), pp. 122–47, and photograph, p. 124.

60 Beck, *Gloves*, pp. 189–97; Totnes Borough Archives, Devon County Record Office (Exeter Branch) MS 1579/A/7/3; Joseph B. Gribble, ed., *Memorials of Barnstaple: A History of that Ancient Borough* (Barnstaple, 1830), p. 292. I am grateful to Mr Michael Berlin for this reference.

61 *Journal of the Architectural, Archeological and Historic [sic] Society for Chester and North Wales*, NS, 20 (1914), frontispiece, captioned as 'The Cross, Chester: Glove Hanging at S.E. Angle of St Peter's Church, from an old print.'

62 Personal Communication from Dr Gary Shaw.

63 Personal observation, June 2001.

64 Peter Clark and Paul Slack, eds, *Crisis and Order in English Towns, 1500–1700* (1972), and *English Towns in Transition, 1500–1700* (1976); Robert Tittler, *The Reformation and the Towns in England: Politics and Political Culture, c. 1540–1640* (Oxford, 1998), chapters 4–8 especially.

65 Norwich Castle Museum and Art Gallery, portrait no. 63:F.

66 Folger Shakespeare Library MS VA 318, Anon., 'A Caveatt for the City of London', fol. 8. My thanks to Dr Erin Blake for affording me access to this image.

67 See above, p. 13.

68 'His picture whom you here see / When he is dead and rotten / By this shall he remembered be / When he should be forgotten'; on-site observation and James Thompson, 'The Heyrick Portraits in the Guildhall, Leicester', *Transactions of the Leicestershire Architectural and Archaeological Society*, 2 (1870), pp. 43–54.

69 Frederick M. Fry, ed., *A Historical Catalogue of the Pictures, Herse-Cloths and Tapestry at Merchant Taylors' Hall* (1907), pp. 97–101 and plate 38.

70 See above, n. 57.

71 'The effigy of Robert Orpwood, Citizen and Goldsmith of London, born in this town of Abingdon, who left perpetual alms to the poor of this hospital in the year of our Lord 1615'; Preston, *Christ's Hospital, Abingdon*, pp. 38–9 and on-site visit, July 2002.

72 'My successors, as often as you succeed in this Hall, let brotherly love be present in your minds', Charles Haskins, *The Salisbury Corporation Pictures and Plate* (Salisbury, 1910), pp. 110–12.

73 Christes Hospitall erected was a passing dede of pittie / What some Sir Richard Dobbs was maior of this most famous citie / Who careful was in government and furthered moche the same / Also a benefactor good, and joyed to see it frame / Whose picture heare his frendes have sett, to put each wight in Minde / To imitate his vertuous dedes as God hathe us assined. Copied from the original in Christ's Hospital, 23 May 2001.

74 Robert Willis, ed., *The Architectural History of the University of Cambridge* (3 vols, Cambridge, 1886, ed., John Willis Clark, repr. 1988), I, p. 65. Literally, 'Interest and pregnant vipers produce similar offspring' or, in effect, 'he who gives benefactions to the worthy avoids the sin of usury'.

75 Francis Little, *A Monument of Christian Munificence, or An Account of the Brotherhood of the Holy Cross, and of the Hospital of Christ in Abingdon* [1627], ed., Claude Delaval Cobham,(Oxford and London, 1871).

76 Poole, ed., *Catalogue of Portraits*, III, p. 211.

77 A.H. Johnson, *The History of the Worshipful Company of Drapers of London* (5 vols, Oxford, 1914–22), III, p. 77, n. 2.

78 Quarter Court Minutes, Guildhall Library MS 16967/2, fol. 6v, 8 August 1604.

79 Daniel Mytens worked in London by 1618 and enjoyed royal patronage from 1624 as one of the most prominent painters on the English scene at that time.

80 Isabelle Finch, 'Portrait of an Ironmonger' (BA Hons thesis, University of East Anglia, 2000), p. 76 and plate 17; Guildhall Library MS 16988/5, p. 7 (Inventory of 6 August 1635) and p. 159.

81 Charles Welch, *History of the Cutlers' Company of London and of the Minor Cutlery Crafts* (2 vols, 1916–23), II, p. 125 and Guildhall Library MS 7147/1, p. 98. The portrait itself is reproduced in Welch, opposite I, p. 213.

82 Suzanne Kuchler and Walter Melion, eds, *Images of Memory: On Remembering and Representation* (Washington, DC, 1991), pp. 3–7.

83 The phrase is Pierre Nora's, in 'Between Memory and History: *Les Lieux de Memoire*', *Representations*, 26 (Spring, 1989), pp. 7–25.

84 Eamon Duffy, *The Stripping of the Altars: Traditional Religion in England, c. 1400–1580* (New Haven and London, 1992), pp. 332–3.

85 See frontispiece of Blatchly, *The Town Library of Ipswich*. The inscription, in which the first letters of each line spell the donor's name, reads as follows: *What can a deede man feede and cloth and holy preecepts give / It can not be ____ tel not me; I know he still dooth live; / Live then sweete Soule in ample rest example to the rest / Like thine his ground most lowe be laid that high wil build his nest / If none think nowe on thanks; if out of sight be oute of minde / Although tis wrong, yet light's thy los that hevenly thank doost finde, / May never yet faire Ipswich trye be foully so unkinde / Schooles, churches, Orphanarye rooms shal keepe yt still in sight / Men, Weemen, Children, Ould and yung shal were the day and night / Alas then not for ye we cri but for our selves alas / Ruing the want of such a wight as al thine adge did pas / This I le poore Man one did moorne; thus gras bewayled gras.*

86 Little, *A Monument of Christian Munificence*, Introduction; Preston, *Christ's Hospital, Abingdon*, pp. 15–29.

87 Little, *A Monument of Christian Munificence*, pp. 94–5.

88 See, for example, Tittler, *The Reformation and the Towns*, pp. 210–20, and 279–82; Woolf, *Social Circulation of the Past*, pp. 280–9.

89 See p. 64, n. 62.

Chapter 6

◆

Audience and display

Given the differences between civic and personal portraits, it readily follows that they should have been intended for different audiences or 'publics'. It is not difficult to fathom what sorts of people were meant to view personal portraiture, and in what circumstances. As Prof. Stone's succinct definition of their purpose would lead us to suspect,[1] most were displayed in prominent places in the country homes of the landed and middling elites: in the great halls and long galleries of the great houses, which became virtual showcases for personal associations, and in the parlours, great chambers and even stairwells of greater and middling houses alike. Other somewhat more intimate portraits tended to be hung in the more private spaces of the house: bedchambers, withdrawing rooms and 'closets'.[2] The most private space of all, of course, would have been found for that small, specialized and very intimate class of the portrait miniature. These would not have been publicly displayed at all, but rather kept, often encased in lockets, in private chests or drawers.

Those in the more public areas of the house were meant to be seen by visitors to these homes, whether monarchs on their progresses through the country estates of the realm or by neighbours, kin and political associates who would visit on one occasion or another. If we think of such visits themselves as forms of social discourse, then the portraits on display, and the interaction between the patron (whether sitter or not), painter, and eventual viewer, form a particular aspect of the whole communicative process. Such portraits identified the patrons or his/her family: they established at a glance his or her claims to family ancestry, personal achievement, political and/or religious loyalties, historical associations, habits of mind or other marks of character. Other portraits, mostly copied and/or printed portraits of figures of state, or of other prominent figures living or deceased, or even of friends, predecessors in office, and colleagues, also came commonly to be acquired and displayed in the homes of a surprisingly wide spectrum of the elite and middling sorts of people by the latter decades of the sixteenth century.[3] They served further to identify the patron by means of association.

We see this at the top end of the social pyramid in the astonishing large collections mounted by prominent figures such as William Herbert, earl of Pembroke; John, Lord Lumley; or Robert Dudley, earl of Leicester, in their grand homes. These collections, often amounting to literally hundreds of works, depicted the leading political figures of the day, both English and foreign, along with biblical and other historical figures.[4] On a more modest scale, some prominent churchmen collected portraits of both their fellow clerics and their predecessors, though here we must assume that collecting was to honour and exemplify the office rather than the collector. As early as the 1530s, Bishop Sherborne of Chichester commissioned a series of no less than fifty-seven roundel portraits of the bishops of Selsey and Chichester from AD 675 to his own time, along with some of the English kings. Archbishop Matthew Parker had collected thirty-six portraits, including seven bishops and seven reformed theologians, at Lambeth by 1575, and particular Oxbridge colleges anticipated Oxford University's famous Restoration era collection of college founders, now in the Bodley, by collecting a series of episcopal portraits after 1600.[5] In addition, some prominent and well-to-do people collected personal portraits and displayed them as talismans of friendship. Launcelot Andrews kept a portrait of his close friend Richard Mulcaster over his study door,[6] and when Thomas Heywood had the character of Alexander Nowell showing off portraits of his friends in his picture gallery, we must assume he was describing a common practice of the era.[7]

In all these cases we see two types of audience or public at work. The first emerged in the form of portrait consumers: the ever-widening circle of those who commissioned or purchased and then displayed portrait images or gave them as gifts. The second public also included this patronal group, whose members obviously viewed the portraits which they displayed, but it extended to that much wider number of people whom these patrons expected to view their acquisitions: the viewing audience. The images themselves linked the two groups providing, as they were meant to do, the discursive medium for interaction between them.

When we turn to the audience for the display of civic portraits, our first tendency is to expect that these images were meant to be seen by all the members of the particular communities for which they were commissioned: by the rank and file as well as the masters of the livery company; by the students as well as the teachers of the school or college; by the residents as well as the governors of the charitable institution; and perhaps even by the entire resident population of a particular town or city as well as by its ruling elite. There are again in all these possibilities two publics involved, the 'consumers' who commissioned or purchased the paintings (in this case institutional bodies rather than individual people on their own accord) and the viewers who saw them. But the latter group could vary in its size and inclusivity and so therefore could the nature of the discourse for which the portrait formed the impetus.

Precisely how large such an audience might be remains open to question. The suggestion of annual, public, outdoor displays of civic portraiture on festive days specific to particular towns and cities has been made with regard to Norwich and its annual Guild Day in the period c. 1580–1620. This implies a mass and completely unregulated audience: one which included anyone at all who may have witnessed the annual mayor-making ceremonial on the streets of that important and populous provincial centre.[8]

Yet this suggestion appears to rest on the evidence of a mid-nineteenth-century print showing details which cannot have applied to the pre–1640 era.[9] We do know that such displays of royal, if not aldermanic, portraits had been launched on a few grand, national celebratory occasions: at the entrance of Mary Tudor and Philip of Spain through the streets of London following their marriage in 1554 or at Elizabeth's passage by the Great Conduit at her entrance into London in January of 1559.[10] But the fragility of panel or canvas portraits and the risks imposed by the English climate must have made such outdoor displays exceptional events. We cannot entirely rule out the prospect that Norwich portraits, and other paintings in the city's possession, may have been displayed on the city's annual Guild Day at some point in the past. But the notion of a mass and unregulated audience which would at some regular interval have observed civic portraits outdoors seems unlikely during the period under consideration here.

On the other hand, the audiences which would have seen the handful of large group portraits on permanent indoor display, such as were intended to mark the founding of a particular school or company, must still have been substantial. Holbein's huge tableau of Henry VIII presiding over the merger of the Barbers and the Surgeons (fig. 12) provides an English prototype of this limited genre. Displayed in the Company Hall where no one who entered could conceivably overlook it, this spectacular canvas served several purposes as we have seen.[11] But by including a range of dignitaries present on the occasion, most of them connected in one way or another to the newly merged company, the tableau identified for all posterity the movers and shakers of each of the founding institutions, perpetuating their fame and the fact of their service to their community. Those generations of Barber-Surgeons and others who have observed this work from its inception to the present day may be seen, metaphorically speaking, to have witnessed an event as well as to have viewed a painting, and to have encountered individually many of the institution's founding fathers. In addition to making the Barber-Surgeons particularly conscious of the role and power of portrait imagery in their institutional culture, it undoubtedly served as a model for the few other grand charter paintings of the mid-century: of Edward VI presenting both to Christ's Hospital London/Horsham and to the Bridewell Hospital in the same year, both of them hanging in similarly large spaces.

Yet large though they may be, none of these paintings can be said to have had an entirely inclusive or unregulated audience. One would have had to be admitted to those interior spaces in order to view these works, and must have possessed some credentials or status for that admission. Then, too, such audiences must have been status-specific and socially stratified rather than socially amorphous in nature: the apprentices, journeymen and masters of the Barber-Surgeons; the masters, staff and residents of the Bridewell; and the student body and masters of Christ's Hospital.

In these cases some of the intent was no doubt to impress, on a daily basis, the rank and file of these civic bodies with the heritage of the institution, the eminence of its foundation and traditions, and the model of civic benefaction represented by its founders and patrons. The image of authority, laconically stated and purposely intimidating, also found its place here, though never as starkly as in Holbein's classic portrait of Henry VIII in Whitehall Palace (1537), which Holbein recycled four years later as part of the Barber-Surgeons' 'Great Picture'.

In addition to Christ's Hospital (Horsham) displaying its foundational group portrait in its main hall where all pupils and staff took their daily meals, nineteenth-century prints and paintings of its original hall also record that it hung conventionally sized portraits of some of its individual worthies and benefactors in spaces which were smaller, more formal and less accessible. The most frequent viewing audience for these portraits seems to have been that more exclusive company of administrative officials, teaching staff and governors themselves, who were presumably meant to be reminded of and were instructed by the visual example of their predecessors.

Along with that more exclusive audience for these smaller, individual portraits, there were three solemn occasions on which pupils of the school were also permitted access even to those inner spaces of the institution: upon admission, when they were taken in by their parent or sponsor and ceremonially clothed with their school uniforms; upon leaving, when they were ceremoniously discharged; and at any time during their residence when they might be disciplined by the master. On these occasions they would have entered a more exclusive and symbolically authoritative space and experienced the full *gravitas* of the institution's major founders and benefactors staring down at them from the walls: the former London Lord Mayors Sir Richard Dobbs, Sir Wolstan Dixie, and Sir John Leman, who was also President of Christ's Hospital (1618–32); Lady Mary Ramsay, substantial benefactress in her own right and wife of Sir Thomas Ramsay, another president of the Hospital (both of whom figured in Heywood's description of Nowell's picture gallery); and perhaps others as well.[12] One may well imagine the solemn impact these images will have had on the youngster brought for admission to the school by his father, or on the laggard schoolboy hauled up for the contemporary equivalent of smoking in the loo!

Another such display to the inmates or residents of a charitable institution may still be seen in the very much smaller and more modest council chamber of Christ's Hospital, Abingdon. As noted in chapter 5, this charity was first established in the early fifteenth century, then dissolved and refounded in the reign of Edward VI. By the early seventeenth century its governing authorities felt the need to commemorate its founding fathers by means of portraits.[13] These were not gathered in a group portrait as with the Barber-Surgeons. Only the painting of 'The Bridge Builders', Geoffrey Barbour and John Howchion, against the scene of one of the bridges being built, is even a double portrait (fig. 14). The rest are individual portraits: of Sir Peter Bessils (who, with Barbour and Howchion, helped establish the pre-Reformation institution), Lionel Bostock, Robert Orpwood, Maud Teasdale, John Parkins and Sir John Mason (fig. 1), with Edward VI, the charter-giving monarch, added for good measure. (Extant portraits of two other founding figures, Thomas Teasdale and William Bostock, were added later.)

Those who dwelt in this Christ's Hospital would not, in the normal course of their daily lives, have had occasion to enter the smallish space – roughly the size of a good university seminar room – in which these were and still are displayed. Yet like the schoolboys of the other Christ's Hospital, they would have had access on particular occasions: on admission to residence at the beginning, on departure from it, and on occasions of discipline or administrative action along the way. On each of these occasions these portraits must have commanded a vivid and often intimidating presence, one enhanced by the fact that they were hung high on the walls of this small room, and were thus seen staring down on those below.

The same must be said for the Norwich civic collection. Roughly nineteen in number by 1640 (an uncertainty created by the lack of precise dating for some), these solemn-toned and grave visages lined the walls of the Guildhall, coming eventually to the courtroom extensions added in the late 1530s. Although as we have seen they were not all commissioned at the same time, they seem by the turn of the seventeenth century to have come to be considered a series. Several seem to have been done by the same hand; they are roughly the same size; all are framed alike. They would have had a similarly impressive and perhaps intimidating effect on those who saw them in that room.

These and other examples suggest that civic portraits were displayed in the halls and council rooms of their patronal institutions, all of which restricted access by the general public to some extent or other, and all of which symbolized the authority of the institutional governing body. In Leicester the portraits of two worthy officers and benefactors, the brothers William (1562–1653) and Robert Heyricke (1540–1618), were painted respectively in 1594 and c. 1618, and long hung on either side of the mayor's chair in the Guildhall Council Chamber. Both men had served the borough as MPs, mayors and benefactors, and it was important to the borough to have their portraits displayed in that particular place so that, as a later observer remarked, they 'looked down in solemn composure ... exercising a kind of tutelary influence over the affairs of that body'.[14] But admission to the Council Chamber of the Leicester Guildhall had almost certainly by c. 1600 become pretty well restricted, as it had in other such halls, to officers of the corporation and others called to that chamber on official business.[15] The Court of the Ironmongers' Company ordered in 1604 that portraits of Anthony Gammage, Mrs Margaret Dane, and others should be displayed in the Company's Common Hall, restricted to members of the livery.[16] Exeter's council ordered in 1606 that portraits of both Lawrence Seldon and his wife, civic benefactors both, be set up in the Council Chamber.[17] The Merchant Taylors wanted the portraits of their benefactors set up in their hall.[18] The Grocers' Company placed their portrait of Sir Stephen Soame, a grocer/Lord Mayor of London in 1598, in their hall by 1619.[19]

In addition it seems clear that portraits on display in civic halls and similar venues may not have been as visible even to their more restricted audiences as we might assume. Quite a few were actually kept covered over, either with silk, taffeta or other cloth curtains hung on metal rods, or even with triptych-like hinged wooden panels or shutters. What is probably the first of at least four portraits of Sir Thomas White, the College's founder, held at St John's College, Oxford, was provided on its first hanging in 1580–81 with curtains and iron curtain rods. Only a few years later these were replaced with hinged wooden shutters.[20] Chester's portrait of that same often-celebrated benefactor had to be provided with a taffeta curtain shortly after its completion in 1593.[21] The portrait of White's fellow merchant taylor Robert Dowe held by that company received similar protection in 1606 or 1607. The Company accounts for that fiscal year record payments for green taffeta, tape rings, and sewing silk for making the curtain 'for Mr Dowe his picture', which would have been hung in the hall where banquets (including a memorial dinner for Dowe himself in 1612) were customarily held.[22] As with the St John's portrait of White, the practice of curtaining portraits seems common in the universities, with payments for similar paraphernalia recorded for portraits at, for example, the Bodleian Library, Lincoln College, and New College, Oxford,[23] while the accounts of the vice-chancellor of Cambridge University in 1612–13 list the outlay of 15s for 'le Curteine stringes and rodd' to cover a newly acquired portrait of Prince Charles.[24]

The prime purpose of this fairly common practice was to keep the paintings from deterioration in the presence of strong light, smoky hearths and candles, random carelessness,[25] or – in the case of those hung in school halls – perhaps the poor aim of schoolboys flinging food. Evidence of such environmental danger to the portraits appears in the frequent payments in company or borough accounts for the 'refreshing' of paintings – obviously a process which involved cleaning – which often entailed an expensive transport to and from what was often a London workshop.

It could, however, be done locally with the right skills. As noted above in chapter 3, this is indicated in the will of Robert Reyce (aka Ryece) of Preston, Suffolk, who left to his friend William Milles, a 'painter and glazier' of nearby Lavenham, a box of paints so that Milles could 'from time to time renew and amend the decays of colours, words, letters, compartments and forms of those tables, writings and inscriptions which he has at any time made for me'.[26] Despite its taffeta curtain, Chester's portrait of White had to be 'refreshed' (by a craftsman with the ironic name of Stephen Darker) in 1648, while St John's College, Oxford (where food was perhaps more likely to be flung) was already sending to London for 'renewing and refreshinge our founder's picture' in 1583–84.[27] The object of such curtaining may well have been practical under the circumstances, and was by no means restricted to civic as opposed to personal portraits.[28] Yet the effect must have been to create of these images something of a totemic or even mysterious quality, making them all the more powerful in their impact on the viewer. In addition, we can only wonder if it reminded some viewers of the occasional pre-Reformation practice of temporarily veiling part of the sanctuary so as to conceal that part of the mass in which transubstantiation took place, and whether it worked to similarly dramatic ends.[29]

The distinction between the main hall and the inner council rooms as venues for portrait display seems to have pertained to livery company halls as well as schools and charities. Again, some interior spaces were preferred over others, the most prestigious and perhaps symbolically more meaningful being those smaller, more intimate spaces reserved for the upper echelons of institutional leadership. We may infer this from the story of the Merchant Taylor master and benefactor John Vernon, who delivered to that Company seven small pictures in 1616 (including one of Henry VIII, one of Elizabeth, and also one of himself) so that they might be displayed in the Company Hall. But in making his presentation, Vernon disingenuously noted that, if the Court of the Company would not think it inappropriate to hang the portrait of such a 'lesse deserving' man as himself in such a space, he would have it hung in the parlour. This more private and prestigious place, usually reserved for the senior officers alone, remained generally less accessible than the hall (in the sense of the main and more public room) of the building. In the parlour of the Merchant Taylors' Hall Vernon noted that his painting would hang alongside those of such particular Company worthies as Sir William Craven, Sir John Swinnerton, and two unnamed members who had served as Sheriffs of

London.[30] The Company seems to have complied with this, serving both its requirements and Vernon's at the same time.

The episode suggests that civic buildings like livery company halls, town halls with their mayor's parlours, and colleges with their master's lodges, resembled country houses in having some spaces reserved for the senior and more prestigious members of the institution. Images displayed in those more intimate spaces were presumably meant for smaller and more specialized 'audiences', often for didactic or inspirational purposes.[31] It also serves to remind us that the sitter's personal motives were not always entirely absent from the acquisition of a portrait by a civic body. Vernon's wishes parallel the evolving social preferences which came to determine spatial design in country houses, where the more personal and arguably totemic objects and paintings were kept in the small, more private interior spaces. It brings us back to the caveat issued in a previous chapter, that not all portraits which deserve to be considered as 'civic' were actually commissioned by the civic body. Some, like Vernon's, were indeed commissioned by the sitter, family or even friends, and then donated to the institution. As we've seen at the outset, it became a 'civic' portrait, albeit of a less pure sort, when that body accepted the painting and displayed it as a civic portrait, sometimes adding an inscription further to connect the figure with the institution.

This personal interest in having one's image displayed as a civic portrait during one's own lifetime (not unlike the common contemporary practice of designing and erecting a funeral monument before death) seems especially vivid among the Barber-Surgeons. Perhaps this was a lingering influence of Holbein's 'Great Painting', in which so many of the founding fathers of the merged livery were individually portrayed (fig. 12). But whatever its origins, this particular company went to great lengths to display images of its masters and benefactors, living as well as deceased.

To meet this demand, and perhaps effectively to stimulate it further, the Barber-Surgeons erected what are described as 'tables' of the portraits of former Company masters hanging in their hall. By the turn of the seventeenth century prominent living members engaged in spirited competition to have images of themselves represented in those tables even if it meant painting (or drawing) them over images which were already there. Depending on which of the sundry meanings of the word was intended,[32] it may well be that these 'tables' were merely sheets of paper or specially prepared wooden boards which could be written or drawn upon, erased and written on again. It is equally likely that they were framed paintings on panel, as several other Company documents refer to tables 'hanging' and 'standing' in the Company Hall.

In 1601 the livery's 'Court of Assistants' felt compelled to order that no member, without permission of that court, should erase or blot out any of the existing pictures so as to replace them with his own image.[33] But this seems not to have stemmed the tide of those who coveted such display. Three years later four of the Assistants were dispatched to confer with no less than John de Critz ('Decreete'), in his first year as Sergeant-Painter to James I, about finishing the tables of pictures which he had been commissioned to produce.[34] In 1627 the Company Court ordered the construction of a large wooden frame, and the employment of a 'picture-maker' to paint on it portraits of two famous members of the Company. And by the mid-1630s, the Barber-Surgeons displayed no fewer than forty-one portraits of former Masters of the Company and Examiners of Surgeons, all apparently displayed in a single, large 'table' framed with wood.[35] From 1634 any newly appointed Master or Examiner was entitled to have his image added to this number by painting it over one of the existing images. Company achives frequently record permission for masters' images to be blotted out or erased and replaced in turn, or admonitions not to erase images without permission. The Company's Assistants also had their table of portraits, created in 1627 to accommodate those whose images were not already on display. That remarkably portrait-conscious company commissioned additional 'tables' from time to time thereafter to accommodate demand.[36]

By at least 1648 and perhaps before, the Painter-Stainers seem to have adopted a somewhat similar rotation of images of their recently admitted officers, known as 'Wardens'. But these images seem to have been displayed only during the term of office of the men so honoured. At the end of that term they were taken down and either moved to a more public place in the Company Hall or actually sold to the member in question.[37]

The creation of these 'tables' of portraits, or even of written documentation of benefactions and their donors, became an increasingly common practice by the late Elizabethan era. Soon after the Grocers' Company displayed the framed portrait of its celebrated benefactor Sir Thomas Lovell, it also erected a 'hanging table' (probably in this context a framed piece of writing) in its jewel house displaying Lovell's will in which such benefactions were described.[38]

Just as a senior member of such an institution signalled his standing in society at large by wearing his civic raiment 'abroad', so did he signal his standing within the more intimate society of the livery by having his image displayed within its rooms. And even if he could not secure a permanent place for that image, as in the case of the Barber-Surgeons, he could at least have his image in plain view for the duration of his active leadership.

Personal desires to have a portrait displayed within a company hall served the institution as well as the individual. When the Goldsmiths' Company decided, in 1618, to commemorate its deceased worthies by displaying the names and arms of all such members in their Common Hall, they noted that they did so

as well for the honour and reputation of those worthy benefactors who are departed this life, as also by their example to imitate and stir up hereafter others to like works of charity and piety.[39]

This didactic motive becomes clearer when we take a close look at institutional perspectives on such display, and the ways in which those perspectives evolved along with attitudes about the cultural entitlements and civic responsibilities of contemporary elites. Several of these factors also afford us a fuller grasp of why these portraits should have been intended primarily for internal consumption.

The first point to consider is the long-standing notion that the prerogative, indeed, the responsibility, of governance naturally fell to the social elites of the day and not to either the middling or 'meaner' sort. But the definition of that elite status, and the relevance of that feudal/chivalric culture with which it had long been associated, shifted markedly over the period at hand.[40] Whereas the expectation of natural leadership traditionally stemmed from factors of birth and inheritance, military prowess and feudal service, it yielded very considerably under Tudor rule to humanistically inspired notions of education, gentility and civility as equally important criteria for governance. These were not attributes of birth, but rather of learning and experience. Their growing value to the monarchy opened the ranks of the ruling elite to the educated 'new men' of whom we read so much in the Tudor era. We see this tide beginning to turn with a few well-educated but common-born men serving Henry VII, flowing more fully with their greater prominence in the government of Henry VIII, and washing very substantially over the role and influence of the traditional, titled aristocracy by the end of the reign of Elizabeth.

This new order emerged through the requirements of Tudor government and the patronage which followed from those requirements, but it was informed, defined and encouraged by a humanist literature of statecraft and civility at every stage. It began with the writings of such seminal figures as, e.g., Machiavelli and Castiglione on the continent. It soon became current in England through translations of those seminal works into English, and by the writings and influence of the Henrician generation of humanists: men like Thomas More, Juan Luis Vives, Thomas Starkey, Richard Morison, John Cheke, Anthony Cooke, Roger Ascham and Thomas Elyot, to be followed thereafter by statesmen and intellectuals like Thomas Smith, Richard Mulcaster, Nicholas Bacon and William Cecil. These men emphasized the virtue of classical learning, and derived their concepts of civility and 'right rule' accordingly. They popularized and put into action principles of civility, comportment, and governance itself. Their perspectives came rapidly to be articulated and further disseminated through a flourishing literature of histories, conduct books and governing manuals, all meant as owners' manuals to the new order, and by the commission of stylistically advanced works of art and architecture.

These voices rose in opposition to the traditional aristocratic, neo-feudal culture. Many of them applied their tastes in the urban rather than the agrarian community, and in the governing bodies, educational foundations and charities of that milieu. The civilizing force of classical societies, after all, had been the cities and not the countryside. The aristocracy of the Roman world, and then of the Renaissance milieu of Italy or the Low Countries, had been oriented more towards the cities than towards landed estates. Sometimes the determination to imitate the ancients in finding a way forward for contemporary life proved an awkward fit. When Thomas Starkey, for example, wrote about cities and urban society in his *Dialogue Between Pole and Lupset*, he did so as if he were more familiar with classical Rome than contemporary Bristol or Norwich. But classical models of behaviour and governance nevertheless found favour with the Tudor monarchy, and so did the hero worship and the civilizing potential of urban life which those models exemplified and encouraged.

As has been suggested in chapter 4, English towns and cities themselves had by no means enjoyed any of the contemporary reputation for civility and cultivation of their Italian counterparts. Yet by the end of the sixteenth century urban society, and its history and government, became worthy subjects for description and analysis, and a more balanced reputation began to emerge.[41] The governance even of provincial towns came in for some more positive discussion, led by the precocious governing manual for Bristol written in the late fifteenth century by Robert Ricart, and taken up in later years by, e.g., John Vowell alias Hooker, for Exeter, Henry Manship for Great Yarmouth, and sundry other writers for specific communities.[42]

Though not written in quite the same vein as the humanist literature on manners and comportment, these works nevertheless strove to educate the ruling elites of local institutions – schools and colleges, livery companies and borough corporations – in several ways. They assumed that governance was a discipline to be learned and not an attribute of birth; they drew on local historical experience in a more critical and didactic manner; and they frequently invoked classical models and virtues as guiding principles for governance and civility.

It is surprising how far down in the social and educational scale, and how widely dispersed from the political centre, such ideas may be found during the era at hand. We might expect such sophistication from a John Hooker of Exeter, who had attended Exeter College, Oxford, studied law in Germany, served as an MP, and wrote both widely and confidently on history and politics. But London's John Stow was but a merchant taylor, and a lesser member of that company, with very little of Hooker's education and few of his experiences. Patrick Collinson reminds us that he 'never darkened the doors of a university, ... had much money, [or] owned a horse', and that 'he had to walk to wherever he wanted to go'.[43] Great Yarmouth's Henry Manship, who proclaimed that his native town was to England as Athens was to Ancient Greece and who freely quoted from Aristotle, Thucydides, Pliny, Horace, Virgil and Cicero as well as such modern writers as Speede, Camden, Holinshed, and Gaspar Contarini, seems not to have had even a grammar school education, travelled abroad, or lived for long periods very far from that East Anglian herring port of his birth.[44]

Given the substantial social and economic pressures of the day, and the increased responsibilities consequently placed on the shoulders of local officials by the crown and parliament, the administrators of all sorts of civic institutions had no choice but to take governance seriously and to draw upon models of governance wherever they could find them. This was all the more true for institutions which were newly incorporated or so recently refounded in and after the mid-sixteenth century.[45]

The familiar figure of the borough Recorder, trained in the law, might whisper instructions in the mayor's ear as the latter – almost always lacking that training – presided over the borough court. But the principles of civic rule by which that mayor tried to govern in his standard one-year term of office, and the virtues of civility which he strove to exemplify, had to be gleaned from other sources and models. So did the notions of the very honour and heritage of the community which he served, and upon which rested his exhortations to civic behaviour.

The emergence of civic portraiture at this time, and of its particular audience among the governing elites of civic institutions, must be understood in this as well as other contexts. John Vernon of the Merchant Taylors and myriad ruling elites of other institutional communities might hope to gain some personal legitimation from displaying their own images to their brethren. But the institution itself gained a more vivid affirmation of its own identity, and enhanced its collective memory, by allowing them to do so. And just as Henry Manship, after many years labouring over his long and laudable history of Great Yarmouth, saw no need to publish the work for dissemination beyond the bounds of the borough's councillors (it remained in dog-eared manuscript until the middle of the nineteenth century) civic portraits need not necessarily have been more publicly displayed in order to serve that prime target audience.

Francis Little had no doubt of this when he described, in his 1627 history of the institution, the intended effect of hanging portraits of its patrons and benefactors in the small hall of Christ's Hospital, Abingdon. As he had been present when most of the portraits had been received and hung, he knew whereof he spoke. So that their memories be preserved, he noted, the governors had caused the pictures to be made and displayed in the hall,

> which precedent posterity should do well to imitate and follow, doing the like for those benefactors that shall come after, preserving also those that be already made, keeping also still their names and works upon record ... It were to be wished that so

many of the [Governors] as God hath enabled would be good examples themselves to draw upon others, by extending and giving out of their estates, ... imitating and following therein the good examples of many that ... was in the like place of the Holy Cross as they are now in the Hospital of Christ.[46]

It remains to be noted that the didactic intent of civic portraits could readily be enhanced by displaying them in close quarters with other symbolically meaningful artefacts so as to form what amounted to a didactic programme within a single, enclosed space. Hanging a portrait of a civic worthy alongside portraits or crests of particular monarchs certainly achieved this effect. This was especially true when an institution derived its authority from the crown, as was the case with most of those considered here. Such proximity celebrated the particular king or queen who chartered the institution and conferred its authority. It visually connected the governing authority of the institution with that of the crown. It signified the institution's loyalty to the reigning monarch. (It remained less common to display portraits of manorial lords, past or present, in the same halls, as they more often than not represented figures who had opposed rather than fostered the emergence of local autonomy. The portrait of Henry Hastings, third earl of Huntingdon in the Leicester Guildhall proves an important exception, but Huntingdon was a particular friend and protector of the borough.)

John Vernon did, as we have noted, donate portraits of Henry VIII and Elizabeth to the Merchant Taylors along with his own. The governors of Christ's Hospital (Abingdon) did hang the portrait of Edward VI, its founding monarch, shoulder to shoulder with those of its own benefactors and masters. The borough council of Dover purchased its portrait of Elizabeth I in 1598 to be set up alongside local imagery in its hall;[47] the borough of Bristol hung crests of both Henry VIII and Elizabeth alongside civic portraits in its Guildhall, even paying to have them 'refreshed' in 1583.[48] The Grocers' Company of London had hung banner portraits of Elizabeth and James I by 1611 close to images of some of its own heroes.[49] Bury St Edmunds hung a portrait of James I in its Guildhall in 1616.[50] The 1639 inventory of paintings held by the Carpenters listed 'tables' of the king's arms (presumably Charles I) and pictures of Charles and his late brother Prince Henry, along with a portrait of its most prominent member, William Portington, who had been Master Carpenter of the Household from 1579 until his death at eighty-four in 1629.[51]

We have already noted how Christ's Hospital, Abingdon, used the strategy of physical proximity to emphasize institutional continuity from pre-Reformation to post-Reformation times. Some institutions engaged in a variation of this strategy, not so much to emphasize institutional continuity as institutional benefaction and civic virtue. They did this by displaying civic portraits in close company with those narrative scenes known in their time as 'history' paintings, usually depicting scenes from the Bible or classical history. A 1635 inventory of the Ironmongers notes a portrait of its benefactor Nicholas Leate hanging in the same room as a painting of the Herodians tempting Christ.[52] But an earlier and much more dramatic work of this type emerged, as noted in chapter 2, in the sixteenth-century tableau commissioned by the Carpenters' Company situating the occupation, and therefore the Company itself, in the context of both Old and New Testament events.[53]

Similar considerations of symbolic proximity were observed on ceremonial occasions, including feasts, company dinners, important holidays and visits of royalty or other dignitaries. The records of several livery companies in particular describe the 'hanging of the hall' for such occasions, in which cloth portrait-banners and all sorts of other ceremonial display could be put out alongside the permanent panel portraits to complete the scene. The Grocers' Company excelled at this. In addition to several panel portraits of its eminent brethren which were hung permanently, it also commissioned cloth portrait banners of Sir Thomas Lovell and three other Company worthies, Masters Lambert, Ryvers and Ramsay, presumably for display on those special occasions which required 'hanging the hall' in preparation. By 1612 there were also banner portraits of six other grocers who had served as Lord Mayors.[54] Though few if any of these cloth portrait banners have survived to the present day, an early nineteenth-century watercolour copy of some of those done for the Council Hall at Bristol show us what they looked like.[55]

Bristol's experience proves especially well documented. The borough's ruling elite undertook an extensive display of visual imagery in the 1620s and 1630s in their Council House, Tolzey and local grammar school, hanging portraits of founders and benefactors, living or deceased, in all three venues. By 1624, as we have seen, posthumous portraits of the former mayors and school-founders Robert and Nicholas Thorne hung in the Council Chamber,[56] with copies of the Thorne portraits added to the Grammar School and one of Sir Thomas White in the following year.[57] White was not a Bristol man himself, though he is easily enough confused with *two* namesakes who were ... and of whom there were also civic portraits. But he was certainly one of the borough's – and indeed the nation's – most spectacular benefactors.[58]

The Thornes' portraits in the Grammar School, done in 1625, permanently associated their memory with the fruits of their principal benefaction, noted above in chapter 2. The hanging of earlier copies of these portraits in 1624 (from originals done in the 1530s)[59] along with White's in the Council Chamber, a 'table' of benefactions,[60] and paintings of biblical scenes hung in the Tolzey, combined to form a powerful visual programme in the civic spaces of the borough. It can only have impressed upon Bristol's leaders for generations to come the virtues of civic benefaction.

Though civic portraits did sometimes serve the personal interests of the sitter, that was not their prime purpose. Nor was it their prime purpose, even if it had been practical to do so, to reach out to the widest possible audience through public and unregulated outdoor display. Portraits of benefactors or former officials no doubt made distinct impressions on the rank and file of those communities, to whom they communicated particular notions of civic behaviour and institutional identity. In that regard we may think of them as one of the numerous expressions of civic political culture which emerged to fill a void left by the Reformation. But perhaps even more importantly, they served as constant reminders of the virtues of civic benefaction, civil comportment, and sage governance for successive generations of the governing elites. And, along with other, more formal instruction manuals in the art of governance, they invoked the history and identity of the institution itself.

NOTES

1   See above, p. 30.

2   I am grateful to Professor Maurice Howard for this insight.

3   The seminal work on the social breadth of portrait ownership in England at this time remains Susan Foister, 'Paintings and Other Works of Art in Sixteenth Century English Inventories', *Burlington Magazine*, 123:938 (May, 1981), pp. 273–82.

4   Lionel Cust, 'The Lumley Inventories', *Walpole Society*, 6 (1918), pp. 15–35; Elizabeth Goldring, 'An Important Early Picture Collection: The Earl of Pembroke's 1561/62 Inventory and the Provenance of Holbein's "Christina of Denmark"', *Burlington Magazine*, 144 (March, 2002), pp. 157–60; and Goldring, 'The Earl of Leicester and the Portraits of the Duc d'Alençon', *Burlington Magazine*, 146 (Feb., 2004), pp. 108–11.

5   John Ingamells, *The English Episcopal Portrait, 1559–1835: A Catalogue* (1981), pp. 14–16.

6   Noted in Nigel Llewellyn, *Funeral Monuments in Post-Reformation England* (Cambridge, 2000), p. 337, albeit with Mulcaster's first name erroneously given as 'Robert'.

7   In 'If You Know Not Me, You Know Nobody', as cited in Lawrence Manley, *Literature and Culture in Early Modern London* (Cambridge, 1995), p. 129. See above, p. 149.

8   Victor Morgan, 'The Norwich Guildhall Portraits: Images in Context', in Andrew Moore and Charlotte Crawley, eds, *Family & Friends: A Regional Survey of British Portraiture* (1992), p. 22.

9   'Street Scene on Guild Day', from *Notices and Illustrations of the Costume Processions, Pageantry, etc., formerly displayed by the Corporation of Norwich* (Norwich, 1850), as reproduced in Morgan, 'Norwich Guildhall Portraits', p. 20, plate 17.

10 J.G. Nichols, ed., *The Chronicle of Queen Jane and Two Years of Queen Mary* (Camden Society 48, 1850), pp. 78–9; John Nichols, *The Progresses and Public Processions of Queen Elizabeth* (3 vols, 1823), I, p. 46.

11 See p. 53.

12 Descriptions of the paintings and inscriptions taken on site, 23 May 2002, and with the helpful comments of Ms Rhona Mitchell, Hospital Archivist at that time. See also Heinz Archive, *vide* Dixie, Dobbs, Leman; and Alfred B. Beaven, *The Aldermen of the City of*

London (2 vols, 1903), *vide* Dixie, Dobbs, Leman and Ramsay.

13   Unless indicated to the contrary, the following is taken from Francis Little, *A Monument of Christian Munificence, or An Account of the Brotherhood of the Holy Cross, and of the Hospital of Christ in Abingdon* [1627], ed., Claude Delaval Cobham (Oxford and London, 1871), pp. xv–xviii, 94, 95–9; Arthur Preston's *Christ's Hospital Abingdon: The Almshouses, the Hall and the Portraits* (Oxford, 1929), *passim*, and from an on-site visit in June 2002, expedited by the efficiency and courtesy of Mr Nigel Hammond, Archivist to the Foundation, to whom I am very grateful.

14   James Thompson, 'The Heyrick Portraits in the Guildhall, Leicester', *Transactions of the Leicestershire Architectural and Archaeological Society*, 2 (1820), p. 48; see also P.W. Hasler, ed., *The House of Commons, 1558–1603* (History of Parliament Trust, 3 vols, 1981), II, pp. 309–10 and Henry Hartopp, ed., *Roll of the Mayors of the Borough and Lord Mayors of the City of Leicester, 1209–1935* (Leicester [1935]), pp. 76–7.

15   For the restriction of admission to guildhalls in general by that time, see Robert Tittler, *The Reformation and the Towns in England: Politics and Political Culture, c. 1540–1640* (Oxford, 1998), pp. 267–9.

16   Quarter Court Minutes, Ironmongers' Company, Guildhall Library MS. 16967 2, fol. 6v (8 August 1604).

17   Exeter Corporation Act Book no. 5, Devon County Record Office (Exeter branch), p. 172 (20 June 1605).

18   Court Records, Merchant Taylors' Company, Guildhall Library, MS. 34010/9, fol. 91v (4 December 1639).

19   Grocers' Company, Wardens' Accounts, 1611–22, Guildhall Library MS. 11571/10, fol. 498v.

20   This is the small panel portrait (17¾ × 14¾") probably done by John Bettes in 1580/81. R.L. Poole, ed., *Catalogue of Portraits in the Possession of the University, Colleges, City and County of Oxford* (3 vols, Oxford Historical Society Publications, vols 57, 1912; 81, 1926; and 82, 1926), III, p. 157.

21   Hugh T. Dutton, *Chester Town Hall and its Treasures* (Chester, 1928), pp. 40–1.

22   Merchant Taylors' Company, Masters' and Wardens' Account Book, vol. 9 (unpaginated) Guildhall Library MS. 34048/9 for 1606–7; Frederick M. Fry, ed., *A Historical Catalogue of the Pictures, Herse-Cloths and Tapestry at Merchant Taylors' Hall* (1907), plate 38 and pp. 97–101.

23   For the portrait of Sir Henry Savile in 1635–36, Poole, ed., *Catalogue of Portraits*, I, pp. xiv and 79; of Richard Fleming at Lincoln College c. 1638, *ibid.*, II, p. 72; for Arthur Lake in 1626–27; *ibid.*, II, p. 153.

24   Cited in Henry Bradshaw, 'On the Collection of Portraits Belonging to the University before the Civil War' [1872], *Collected Papers of Henry Bradshaw* (Cambridge, 1889), p. 292.

25   My thanks for their comments on this issue to Maurice Howard, Catherine MacLeod, and especially Karen Hearn.

26   Will of Robert Ryece, gent., of Preston, Suffolk, 7 February, 1637/38; Nesta Evans, ed., *Wills of the Archdeaconry of Sudbury, 1636–1638* (Suffolk Record Society 35, 1993), p. 223.

27   This came at a cost of 18s 11d which might have paid for the picture itself. St John's College, Oxford MSS., '*Compotus Animus*' for 1583–84, fol. 21v. I am grateful to Dr

Malcolm Vale for affording me access to the College archives.

28 Remnants of such curtaining may often be seen in well-preserved personal portraits and other paintings of this time, as in the portrait of Sir Henry Unton (1586) in Tate Britain, where eye bolts for the curtain rods may still be seen affixed on to the picture frame. Tate Britain catalogue no. T00402. My thanks to Karen Hearn for pointing this out to me.

29 Eamon Duffy, *The Stripping of the Altars: Traditional Religion in England, c. 1400–1580* (London and New Haven, 1992), p. 111.

30 Cited in Fry, ed., *Catalogue*, p. 67–9, from Court Minutes of the Merchant Taylors' Company, now available as Guildhall Library microfilm, 328/7, fols, 244–6.

31 John Bold, 'Privacy and the Plan', in John Bold and Edward Chaney, eds, *English Architecture, Public and Private: Essays for Kerry Downs* (1993), pp. 109–112; Robert Tittler, *Architecture and Power: The Town Hall and the English Urban Community, c. 1500–1640* (Oxford, 1991), pp. 117–19.

32 See the full discussion in chapter 3, note 70, above.

33 Sidney Young, *The Annals of the Barber-Surgeons of London* (1890), p. 508.

34 It sounds as if de Critz undertook the commission before his elevation in the King's service, and then had no time to complete it expeditiously thereafter. *Ibid.*, p. 508.

35 *Ibid.*, p. 509.

36 *Ibid.*, pp. 509–10.

37 W.A.D. Englefield, *The History of the Painter-Stainers' Company of London* (1923), *Addenda*, p. vii.

38 Grocers' Company, Wardens' Accounts, 1557–58, Guildhall Library MS. 11571/6, fol. 80v.

39 Cited in Sir Walter Sherburne Prideaux, *Memorials of the Goldsmiths' Company* (2 vols, 1896), I, p. 129.

40 The following discussion has been informed by Anna Bryson, *From Courtesy to Civility: Changing Codes of Conduct in Early Modern England* (Oxford and New York, 1998), especially pp. 7, 24–35, 49–53, and 61–71.

41 Manley, *Literature and Culture, passim*. See also above, chapter 4, pp. 101–4.

42 Hooker, alias John Vowell, *The Description of the Citie of Excester* ... [c. 1575], eds, W.J. Harte, et al. (Devon and Cornwall Record Society, 3 vols, 1919–47); Henry Manship, *The History of Great Yarmouth*, [c. 1619], ed., Charles John Palmer (Great Yarmouth, 1854).

43 Patrick Collinson, 'Foreword' to Ian Gadd and Alexandra Gillespie, eds, *John Stow (1525–1605) and the Making of the English Past* (2004), p. xiii.

44 For biographical information see especially Hasler, ed., *House of Commons, 1558–1603*, II, pp. 333–5, *vide* Hooker; and Robert Tittler, 'Henry Manship: Constructing the Civic Memory in Great Yarmouth', in *Townspeople and Nation: English Urban Experiences, 1540–1640* (Stanford, 2001), pp. 121–39.

45 For the challenges facing local governing institutions, and especially towns, in the wake of the Reformation, see Tittler, *The Reformation and the Towns*, especially parts I and II.

46 Little, *A Monument to Christian Munificence*, pp. 94–9.

47 Susan Doran, ed., *Elizabeth: The Exhibition at the National Maritime Museum* (Greenwich, 2003), fig. 200 and pp. 196–8.

48 Audit Book for 1580–, Bristol Record Office MS. F/Au/1/12, p. 159.

49 Wardens' Accounts, Grocers' Company, Guildhall Library MS. 11571/10, annual inventory of 1611–1612, fol. 44v.

50 Margaret Statham, ed., *Accounts of the Feoffees of the Town Lands of Bury St Edmunds, 1569–22* (Suffolk Record Society 46, 2003), pp. iii and 239.

51 Prideaux, *Goldsmiths' Company*, I, p. 129; Inventory of the Company Hall, 1639, Guildhall MS. 4329A, fol. A. (This page, paginated by letters and not numbers, has been written upside down and beginning at the end of the volume moving towards the beginning.); Howard Colvin, ed., *A History of the King's Works* (6 vols, 1963–82), III, pp. 101 and 133.

52 Freemen's Registers and Inventories, Ironmongers' Company, Guildhall Library MS. 16988/5, p. 7 (6 August 1635).

53 Aside from an obvious sixteenth-century provenance, it is not clear whether this is the work for which 'Baker the painter' was allowed eleven yards of canvas for making 'The Story' in the Parlour of the hall in 1571, or an earlier work on display by 1561. There may indeed have been two such works, one of 1561 and one of a decade later. B.W.F. Alford and T.C. Barker, *A History of the Carpenters' Company* (1968), pp. 62, 150, 225–7.

54 Grocers' Company, Wardens' Accounts, 1566–67, Guildhall Library MS. 11571/6, fol. 44v and (for 1611–12) 11571/10, fols 42v–44v. See also references to repairing a banner of the former London Lord Mayor and goldsmith Sir Martin Bowes by that company in 1577 and 1606, and the extensive expenditure for banners and streamers by the Saddlers' Company to celebrate the accession of James I in 1603. Prideaux, *Goldsmiths' Company*, I, pp. 82 and 107, and Saddlers' Company, Wardens' Accounts, Guildhall Library MS. 5384, fol. 59r.

55 By Joseph Manning, c. 1828, Breckonridge Topographical Collection, Bristol City Museum Art Gallery. I am grateful to Ms Sheena Stoddart, Curator of the Bristol City Museum and Art Gallery, for pointing me to this and other sources on my visit of 15 July 2002.

56 Bristol Record Office MS. F/AU/1/19, pp. 294 and 296.

57 Bristol Record Office MS F/AU/1/20, p. 25 and 44; Jean Vanes, *Education and Apprenticeship in Sixteenth Century Bristol* (Bristol, 1982), unpaginated.

58 Even contemporaries found it difficult to sort out the three Thomas Whites who made their mark in sixteenth-century Bristol. Thomas White, mayor of Bristol in 1531, was a contemporary of the Thornes. When in 1625 the borough chamberlain sent to Coventry for a copy of what he thought was this White's picture, as he tells us in the audits for that year, he got one instead of Sir Thomas White, the London philanthropist; Bristol Record Office MS. F/AU/1/20, p. 44. The borough acquired the intended White image shortly thereafter. These two joined a portrait of Dr Thomas White, so that by about 1630 there were three portraits of men bearing that name. Those of the physician and the mayor still survive in the City Museum and Art Gallery, though the latter, on panel, is in poor condition and has broken into two pieces. The portrait of Sir Thomas White seems no longer to exist, though a 1828 watercolour copy of it, by Joseph Manning, may be found in the Breckonridge Collection.

59 Bristol Record Office MS. F/AU/1/19, pp. 294 and 296.

60 Bristol Record Office MS. F/AU/1/20, p. 37.

Conclusion

◆

O ne of the key themes to the political and social life of the Tudor and early Stuart age is the need for defining and establishing legitimacy. The accession of the Tudor dynasty itself, by battle at Bosworth Field rather than by peaceful succession, created an instant need for political and constitutional legitimacy. The Reformation and the royal supremacy over the Church created a crisis of both spiritual and constitutional legitimacy. The rapid rise of new groups up the social ladder, and of individual families within those groups, saw the same need among the landed and urban elites.

One of the solutions fixed upon by all these groups and institutions was legitimation by various forms of cultural expression: not merely by the ownership of a painting or the construction of a country house as a symbol of status and wealth, though those had their uses, but by the particular imagery which such material acquisitions could convey to those who perceived them. The Tudor monarchy understood this right from the start, though it was Henry VIII rather than his father who most emphatically acted on that recognition. By the end of his reign, and thanks to Holbein's understanding of 'Renaissance monarchy' as practised elsewhere and to his own manifest genius, Henry was able to become a visual icon as well as an imperious monarch. The landed and urban elites understood this too, with country houses, portraits, and fashionable clothing all bearing witness to that perception. It should not then surprise us that civic institutions followed suit, albeit slightly later, with far lesser resources and with somewhat different motivations. The town and guildhall, the civic regalia, the civic history, and the civic portrait all flourished under those circumstances; all spoke to the same need.

Part of this effort of legitimation consisted in the rush to retrieve the relevant past: Stone's 'frenzied ancestor worship of the age'. The extraordinary efforts of Elizabeth I exemplify this especially well. Having good cause to ponder her own legitimacy as queen, she had the heralds trace her genealogy back to Rollo, King of Normandy,[1] thereby setting the scene for equally audacious, or at least earnest, efforts down through the ranks of contemporary social elites. William Cecil had William Camden and other genealogists work on constructing a pedigree which threatened to become almost as long as his queen's, and many others undertook a similar quest.[2]

Portraiture was very much a part of this genealogical turn, sometimes almost literally so. Nicholas Bacon, Elizabeth's Lord Keeper of the Great Seal and Cecil's brother-in-law, found it much more difficult to indulge in extensive genealogies: his father was merely the sheep-reeve for the abbot of Bury St Edmunds. And yet, as presiding officer over the House of Lords, social acceptance can never have been far from his mind. Towards the end of his life he had a family tree drawn nonetheless, distinguished not with the heraldic shields which were conventional among his better-born colleagues, but with miniature portraits of recent generations hanging like apples from the branches of the drawn tree.[3] A quarter-century later James I had a similar portrait genealogy done so as to assert his descent from Margaret Tudor, and therefore his claim to the English throne.[4]

Civic institutions, often run by men actively striving for new social heights themselves, also took up portraiture as a means of legitimation. Those, like Gloucester, Exeter and Chester, with extensive traditions of such visual imagery and local craftsmen experienced in producing it, did so more readily than others. So did those, perhaps like Norwich, King's Lynn and Bristol, with easier access to continental models for its deployment. Just as written mayoral lists, reaching far back into the historic past of many towns and boroughs, came increasingly often to be compiled where records permitted, so portraits were commissioned by all types of civic institution towards the same end. Though some of the livery companies do seem to have attempted something of the sort on a limited and miniature scale in their 'tables' of multiple portraits, complete portrait runs of all former mayors, masters, and similar officials would ordinarily have been far too expensive, space-consuming and difficult to compile, especially when the written record of past officials tended to be so patchy. But portraits of selected and heroic figures, founders and benefactors, retrieved and perpetuated the memory of key points and people in the civic past. Especially when several were displayed together, whether intended (as in Norwich) as a formal series or (probably as in Abingdon) not, they effectively recreated an official genealogy of the institution, a family tree of the civic body.

Politics and the political process, in which the projection of imagery of authority was an integral part, are by no means issues which should be investigated exclusively at the pinnacle of the political system. It is a pervasive relationship, occurring at various levels of the body politic, and one which would not have been understood at the highest level if it had not been familiar at the lowest. Though one may well question the extent of the viewing audience for any of these portraits,[5] it is entirely likely that, over the course of time, far more people would have viewed the image of a provincial mayor, or of a college and school founder, and viewed it at closer range, than would have seen Rubens's 'Apotheosis of James I' in the ceiling at Whitehall. Along with other ceremonial and mimetic activites deployed to the same end, civic portraits helped frame the identity of the borough corporation and the college or livery company or the school and college just as much, and just in the same way, as Holbein's iconic image of Henry VIII served the monarchy. To contemporaries at least, such a portrait did indeed serve as the face of the institution.

NOTES

1 BL Kings MS 396, fols 3v–4r, as reprinted in Susan Doran, ed., *Elizabeth: The Exhibition at the National Maritime Museum* (Greenwich, 2003), fig. 100, p. 105.

2 *ODNB*, *vide* Cecil, Wiliam; Daniel Woolf, 'Senses of the Past in Tudor Britain', in Robert Tittler and Norman Jones, eds, *A Companion to Tudor Britain* (Oxford, 2004), p. 410.

3 Held privately, but reprinted with permission in Robert Tittler, *Nicholas Bacon: The Making of a Tudor Statesman* (London and Athens, Ohio, 1976), opposite p. 129.

4 Reprinted in Doran, ed., *Elizabeth*, fig. 266 and pp. 249–50.

5 See T.K. Rabb, 'Play not Politics: Who Really Understood the Symbolism of Renaissance Art?', *Times Literary Supplement* (10 Nov., 1995), pp. 18–20; Sidney Anglo, *Spectacle, Pageantry and Early Tudor Policy* (2nd edn, 1997), Preface, and Anglo, *Images of Tudor Kingship* (1992), as cited in Kevin Sharpe, *Remapping Early Modern England: The Culture of Seventeenth-Century Politics* (Cambridge, 2000), chapter 12 and especially pp. 456–9.

Appendix A

Civic portraits painted or acquired,
1500–1640

NB: This Appendix lists those portraits which have been confidently identified as meeting all the definitional criteria for civic portaiture prior to 1640 as laid out in chapter 1 above. Every effort has been made to identify and verify as many such works as possible. Numerous portraits have been omitted, some perhaps surprisingly so, as not verifiably meeting all the definitional requirements of civic portraiture prior to 1640. Still, this cannot claim to be a comprehensive list. Information about additional civic portraits or documented corrections to those listed here will be gratefully received. Both surviving and non-surviving portraits have been listed as verification deemed appropriate, with the latter being identified archivally. The list records, in order, the sitter(s), institution, date of acquisition when at least highly probable or certain, and painter if known.

A key to abbreviations of the most frequently cited works is as follows:

Harding 'List': George Perfect Harding, 'A List of Portraits, Pictures in Various Mansions of the United Kingdom', unpublished manuscript Heinz Archive, National Portrait Gallery (3 vols, 1804).

Heinz Archive: National Portrait Gallery Heinz Archive.

ODNB : H.C.G. Matthew and Brian Harrison, eds, *Oxford Dictionary of National Biography* (2004).

Poole: R.L. Poole, ed., *Catalogue of Portraits in in the Possession of the University, Colleges, City and County of Oxford* (3 vols, Oxford Historical Society Publications, vols 57, 1912; 81, 1926; and 82, 1926).

Willis: Robert Willis, ed., *The Architectural History of the University of Cambridge* (3 vols, Cambridge, 1886, ed., John Willis Clark, repr. 1988).

A.1 UNIVERSITY COLLEGES

Alcock, Bishop John, Jesus College, Cambridge; 1598 (?); anon.[1]
Allen, Thomas, Trinity College, Oxford; c. 1633; anon.[2]
Balsham, Hugh de, Peterhouse, Cambridge; c. 1565; anon.[3]
Beaufort, Lady Margaret, Christ's College, Cambridge; 1511–13; Maynarde Vewicke.[4]

Beaufort, Lady Margaret, Christ's College, Cambridge; c. 1530–40s; anon.[5]
Beaufort, Lady Margaret, Cambridge University; presented c. 1580; anon.[6]
Beaufort, Lady Margaret, Christ's College, Cambridge; c. 1580–90s; anon.[7]
Beaufort, Lady Margaret, Cambridge University; presented 1580; anon.[8]
Beaufort, Lady Margaret, St John's College, Cambridge; 1598; Rowland Lockey.[9]
Bennet, Simon, University College, Oxford; 1628, anon.[10]
Bennet, Simon, University College, Oxford; after 1628; anon.[11]
Bisse, Philip, Wadham College, Oxford; c. 1613; anon.[12]
Blythe, John, Peterhouse, Cambridge; 1617; John Newman (?).[13]
Bodley Frieze, Bodleian Library, Oxford (202 fresco portraits), 1618–20; John Clarke and Thomas Knight.[14]
Bodley, Sir Thomas, Bodleian Library, Oxford; purchased 1634/35; anon.[15]
Bodley, Sir Thomas, Bodleian Library, Oxford; 1636/37; 'a French painter'.[16]
Burghley, William Cecil, Lord, Cambridge University; by 1603; anon.[17]
Burgoyne, Thomas, Peterhouse, Cambridge; c. 1565; anon.[18]
Burton, Robert, Brasenose College, Oxford; 1635; Gilbert Jackson.[19]
Camden, William, Bodleian Library; presented between 1622 and 1647 (?); Marcus Gheeraerts the Younger (?).[20]
Camden, William, Worcester College, Oxford; presented 1622; anon.[21]
Castro-Bernard, Thomas de, Peterhouse, Cambridge; c. 1565; anon.[22]
Cecil, Robert, Cambridge University; c. 1603; anon.[23]
Charles, Prince of Wales, Cambridge University; acquired 1612–13; Robert Peake.[24]
Chichele, Henry, All Souls, Oxford; 1609; Sampson Strong.[25]
Cosins, Joseph, Peterhouse, Cambridge; 1634; anon.[26]
Denman, Thomas, Peterhouse, Cambridge; c. 1565; anon.[27]
Devorguilla, Lady, Balliol College, Oxford; pre–1600; anon.[28]
Devorguilla, Lady, Balliol College, Oxford; 1604/5; anon.[29]
Edmondes, John, Peterhouse, Cambridge; c. 1565; anon.[30]
Edward I, Peterhouse, Cambridge; c. 1565; anon.[31]
Elizabeth I, Cambridge University; 1588–89; Mr Skinner.[32]
Elizabeth I, Cambridge University; by 1603; anon.[33]
Fleming, Richard, Lincoln College, Oxford; 1638; anon.[34]
Fox, Richard, Corpus Christi College, Oxford; c. 1528–32; Jan Rav (Johannes Corvus).[35]
Fox, Richard, Corpus Christi College, Oxford; presented 1579; anon.[36]
Fox, Richard, Corpus Christi College, Oxford; 1604; Sampson Strong.[37]
Frankland, Joyce, Gonville and Caius, Cambridge; 1586; anon.[38]
Frankland, Joyce, Brasenose College, Oxford; c. 1586/87; anon.[39]
Frankland, Joyce, Brasenose College, Oxford; after 1586/87; anon.[40]
Frankland, Joyce, Emmanuel College, Cambridge; after 1586; anon.[41]
Frankland, Joyce, Brasenose College, Oxford; c. 1638; Gilbert Jackson (?).[42]
Godwin, Francis, Christ Church, Oxford; 1613; anon.[43]
Hanson, Edmund, Peterhouse, Cambridge; c. 1565; anon.[44]
Henry VI, All Souls, Oxford; late 16th/early 17th C.; anon.[45]
Henry VIII, Trinity, Cambridge; given by Henry Beaumont; 1567; anon.[46]
Heton, Martin, Christ Church, Oxford; 1609; anon.[47]
Holbroke, John, Peterhouse, Cambridge; c. 1565; anon.[48]

Hornbie, Henry, Peterhouse, Cambridge; c. 1565; anon.[49]
James I, Cambridge University; acquired 1611–12; anon.[50]
James, Thomas, Bodleian Library, Oxford; betwen 1622 and 1643; Gilbert Jackson (?).[51]
King, John, Christ Church, Oxford; 1620; Nicholas Lockey (?).[52]
King, John, Christ Church, Oxford; 1622; Daniel Mytens (?).[53]
Lake, Arthur, New College, Oxford; 1626/27; Richard Greenbury.[54]
Lane, Thomas, Peterhouse, Cambridge; c. 1565; anon.[55]
Langham, Bishop Simon, Peterhouse, Cambridge; c. 1565; anon.[56]
Leicester, Robert Dudley, Earl of, Cambridge University; presented 1580; anon.[57]
Lownde, Mr, Peterhouse, Cambridge; c. 1565; anon.[58]
Martin, William, Peterhouse, Cambridge; c. 1565; anon.[59]
Matthew, Tobias, Christ Church, Oxford; 1610/11; anon.[60]
Mildmay, Sir Walter, Emmanuel, Cambridge; 1588; anon.[61]
Montacute, Simon de, Peterhouse, Cambridge; c. 1565; anon.[62]
Montague, James, Sidney Sussex, Cambridge; between 1616 and 1639; anon.[63]
Mordaunt, John, Baron, Brasenose College, Oxford; between 1564 and 1638; anon.[64]
Mordaunt, John, Baron, Brasenose College, Oxford; 1638; Gilbert Jackson.[65]
North, Sir Edward, Peterhouse, Cambridge; c. 1565; anon.[66]
Nowell, Alexander, Brasenose College, Oxford; pre–1640; anon.[67]
Paddy, Sir William, St John's College, Oxford; c. 1600; Marcus Gheeraerts (?).[68]
Parker, Matthew, Cambridge University; presented 1580; anon.[69]
Pate, Richard, Corpus Christi College, Oxford; 1550; anon.[70]
Perkins, William, Sidney Sussex, Cambridge; by 1639; anon.[71]
Perne, Andrew, Peterhouse, Cambridge; 1589; anon.[72]
Petre, Sir William, Exeter College, Oxford; 1567; anon.[73]
Pope, Lady Elizabeth, Trinity College, Oxford; 1612/13; anon.[74]
Pope, Thomas, Trinity College, Oxford; acquired 1596; anon.[75]
Pope, Thomas, Trinity College, Oxford; c. 1637; anon.[76]
Ravis, Thomas, Christ Church, Oxford; 1609–10; anon.[77]
Savile, Henry, Oxford University; given 1622; anon.[78]
Shirton, Dr, Peterhouse, Cambridge; c. 1565; anon.[79]
Sidney, Frances, Countess of Sussex, Sidney Sussex, Cambridge; painted c. 1565, acquired by 1590s; Steven van de Meulen.[80]
Sidney, Frances, Countess of Sussex, Sidney Sussex, Cambridge; painted c. 1575, acquired by 1590s; George Gower.[81]
Sidney, Frances, Countess of Sussex, Sidney Sussex, Cambridge; acquired 1601; anon.[82]
Slade, Robert, Peterhouse, Cambridge; 1616; John Newman (?).[83]
Smith, Robert, Peterhouse, Cambridge; c. 1565; anon.[84]
Smyth, William, Wadham College, Oxford; 1635; Gilbert Jackson.[85]
Wainfleet, William of, New College, Oxford; given pre–1613; anon.[86]
Wainfleet, William of, Magdalen College, Oxford; 1638; Richard Greenbury.[87]
Warkeworth, John, Peterhouse, Cambridge; c. 1565; anon.[88]
Westphaling, Herbert, Jesus College, Oxford; 1601; anon.[89]
Whitgift, Archbishop John, Peterhouse, Cambridge; c. 1589; anon.[90]
White, Sir Thomas, St John's College, Oxford; 16th C.; anon.[91]

White, Sir Thomas, St John's College, Oxford; 1580/81 (?); John Bettes (?).[92]
White, Sir Thomas, St John's College, Oxford; 1580/81; anon.[93]
White, Sir Thomas, St John's College, Oxford; 1583/84; anon.[94]
Wilshawe, Henry, Peterhouse, Cambridge; c. 1589; anon.[95]
Wolfe, Mrs Tabitha, Peterhouse, Cambridge; c. 1565; anon.[96]
Wolsey, Cardinal Thomas, Christ Church, Oxford; early/mid-16th C.; anon.[97]
Wolsey, Cardinal Thomas, Christ Church, Oxford; 1610–11; Sampson Strong.[98]
Wolsey, Cardinal Thomas, Magdalen College; Oxford; by 1618; Sampson Strong (?).[99]
Woodville, Elizabeth, Queen's College, Oxford; 16th C., anon.[100]
Wright, Robert, Trinity College, Oxford; 1632; anon.[101]
Wright, Robert, Wadham College, Oxford; c. 1632; anon.[102]
Wyckham, William of, New College, Oxford; 1596; Sampson Strong.[103]
Wyckham, William of, New College, Oxford; by 1611 if by Strong; Sampson Strong (?).[104]
Wyckham, William of, New College, Oxford; bequeathed by Dr Ryves, by 1613; anon.[105]

A.2 PROVINCIAL TOWNS AND CITIES

Anon. Alderman, Bristol; 1583; anon.[106]
Atkin, William, King's Lynn; c. 1619; anon.[107]
Atwell, Lawrence, Exeter; painted 1588, purchased 1599; anon.[108]
Bell, Sir Thomas, Gloucester; c. 1600; anon.[109]
Blackaller, John, Exeter; c. 1560s; anon.[110]
Bright, Thomas, Bury St Edmunds; 1616; Mr Fenn.[111]
Borough, Walter, Exeter; 1626; anon.[112]
Coke, Sir Edward, Norwich; c. 1587; anon.[113]
Cole, Edward, Winchester; c. 1617; anon.[114]
Cooke, John and Joan, Gloucester; c. 1590–c. 1620; anon.[115]
Crew, Philip, Salisbury; c. 1638, anon.[116]
Davenport, Christopher, Coventry; early 17th C.[117]
Denny, William (?), Norwich; c. 1619; anon.[118]
Drake, Sir Francis, Plymouth; 1616; anon.[119]
Elizabeth I, Dover; 1598; anon.[120]
Falkner, John, Gloucester; c. 1600; anon.[121]
Fawcett, Henry, Norwich; 1608; anon.[122]
Flexney, Ralph, Oxford City; *tempus* James I; anon.[123]
Godiva, Lady, Coventry; 1586; Adam van Noort(?).[124]
Goldston, Joan, Gloucester; c. 1600; anon.[125]
Goldston, William, Gloucester; c. 1600; anon.[126]
Green, Joshua, King's Lynn; early 17th C., anon.[127]
Grobham, Sr. Richard, Salisbury; c. 1630; anon.[128]
Harrington, George, Bristol; 1630; anon.[129]
Haydon, John, Gloucester; late 16th C.; anon.[130]
Hernsey/Hornsey, Robert (?), Norwich; 1630s; anon.[131]
Heyricke, Robert, Leicester; by 1618; anon.[132]
Heyricke, William, Leicester; 1594; anon.[133]
Hobart, Sir Henry (?), Norwich; early 17th C.; anon.[134]

Hooker, John Vowell, alias, Exeter; late 16th/early 17th C.; anon.[135]
Huntingdon, Henry Hastings, third earl of; Leicester; 1623; Christopher Carter.[136]
Hurst, William, Exeter; 1568 (?); anon.[137]
James I, Bury St Edmunds; 1616; Mr Fenn.[138]
Jannys, Robert, Norwich; early 17th C.; anon.[139]
Jesson, Thomas, Coventry; 1636; anon.[140]
Kendrick, John, Reading; 1624; anon.[141]
King, Thomas, Norwich; early 17th C.; anon.[142]
Kitchen, Robert, Bristol; c. 1594; anon.[143]
Layer, Thomas, Norwich; 1606; anon.[144]
Marsham, John, Norwich; early 17th C. (?); anon.[145]
Moundford, Francis (?), Norwich; 16th C; anon.[146]
Offley, William, Chester; early 17th C.; anon.[147]
Pate, Richard, Gloucester; c. 1600; anon.[148]
Pembroke, Philip Herbert, fourth earl of, Bristol; c. 1627; anon.[149]
Percy, Alan, Norwich; 1549 (?); anon.[150]
Periam, John, Exeter; 1616; John Browke/Brooke (?).[151]
Pettus, Sir John, Norwich; 1612; anon.[152]
Popley, Joan, Salisbury; late 16th C., anon.[153]
Poulton, Thomas, Gloucester, c. 1600; anon.[154]
Rede, Mrs Anne, Norwich; late 16th C., anon.[155]
Rede, Sir Peter, Norwich; 1568; anon.[156]
Seldon, Lawrence, Exeter; 1606; anon.[157]
Smith, Mrs Joanna, Norwich; 1594; anon.[158]
Smyth, Jankyn, Bury St Edmunds; 1616; Mr Fenn.[159]
Snelling, Thomas, King's Lynn; c. 1622 (?); anon.[160]
Steward, Augustine, Norwich; late 16th C; anon.[161]
Stonyng, Gregory, Lichfield; mid–16th C.; anon.[162]
Thorne, John, Gloucester; 1618; anon.[163]
Thorne, Nicholas, Bristol; 1530; anon.[164]
Thorne, Nicholas, Bristol; 1624; 'the Dutch Painter'.[165]
Thorne, Nicholas, Bristol; 1625; 'the Dutch Painter'.[166]
Thorne, Robert, Bristol; 1536; anon.[167]
Thorne, Robert, Bristol; 1624; 'the Dutch Painter'.[168]
Thorne, Robert, Bristol; 1625; 'the Dutch Painter'.[169]
Tooker, Giles, Salisbury; 1619; anon.[170]
Tuckfield, Joan, Exeter; 1573; anon.[171]
Vernon, John, Chester; 1616; anon.[172]
Wetherstone, Isabel, Gloucester; c. 1600; anon.[173]
Wheatley, Thomas, Coventry; by 1597; anon.[174]
White, Thomas, (Mayor of) Bristol; 16th C.; anon.[175]
White, Dr Thomas, Bristol; 1625; anon.[176]
White, Sir Thomas, Bristol; 1566; anon.[177]
White, Sir Thomas, Bristol; 1625; 'John the painter'.[178]
White, Sir Thomas, Canterbury; acquired 1608; anon.[179]
White, Sir Thomas, Chester; by 1593; anon.[180]

White, Sir Thomas, Coventry; hung 1593; anon.[181]
White, Sir Thomas, Exeter; 1566 (?); anon.[182]
White, Sir Thomas, Gloucester; pre–1640; anon.[183]
White, Sir Thomas, Leicester; pre-1640; anon.[184]
White, Sir Thomas, Lincoln; pre–1640; anon.[185]
White, Sir Thomas, Norwich; 16th C.; anon.[186]
White, Sir Thomas, Oxford City; 1597; Sampson Strong.[187]
White, Sir Thomas, Oxford City; 1633; anon.[188]
White, Sir Thomas, Reading; 1566 (?); anon.[189]
White, Sir Thomas, Salisbury; late 16th/early 17th C.; anon.[190]
White, Sir Thomas, Winchester; c. 1600; anon.[191]
Willsheire, Gregory, Gloucester; c. 1600; anon.[192]
Wyndham, Francis, Norwich; 1592; anon.[193]
Yarham, Robert, Norwich; 1591; anon.[194]

APPENDIX A.3 LONDON LIVERY COMPANIES

Adams, William, Haberdashers, hung c. 1598; anon.[195]
Aldersay, Thomas, Haberdashers, hung c. 1598; anon.[196]
Aske, Robert, Haberdashers, hung c. 1598; anon.[197]
Babb, Thomas, Painter-Stainers (see Pargeter below).
Barber-Surgeons (Group Portrait); 1543; Hans Holbein the Younger.[198]
Buck, [John], Drapers; by 1620; anon.[199]
Bunce, James, Leathersellers; by 1631; anon.[200]
Campbell, Sir James, Ironmongers; c. 1640; Edward Cooke.[201]
Carleton, Thomas, Painter-Stainers (see 'Potkyn' below).
Charles, Prince of Wales, Merchant Taylors; c. 1603–7, John de Critz.[202]
Crathorne [Craythorne/Cawthorne], Mrs Margaret, Cutlers; 1569; anon.[203]
Craven, Sir William, Merchant Taylors, early 17th C.; anon.[204]
Dane, Mrs Margaret, Ironmongers; painted 1579; acquired 1604; anon.[205]
Denham, Sir William, Ironmongers, c. 1640; Edward Cooke.[206]
Dowe, Robert, Merchant Taylors; c. 1606; John de Critz.[207]
Dummer, Mr, Drapers; by 1620; anon.[208]
Elizabeth I, Merchant Taylors; 1616; anon.[209]
Gammage, Anthony, Ironmongers; 1604; anon.[210]
Gray, Robert, Merchant Taylors; painted 1633, hung 1639; Cornelius Janssen (?).[211]
Gwin [Gwyn, Gwynn, Gwinn], Dr [Matthew], Barber-Surgeons; 1627/28; anon.[212]
Hallwood, Thomas, Ironmongers; 1640; Edward Cooke.[213]
Heylin, Rowland, Ironmongers; c. 1640; Edward Cooke.[214]
Hyde, Bernard, Salters; by 1640 (?); Edward Cooke.[215]
Jolles, Sir John, Drapers; by 1620; anon.[216]
Jones, William, Haberdashers; hung c. 1598; anon.[217]
Leat(e), Nicholas, Ironmongers; painted by 1631, presented 1631; Daniel Mytens.[218]
Lee, Sir Henry, Armourers and Brasiers'; c. 1602; Marcus Gheerearts the Younger.[219]
Lewen [Lewin], Thomas, Ironmongers; 1640; Edward Cooke.[220]
Lovell, Sir Thomas, Grocers; by 1566/67; anon.[221]

Myddleton, Sir Hugh, Goldsmiths; painted 1628, presented 1633; Cornelius Janssen.[222]

Mitchell [Michell], Thomas, Ironmongers; 1640; Edward Cooke.[223]

Owen, Dame Alice, Brewers; 1610 (?); anon.[224]

Pargeter, Clement, with William Peacock and Thomas Babb, Painter-Stainers; 1623/24; Cornelius Janssen (?).[225]

Peacock, William, Painter-Stainers (see 'Pargeter' above).

Platt, Richard, Brewers; dated 1600; anon.[226]

Portington, William, Carpenters; dated 1626; listed 1639; anon.[227]

Potkyn, John, with Thomas Carleton and John Taylor, Painter-Stainers; 1631; anon.[228]

Robson, William, Salters; by c. 1640; Edward Cooke.[229]

Russell, Sir Thomas, Drapers; by 1620; anon.[230]

Soame, Sir Stephen, Grocers; hung by 1619; anon.[231]

Southern, Nowell, Merchant Taylors; 1608; John de Critz.[232]

Swinnerton, Sir John, Merchant Taylors; pre-1616; anon.[233]

Taylor, John, Painter-Stainers (see Potkyn above).

Thorold, Thomas, Ironmongers; 1637; Cornelius Janssen.[234]

Vernon, John, Merchant Taylors, presented by sitter, 1616; anon.[235]

White, Sir Thomas, Merchant Taylors, 1606; John de Critz.[236]

Whitmore, Sir George, Haberdashers; hung c. 1598; anon.[237]

A.4 CHARITABLE INSTITUTIONS (INCLUDING SCHOOLS)

Abbot, George, Abbot's Hospital, Guildford, Surrey; between 1609 and 1623; anon.[238]

Barbour, Jeffrey, with John Howchion ('The Bridge Builders'), Christ's Hospital, Abingdon; 1607; Sampson Strong (?).[239]

Bessils, Sir Peter, Christ's Hospital, Abingdon; 1607; Sampson Strong (?).[240]

Bostock, Lionel, Christ's Hospital, Abingdon; c. 1607; Sampson Strong (?).[241]

Bridewell Hospital, London (Group Portrait); shortly after 1553; anon.[242]

Christ's Hospital (London/Horsham) (Group Portrait); shortly after 1553; anon.[243]

Dixie, Sir Wolstan, Christ's Hospital (London/Horsham); 1593; anon.[244]

Dobbs, Sir Richard, Christ's Hospital (London/Horsham); c. 1560s; anon.[245]

Edward VI, Christ's Hospital, Abingdon; c. 1600–10; attrib. Simon van de Pass.[246]

Foxe, John, Trinity Hospital, Guildford; late 16th C.; anon.[247]

Knevit, Alice, Free School and Alms House at Radcliffe; between 1539 and 1598; anon.[248]

Leman, Sir John, Christ's Hospital (London/Horsham); by 1640; anon.[249]

Mason, Sir John, Christ's Hospital, Abingdon; 1607; Sampson Strong.[250]

Orpwood, Robert, Christ's Hospital, Abingdon; presented 1615; Sampson Strong (?).[251]

Parkins, John, Christ's Hospital, Abingdon; 1607; Sampson Strong (?).[252]

Platt, Richard, Aldenham Grammar School; painted 1600, presented 1611; anon.[253]

Ramsay, Lady Mary, Christ's Hospital (London/Horsham); by 1640; anon.[254]

Sutton, Thomas, Charterhouse; painted c. 1590s, presented 1622; anon.[255]

Teasdale, Maud, Christ's Hospital, Abingdon; 1612; anon. Sampson Strong (?).[256]

Appendix A

NOTES

1 Communication from Ms Frances Willmoth and Dr Rod Mengham of Jesus College, to whom I am very grateful, based on records in the College audit book for the years 1569–98. This is likely to be a copy of an earlier portrait done at the beginning of the sixteenth century.

2 Poole, *Catalogue*, III, p. 125.

3 Heinz Archive, *vide* 'Collections for Peterhouse'; Willis, I, p. 64.

4 Frederick Hepburn, 'The Portraiture of Lady Margaret Beaufort', *Antiquaries Journal*, 72 (1992), pp. 118–20, 130, 136; Roy Strong, *Tudor and Jacobean Portraits*, (2 vols, 1969), I, p. 20; C.H. Cooper, *Memoir of Margaret, Countess of Richmond and Derby* (1874). Neither this nor other near-contemporary portraits of Margaret are now thought to have survived.

5 Hepburn, 'Portraiture of Lady Margaret Beaufort', p. 131 and fig. 7.

6 Henry Bradshaw, 'On the Collection of Portraits Belonging to the University before the Civil War' [1872], *Collected Papers of Henry Bradshaw* (Cambridge, 1889), p. 287.

7 Hepburn, 'Portraiture of Lady Margaret Beaufort', pp. 128–9. This had previously been mis-identifed as a c. 1504 portrait, but tree-ring dating has confirmed the mid- to late Elizabethan date instead.

8 J.W. Goodison, ed., *Catalogue of Cambridge Portraits*, I., *The University Collection* (Cambridge, 1955), p. xvii.

9 Hepburn, 'Portraiture of Lady Margaret Beaufort', pp. 122–3; Strong, *Tudor and Jacobean Portraits*, I, pp. 21–2; *ODNB*, *vide*, Lockey, Rowland.

10 Poole, *Catalogue*, II, p. 2.

11 A copy of the 1628 portrait. *Ibid.*, II, p. 2.

12 Commissioned by Bisse's widow for the College after his death; *ibid*, III, p. 211.

13 T.A. Walker, *A Biographical Register of Peterhouse Men* (2 vols, Cambridge, 1927 and 1930), II, p. 294; Heinz Archive, *vide* 'Collections for Peterhouse'; Willis, I, p. 68.

14 J.N.L. Myres, 'The Painted Frieze in the Picture Gallery', *Bodleian Library Record*, 3 (1950–51), pp. 82–90; J.N.L. Myres and E. Clive Rouse, 'Further Notes on the Painted Frieze and Other Discoveries in the Upper Reading Room and the Tower Room', *Bodleian Library Record*, 5 (Oct., 1956), pp. 290–308; J.N.L. Myres, 'Thomas James and the Painted Frieze', *Bodleian Library Record*, 4 (1952–53), pp. 30–51; M.R.A. Bullard, 'Talking Heads: The Bodleian Frieze, its Inspiration, Sources, Design and Significance', *Bodleian Library Record*, 14:6 (Apr., 1994), pp. 461–83.

15 Purchased for 30s; Poole, *Catalogue*, I, p. 29.

16 Purchased for £2; *ibid.*, I, p. 29

17 Goodison, ed., *Catalogue of Cambridge Portraits*, I, p. xx; Bradshaw, 'On the Collection of Portraits', p. 291.

18 Heinz Archive, *vide* 'Collections for Peterhouse'; Willis, I, p. 64.

19 Poole, *Catalogue*, II, p. 251.

20 *Ibid.*, I, pp. 32–3.

21 *Ibid.*, III, p. 256.

22 Heinz Archive, *vide* 'Collections for Peterhouse'; Willis, I, pp. 64–5.

23 This was presumably acquired to mark Cecil's appointment as Chancellor of the University in 1601/2; Bradshaw, 'On the Collection of Portraits', p. 292; Goodison, ed., *Catalogue of Cambridge Portraits*, p. xx.

24 Bradshaw, 'On the Collection of Portraits', p. 292.

25 Poole, *Catalogue* II, p. 181.

26 Heinz Archive, *vide* 'Collections for Peterhouse'; Willis, I, p. 64.

27 Heinz Archive, *vide* 'Collections for Peterhouse'; Willis, I, p. 65.

28 Poole, *Catalogue*, II, p. 18.

29 *Ibid.* II, pp. 17–18.

30 Heinz Archive, *vide* 'Collections for Peterhouse'; Willis, I, p. 66.

31 Heinz Archive, *vide* 'Collections for Peterhouse'; Willis, I, p. 63.

32 Bradshaw, 'On the Collection of Portraits', p. 292.

33 Goodison, ed., *Catalogue of Cambridge Portraits*, I, p. xx; possibly that given by a Mr Skinner, c. 1588–89; Bradshaw, 'On the Collection of Portraits', p. 292.

34 Poole, *Catalogue*, II, p. 172.

35 *Ibid.*, II, pp. 261–3, misdating it to as early as 1518; Strong, *Tudor and Jacobean Portraits*, I, p. 125; *ODNB*, *vide* Fox, Richard.

36 Poole, *Catalogue*, II, p. 263–4; Strong, *Tudor and Jacobean Portraits*, I, p. 126.

37 Poole, *Catalogue*, II, pp. 263–4; Strong, *Tudor and Jacobean Portraits*, I, p. 126.

38 Poole, *Catalogue*, II, pp. 248–9; Heinz Archive, *vide* Frankland, Joyce.

39 Considered to be modelled on the original at Gonville and Caius, Cambridge; Poole, *Catalogue*, II, pp. 248 (no. 11).

40 *Ibid.*, II, pp. 248–9 (no. 12).

41 Heinz Archive, *vide* Frankland, Joyce.

42 Poole, *Catalogue*, II, p. 248 (no. 13).

43 *Ibid.*, III, p. 22.

44 Heinz Archive, *vide* 'Collections for Peterhouse'; Willis, I, p. 65.

45 Strong, *Tudor and Jacobean Portraits*, I, p. 147; Poole, *Catalogue*, II, p. 180.

46 Goodison, ed., *Catalogue of Cambridge Portraits*, I, p. xviii.

47 Poole, *Catalogue*, III, p. 17.

48 Heinz Archive, *vide* 'Collections for Peterhouse'; Willis, I, p. 65.

49 Heinz Archive, *vide* 'Collections for Peterhouse'; Willis, I, p. 65.

50 Bradshaw, 'On the Collection of Portraits', p. 292.

51 James stepped down as Bodley Librarian in 1622 and died in 1629; Jackson, to whom this is usually attributed, died in 1643. Poole, *Catalogue*, I, p. 36; *ODNB*, *vide* James, Thomas and Jackson, Gilbert.

52 Poole, *Catalogue*, III, pp. 19–20.

53 *Ibid.*, III, p. 20.

54 The extant painting may be a copy of the original by Greenbury, but the date and authorship of that original is documented in the College archives as cited in Poole, *Catalogue*, II, pp. 153–5.

55 Heinz Archive, *vide* 'Collections for Peterhouse'; Willis, I, p. 65.

56 Heinz Archive, *vide* 'Collections for Peterhouse'; Willis, I, p. 64.

57 Goodison, ed., *Catalogue of Cambridge Portraits*, I, p. xvii; Henry Bradshaw, 'On the Collection of Portraits', p. 287.

58 Heinz Archive, *vide* 'Collections for Peterhouse'; Willis, I, p. 66.

59 Heinz Archive, *vide* 'Collections for Peterhouse'; Willis, I, p. 66.

60 Poole, *Catalogue*, III, pp. 20–1.

61 *ODNB*, *vide* Mildmay, Sir Walter. Two other portraits in the College's possession, dated 1574 and 1579, cannot be verified as acquired by the College in this era.

62 Heinz Archive, *vide* 'Collections for Peterhouse'; Willis, I, p. 66.

63 J.W. Goodison, ed., *Catalogue of the Portraits in Christ's, Clare and Sidney Sussex Colleges* (Cambridge, 1985), pp. 81–2.

64 Poole, *Catalogue*, II, p. 247.

65 *Ibid.*, II, p. 247.

66 Heinz Archive, *vide* 'Collections for Peterhouse'; Willis, I, p. 67.

67 Poole, *Catalogue*, II, p. 249–50.

68 *Ibid.*, III, pp. 163–4.

69 Goodison, ed., *Catalogue of Cambridge Portraits*, I, p. xvii; Bradshaw, 'On the Collection of Portraits', p. 287.

70 Poole, *Catalogue*, II, pp. 267–8; A.L. Browne, 'Richard Pates, MP for Gloucester', *Transactions of the Bristol and Gloucestershire Archeological Society*, 56 (1935 for 1934), p. 221 and plate opp. p. 201.

71 Goodison, *Catalogue of the Portraits in Christ's, Clare and Sidney Sussex Colleges*, p. 84.

72 Heinz Archive, *vide* 'Collections for Peterhouse'; Willis, I, p. 66; R.J. Skaer, 'The Panel Portrait of Andrew Perne', *Peterhouse: a Record* (volume for 1997–98, published 1999), pp. 38–41.

73 Poole, *Catalogue*, II, p. 65.

74 *Ibid.*, III, pp. 122–3.

75 Copied from an earlier, 1558, personal portrait; Poole, *Catalogue*, III, pp. 117–18.

76 *Ibid.*, III, p. 119.

77 *Ibid.*, III, p. 17.

78 *Ibid.*, I, pp. xiv and 32.

79 Heinz Archive, *vide* 'Collections for Peterhouse'; Willis, I, p. 66;

80 Goodison, ed., *Catalogue of the Portraits in Christ's, Clare and Sidney Sussex Colleges*, pp. 86–7.

81 *Ibid.*, p. 87.

82 *Ibid.*, p. 87.

83 Heinz Archive, *vide* 'Collections for Peterhouse'; Willis, I, p. 68; T.A. Walker, *A Biographical Register of Peterhouse Men* (2 vols, Cambridge, 1927 and 1930), II, p. 294.

84 Heinz Archive, *vide* 'Collections for Peterhouse'; Willis, I, p. 67.

85 Poole, *Catalogue*, III, p. 216.

86 *Ibid.*, II, pp. 149; will of Warden Ryves, 1613, National Archives, Family Record Centre, PROB 11/121, fol. 4r.

87 *Ibid.*, II, pp. xix, 149 and 209.

88 Heinz Archive, *vide* 'Collections for Peterhouse'; Willis, I, p. 65.

89 Poole, *Catalogue*, III, p. 191.

90 Heinz Archive, *vide* 'Collections for Peterhouse'; Willis, I, p. 67.

91 On panel, 32¼ × 25". It is this which served as the model for Faber's engraving of 1712; Poole, *Catalogue*, III, pp. 155–6.

92 On panel, 17¾ × 14¾". Probably that for which John Bettes was paid in 1580/81, and which was recorded as extant in 1597; Poole, *Catalogue*, III, p. 157; W.H. Stevenson and H.E. Salter, *The Early History of St John's College* (Oxford Historical Society Publications, 1939), p. 386.

93 The second of the 'two counterfaytes of our Founder' which are cited in Stevenson and Salter, *The Early History of St John's College*, p. 386.

94 A lost painting of 1583–84 cited in the College's Bursar's Accounts by Poole, *Catalogue*, III, p. 159.

95 Heinz Archive, *vide* 'Collections for Peterhouse'; Willis, I, p. 67.

96 Heinz Archive, *vide* 'Collections for Peterhouse'; Willis, I, p. 67.

97 Considered the earliest Wolsey portrait held by the College; Poole, *Catalogue*, III, p. 4.

98 *Ibid.*, III, pp. 4–5.

99 *Ibid.*, II, pp. 211–12.

100 The one portrait of Woodville known to have been held by Queen's College prior to 1640 may be a copy of the late fifteenth-century work; *To Prove a Villain, the Real Richard III*, exhibition at the Royal National Theatre (1991), with commentary by Pamela Tudor-Craig; www.r3.org/rnt1991/paintedqueen.html.

101 Poole, *Catalogue*, III, p. 126.

102 *Ibid.*, III, pp. 214–15.

103 *Ibid.*, II, p. 147.

104 *Ibid.*, II, pp. 146–7; possibly based on Strong's 1596 painting.

105 *Ibid.*, II, p. 147.

106 Richard Quick, ed., *Catalogue of the Second Loan Collection of Pictures held in the Bristol Art Gallery* (Bristol, 1905), no. 227.

107 Information provided by R.W. Edwards, Head of Design Services, Borough of King's Lynn, letter of 25 July 1991, and on-site visit facilitated by Mr David Pitcher; I am grateful to both for this information.

108 Exeter Corporation Act Book no. 5, Devon County Record Office (Exeter Branch), p. 432; George Oliver, *History of the City of Exeter* (1861) p. 219; Hugh Lloyd Parry, *The History of the Exeter Guildhall and the Life Within* (Exeter, 1936), p. 153.

109 Brian Frith, *Twelve Portraits of Gloucester Benefactors* (Gloucester, 1972), pp. 11–12.

110 S.T. Bindoff, ed., *The House of Commons 1509–1558* (History of Parliament Trust, 3 vols, 1982), I, p. 439; Hooker, alias, John Vowell, *The Description of the Citie of Excester* ... [c. 1575], eds, W.J. Harte, et al. (Devon and Cornwall Record Society, 3 vols, 1919–47), I, p. 67.

111 Margaret Statham, ed., *Accounts of the Feoffees of the Town Lands of Bury St Edmunds, 1569–1622* (Suffolk Record Society 46, 2003), pp. lii and 239, plate II.

112 Oliver, *History of Exeter*, p. 219; Lloyd Parry, *Exeter Guildhall*, p. 154.

113 Virginia Tillyard, 'Civic Portraits Painted for, or Donated to, the Council Chamber of Norwich Guildhall before 1687 with Documentary Evidence relating to the Artistic Background of the City' (MA thesis, Courtauld Institute, 1978), pp. 47–8 (hereafter Tillyard, Thesis); Andrew Moore and Charlotte Crawley, eds, *Family & Friends: A Regional Survey of British Portraiture* (1992), p. 199.

114 Tom Atkinson, *Elizabethan Winchester* (1963) plate 4, p. 70.

115 Frith, *Gloucester Benefactors*, pp. 8–9; Robert Tittler, 'John and Joan Cooke: Civic Portraiture and Urban Identity in Gloucester', in *Townspeople and Nation: English Urban Experiences, 1540–1640* (Stanford, 2001), pp. 81–99.

116 Charles Haskins, *The Salisbury Corporation Pictures and Plate* (Salisbury, 1910) pp. 110–12.

117 J.C. Lancaster, *St Mary's Hall, Coventry* (1981), p. 71; on-site examination.

118 Tillyard, 'Thesis', p. 50; Moore and Crawley, *Family & Friends*, p. 201.

119 Poole, *Catalogue*, I, p. 168.

120 E. Wollaston-Knocker, *An Account of the Corporation Insignia, Seals and Corporate Plate* (Dover, 1898), p. 46; Susan Doran, ed., *Elizabeth: the Exhibition at the National Maritime Museum* (Greenwich, 2003), pp. 196–8.

121 Frith, *Gloucester Benefactors*, pp. 10–11.

122 Tillyard, 'Thesis', p. 51; Moore and Crawley, eds, *Family & Friends*, p. 199.

123 Poole, *Catalogue*, I, p. 245.

124 Thomas Sharp, *Illustrative Papers on the History and Antiquities of the City of Coventry* (Birmingham, 1871), p. 211; Ronald Aquila Clarke and P.A.E. Day, *Lady Godiva: Images of a Legend in Art and Society* (Coventry, 1982), *passim*; I am grateful to Ron Clarke for his help in interpreting this painting and allowing me to see it on site.

125 Frith, *Gloucester Benefactors*, pp. 16–17.

126 *Ibid.*, p. 16.

127 Information provided by Mr R.W. Edwards, Head of Design Services, Borough of King's Lynn and Mr David Pitcher at an on-site visit.

128 Haskins, *Salisbury Pictures*, pp. 147–50.

129 Quick, ed., *Catalogue of Pictures*, no. 216; Bristol Record Office MS F/AU/1/21, p. 29.

130 Frith, *Gloucester Benefactors*, p. 15.

131 Tillyard, 'Thesis', pp. 50–1; Moore and Crawley, eds, *Family & Friends*, p. 201.

132 Henry Hartopp, ed., *Roll of the Mayors of the Borough and Lord Mayors of the City of Leicester, 1209–1935* (Leicester [1935]), pp. 76–7; James Thompson, 'The Herrick Portraits in the Guild Hall, Leicester', *Transactions of the Leicestershire Architectural and Archaeological Society*, 2 (1870), pp. 43–54.

133 Thompson, 'The Herrick Portraits', pp. 43–54; John Nichols, *The History and Antiquities of the County of Leicester* (4 vols, 1804–1815), I, p. 354.

134 Tillyard, 'Thesis', p. 52.; Moore and Crawley, *Family & Friends*, p. 199.

135 Lloyd Parry, *Exeter Guildhall*, p. 153.

136 Catherine F. Patterson, *Urban Patronage in Early Modern England: Corporate Boroughs, the Landed Elite and the Crown, 1580–1640* (Stanford, 1999), p. 200; Leicester Museum, *Catalogue of Local Portraits* (Leicester, 1956), pp. 12–13; Helen Stocks and W.H. Stevenson, eds, *Records of the Borough of Leicester* (Cambridge, 1923), p. 217.

137 Lloyd Parry, *Exeter Guildhall*, p. 152; Oliver, *History of Exeter*, p. 218.

138 Statham, ed., *Accounts*, p. 239.

139 Basil Cozens-Hardy and E.A. Kent, eds, *The Mayors of Norwich* (Norwich, 1938), p. 42; Tillyard, 'Thesis' pp. 21 and 42; Moore and Crawley, eds, *Family & Friends*, p. 197.

140 Lancaster, *St Mary's Hall, Coventry*, p. 26. A nineteenth-century watercolour copy of this is in the Aylesford Collection, Birmingham Central Library, Portrait Volume, fol. 193.

141 On-site examination; John Man, *The History and Antiquities of the Borough of Reading* (Reading, 1816), p. 128.

142 Tillyard, 'Thesis' p. 42.; Moore and Crawley, eds, *Family & Friends*, p. 201.

143 Quick, ed., *Catalogue of Pictures*, p. 68, no. 212.

144 Tillyard, 'Thesis', p. 40; Moore and Crawley, eds, *Family & Friends*, p. 199.

145 Tillyard, 'Thesis', pp. 22 and 43; Moore and Crawley, eds, *Family & Friends*, p. 197.

146 Tillyard, 'Thesis', p. 48; Moore and Crawley, eds, *Family & Friends*, p. 194.

147 Hugh T. Dutton, *Chester Town Hall and its Treasures* (Chester, 1928), pp. 15–16 and Heinz Archieves, *vide* Offley, William.

148 Frith, *Gloucester Benefactors*, pp. 12–13.

149 John Latimer, *The Annals of Bristol in the Seventeenth Century* (Bristol, 1900), pp. 91 and 97.

150 Tillyard, 'Thesis', p. 52; Moore and Crawley, eds, *Family & Friends*, p. 197.

151 Oliver, *History of Exeter*, p. 219, n. 5; Lloyd Parry, *Exeter Guildhall*, p. 152.

152 Cozens-Hardy and Kent, eds, *Mayors of Norwich*, p. 69; Moore and Crawley, eds, *Family & Friends*, p. 199.

153 Haskins, *Salisbury Pictures*, pp. 142–5.

154 Frith, *Gloucester Benefactors*, p. 19.

155 Tillyard, 'Thesis', pp. 45–6; Moore and Crawley, eds, *Family & Friends*, p. 197.

156 Tillyard, 'Thesis', p. 45; Moore and Crawley, eds, *Family & Friends*, p. 197.

157 Exeter Corporation Act Book no. 5, Devon County Record Office (Exeter Branch), p. 172. No longer extant.

158 Moore and Crawley, eds, *Family & Friends*, p. 199.

159 Erroneously labelled 'mid–16th C.' in the Witt Archive, Courtauld Institute, *vide* Smith and Bright; Statham, ed., *Accounts*, pp. lii, 239.

160 Information provided by R.W. Edwards, Head of Design Services, King's Lynn, letter of 25 July 1991, and on-site visit facilitated by Mr David Pitcher.

161 Cozens-Hardy and Kent, eds, *Mayors of Norwich*, pp. 48–9; Tillyard, 'Thesis', pp. 22 and 46; Moore and Crawley, eds, *Family & Friends*, p. 197.

162 *Victoria History of the Counties of England, Staffordshire*, XIV (1990), plate 21 (b), pp. 78, 83, 129.

163 Frith, *Gloucester Benefactors*, pp. 19–20.

164 Copied by the local watercolourist Edward Cashin in 1825, and described shortly thereafter in 'Alderman Haythorne's Manuscript' (*vide* Bristol City Museum catalogue entry E 183; registration number M2537), held in the Bristol City Museum.

165 The Corporation of Bristol paid for one portrait each of both Nicholas and Robert Thorne to hang in the Council Chamber in 1624, and another portrait of each for the Grammar School in 1625. Payments for the 1624 commissions are recorded in Bristol Record Office MS F/Au/1/19, p. 294; for the 1625 pair, see F/Au/1/20, p. 25. See also Quick, ed., *Catalogue of Pictures*, no. 202, p. 61; J.F. Nicholls, *The Free Grammar School of Bristol and the Thorns [sic], its Founders* (St Peter's Port, Guernsey, 1984), pp. 5, 8 and 11.

166 See note 165.

167 Quick, ed., *Catalogue of Pictures*, no. 201, currently catalogued in the Bristol City Museum as K4462. Photographs of it have been published in Jean Vanes, *Education and Apprenticeship in Sixteenth Century Bristol* (Bristol, 1982), plate I, and C.P. Hill, *A History of Bristol Grammar School* (Gloucester, 1951), frontispiece.

168 See note 165.

169 See note 165.

170 Haskins, *Salisbury Pictures*, pp. 9–12.

171 Oliver, *History of Exeter*, p. 218; Lloyd Parry, *Exeter Guildhall*, p. 153.

172 BL Harleian MS 2150, fol. 180r and 181r. He left the painting to the town in his will, to hang in the Pentice.

173 Frith, *Gloucester Benefactors*, p. 18.

174 Lancaster, *St Mary's Hall, Coventry*, p. 71.

175 Quick, ed., *Catalogue of Pictures*, no. 204; Bristol Record Office MS F/Au/1/20, p. 44. The picture exists in two fragments, barely visible, but was copied in a watercolour by Joseph Manning, c. 1828, and this may be seen in the City Museum store room, Breckonridge Collection, no. M 4076.

176 Quick, ed., *Catalogue of Pictures*, p. 63 and no. 207; Bristol Record Office MS F/AU/1/20, p. 30.

177 Robert Tittler, 'Sir Thomas White of London: Civil Philanthropy and the Making of the Merchant Hero', in *Townspeople and Nation*, pp. 106–8.

178 Quick, ed., *Catalogue of Pictures*, no. 206; Bristol Record Office MS F/AU/1/20, p. 44.

179 Heinz Archive, *vide* 'Canterbury Corporation'; Edward Hasted, *The History and Topographical Survey of the County of Kent* (12 vols, Canterbury, 1797–1801), XII, p. 642.

180 Hugh T. Dutton, *Chester Town Hall and its Treasures* (Chester, 1928), p. 16.

181 Lancaster, *St Mary's Hall, Coventry*, p. 71; on-site examination.

182 Oliver, *History of Exeter*, p. 219, n. 5; Lloyd Parry, *Exeter Guildhall*, pp. 152–3.

183 Frith, *Gloucester Benefactors*, p. 14.

184 Leicester Museum and Art Gallery, *Catalogue of Local Portraits* (Leicester [1956]), *vide* White, Sir Thomas; Nichols, *History and Antiquities of Leicester*, I, part ii, pp. 353–4; Oliver, *History of Exeter*, p. 218.

185 Historical Manuscripts Commission, *Report on the Manuscripts of the Corporation of Lincoln* (1895), p. 206.

186 Tillyard, 'Thesis', p. 44; Moore and Crawley, eds, *Family & Friends*, p. 197.

187 Poole, *Catalogue*, I, pp. 244–5; Stevenson and Salter, *Early History of St John's College*, p. 386; H.E. Salter, ed., *Oxford Council Acts, 1583–1626* (Oxford Historical Society Publications, 1928), p. 378.

188 M.G. Hobson and H.E. Salter, eds, *Oxford Council Acts, 1626–1665* (Oxford Historical Society Publications, 1933), p. 33.

189 Heinz Archive, *vide* White, Sir Thomas; on-site examination; Historical Manuscripts Commission, *Report on the Manuscripts of the Borough of Reading* (1888), p. 206; Man, *History and Antiquities of Reading*, pp. 396–8; H.B. Wheatley, *Historical Portraits: Some Notes on the Painted Portraits of the Celebrated Characters* (London, 1897), p. 252.

190 Haskins, *Salisbury Pictures*, pp. 93–95.

191 Examined on site; Winchester Museums Service, catalogue no. WINCM: A.1498. Communication from Ross Turl of the WMS, to whom I am grateful.

192 Frith, *Gloucester Benefactors*, pp. 17–18.

193 Tillyard, 'Thesis', p. 40; Moore and Crawley, eds, *Family & Friends*, p. 199.

194 Cozens-Hardy and Kent, eds, *Mayors of Norwich*, p. 65; Tillyard, 'Thesis', p. 50; Moore and Crawley, eds, *Family & Friends*, p. 199.

195 Ian Archer, *History of the Haberdashers' Company* (Chichester, 1991), p. 74.

196 Archer, *History of the Haberdashers' Company*, p. 74; Harding, 'List', II, p. 153.

197 Archer, *History of the Haberdashers' Company*, p. 74.

198 Jessie Dobson and R. Milnes Walker, *Barbers and Barber-Surgeons: A History of the Barbers and Barber-Surgeons Company* (Oxford, 1979), pp. 118–20; Roy Strong, 'A Preliminary Cartoon for the Barber-Surgeons' Group Rediscovered: a Preliminary Report', in Strong, *The Tudor and Stuart Monarchy*, I, pp. 55–71; Paul Ganz, *The Paintings of Hans Holbein* (1950), p. 290; Susan Foister, *Holbein and England* (2004), pp. 65–7.

199 The Company court ordered that Buck's portrait be displayed in 1605, but had to do so again in 1618 and 1620. A.H. Johnson, *The History of the Worshipful Company of Drapers of London* (5 vols, Oxford, 1914–22), III, p. 77 and n. 2.

200 Penelope Hunting, *The Leathersellers' Company: A History* (1994), pp. 94–5.

201 Anon., *A Glance at the Pictures in the Hall of the Worshipful Company of Ironmongers* (1847), p. 13; John Nicholl, *Some Account of the Worshipful Company of Ironmongers* (1851), *vide* Campbell; Isabelle Finch, 'Portrait of an Ironmonger' (BA Hons. thesis, University of East Anglia, 2000), p. 63 and plate 4; Harding, 'List', II, p. 149; Inventory, 1640, Ironmongers' Company, Guildhall MS 16988/5, 30 July 1640.

202 Masters' and Wardens' Account Book, vol. 9 (unpaginated), Merchant Taylors' Company, Guildhall Library MS 34048/9, microfilm frame no. 915.

203 Charles Welch, *History of the Cutlers' Company of London and of the Minor Cutlery Crafts* (2 vols, 1916–23) I, opp. p. 213 plate; I, pp. 213–14 and II, p. 125; Accounts and Minutes of the Cutlers' Company, Guildhall Library MS 7147/1, p. 98; illustrations of two portraits of her are held by the Heinz Archive.

204 Frederick M. Fry, ed., *A Historical Catalogue of the Pictures, Herse-Cloths and Tapestry at Merchant Taylors' Hall* (1907), pp. 76–8; Tarnya Cooper, '*Memento Mori* Portraiture: Painting, Protestant Culture and the Patronage of Middle Elites in England and Wales' (Ph.D thesis, University of Sussex, 2001), p. 384. I am grateful to Dr Cooper for allowing me to read her thesis.

205 Nicholl, *Some Account*, p. 474; Quarter Court Minutes, Ironmongers' Company, Guildhall Library MS 16967/2, fol. 6v.; Anon., *A Glance at the Pictures*, p. 8.

206 Anon., *A Glance at the Pictures*, p. 7; Nicholl, *Some Account*, p. 474. Harding, 'List', II, p. 149.

207 Fry, *Catalogue*, pp. 97–101 and plate 38; Robert Tittler, 'Three Portraits by John de Critz for the Merchant Taylors' Company', *Burlington Magazine*, 147:1228 (July, 2005), pp. 491–3.

208 The Company court ordered that Dummer's portrait be displayed in 1605, but had to do so again in 1618 and 1620. Johnson, *History of the Drapers*, III, p. 77 and n. 2.

209 Presented by John Vernon; Fry, *Catalogue*, p. 67–9, from Court Minutes of the Merchant Taylors' Company, now available as Guildhall Library microfilm, 328/7, fols, 244–6.

210 Elizabeth Glover, *A History of the Ironmongers' Company* (1991), p. 61; Quarter Court Minutes, Ironmongers' Company, Guildhall Library MS 16967/2, fol. 6v.

211 Fry, *Catalogue*, pp. 89–91 and plate 36; Court Records, Merchant Taylors' Company, Guildhall Library MS 34010/9, fol. 91v.

212 Sidney Young, *The Annals of the Barber-Surgeons of London* (1890), pp. 210, 334–5, 338, 509; Dobson and Walker, *Barbers and Barber-Surgeons*, p. 139.

213 Anon., *A Glance at the Pictures*, p. 10; Finch, 'Thesis', p. 71.

214 Anon., *A Glance at the Pictures*, p. 12; Nicholl, *Some Account*, pp. 473–4.

215 J. Steven Watson, *History of the Salters' Company* (1963), pp. 123–4.

216 Johnson, *History of the Drapers*, III, p. 77. The Company court ordered that Jolles' portrait be displayed in 1605, but had to do so again in 1618 and 1620.

217 Archer, *History of the Haberdashers' Company*, p. 74.

218 Freemen's Registers and Inventories, Ironmongers' Company, Guildhall Library MS 16988/5, p. 7; Anon., *A Glance at the Pictures*, p. 11; Nicholl, *Some Account*, p. 473.

219 *ODNB*, *vide* Lee, Sir Henry.

220 Quarter Court Minutes, Ironmongers' Company, Guildhall Library MS 16967/2, p. 306; Anon., *A Glance at the Pictures*, p. 6; Nicholl, *Some Account*, p. 474.

221 Wardens' Accounts, Grocers' Company, Guildhall Library MSS 11571/6, fol. 205v and 11571/10, fol. 44v. An account for 1601 records that the painting hung in the upper end of the Grocers' Hall near the bay window, an extremely prominent place; MS 11571/8, fol. 706r.

222 Given to Goldsmiths' Company by Lady Myddleton, 1633; Richard Ormerod and Malcolm Rogers, eds, *Dictionary of British Portraiture* (4 vols, 1979–81), *vide* Myddelton, which dates this painting to 1628; Sir Walter Sherburne Prideaux, *Memorials of the Goldsmiths' Company* (2 vols, 1896), I, pp. 159 and 136, which dates this to 1631. At least six other panel portraits of Myddleton are known, of which the original from which some of the others were copied is said to be that in the Baltimore Museum of Art; Heinz Archive, *vide* Myddelton, Sir Hugh.

223 Quarter Court Minutes, Ironmongers' Company, Guildhall Library MS 16967/2, p. 306; Nicholl, *Some Account*, p. 473; Harding, 'List', II, p. 149; Finch, 'Thesis', p. 78, plate 19.

224 The portrait is dated 1610 and, though not mentioned in the Company records until 1691, it is presumed to have been acquired by the Company at or near this date. Harding, 'List', II, p. 145; Heinz Archive, *vide* Owen, Alice; Ordinances of the Brewers' Company, Guildhall Library MS 5458, fol. 12v.

225 Court Minutes, Painter-Stainers' Company, Guildhall Library MS 5667/1, pp. 14–16; Heinz Archive, *vide* Pargeter, Clement; Harding, 'List', II, p. 137.

226 Inventory of 1691, Brewers' Company, Guildhall Library MS 5458, fol. 12v; Heinz Archive, *vide* Platt, Richard; Harding, 'List', II, p. 145; *ODNB*, *vide* Platt, Richard.

227 B.W.F. Alford and T.C. Barker, *A History of the Carpenters' Company* (1968), p. 225; Inventory of 1639, Memorandum Book, Carpenters' Company, Guildhall Library MS 4329A, fol. A.

228 Court Minutes, Painter-Stainers' Company, Guildhall Library MS 5667/1; Oliver Millar, *The Age of Charles I: Painting in England 1620–1649* (1972), p 92.

229 Watson, *History of the Salters' Company*, pp. 69–72, 122–3; Harding, 'List', II, p. 155.

230 The Company resolved in 1605 that the portrait be displayed, but had to do so again in 1618 and 1620; Johnson, *History of the Drapers*, III, p. 77 and n. 2.

231 Wardens' Accounts, Grocers' Company, Guildhall Library MS 11571/10, fol. 410v, 458r, and 498v, and 11571/11, fol. 439v. His portrait hung with his arms on the south side of the Grocers' Hall, near that of Sir Thomas Lovell. By 1642 there were still only these two portraits on display in the Hall; MS 11571/12, fol. 459r.

232 Heinz Archive, *vide* 'Southern, Nowell'; Ann Saunders and Matthew P. Davies, *History of the Merchant Taylors' Company* (2 vols, 2004), I, p. 270. Though this portrait is not listed in the several lists of Merchant Taylors' portraits made through the years, de Critz is known to have done other Merchant Taylors portraits at that time and the Company holds the portrait today. It is thus likely that de Critz did the portrait for the Company, that it soon passed into other hands, and was re-acquired by the Company at a later date.

233 Cited in Fry, *Catalogue*, pp. 67–9, from Court Minutes of the Merchant Taylors' Company, now available as Guildhall Library microfilm, 328/7, fols 244–6.

234 Nicholl, *Some Account*, p. 473; Finch, 'Thesis', p. 85 and plate 26.

235 Court Minute Books, Merchant Taylors' Company, Guildhall Library Microfilm 328/7, fols 244–6; Fry, *Catalogue*, p. 67 and pl. 31.

236 Fry, *Catalogue* pp. 1, 93–94; Tittler, 'Three Portraits by John de Critz, pp. 491–3.

237 Archer, *History of the Haberdashers' Company*, p. 74.

238 Strong, *Tudor and Jacobean Portraits*, I, p. 1; Thomas Whitburn, *Local Pictures as Landmarks of History* (Guildford, 1888), p. 38.

239 Arthur E. Preston, *Christ's Hospital Abingdon: The Almshouses, the Hall and the Portraits* (Oxford, 1929), pp. 49–51.

240 *Ibid.*, pp. 36–7.

241 *Ibid.*, p. 56.

242 L.M.N. Surry, *The Portraits of Edward VI* (Portsmouth, n.d.), pp. 89–91; Heinz Archive, *vide* Bridewell.

243 Heinz Archive, *vide* Christ's Hospital.

244 This is the original from which the better known Dixie portrait at Emmanuel College, Cambridge was copied. Ormerod and Rogers, *Dictionary of British Portraiture*, *vide* Dixie; *ODNB*, *vide* Dixie, Sir Wolstan; G.P. Harding, *A List of Portraits in Christ's Hospital* (2 vols, 1804), II, p. 123; Heinz Archive, *vide*, Dixie, Sir Wolstan; Frank Stubbings, *A Catalogue of Portraits at Emmanuel College* (Cambridge, n.d. [1988]), *vide* Dixie.

245 On-site observation of the painting and its explanatory inscription.

246 Berkshire Record Office MS D/EP 7/55.

247 Strong, *Tudor and Jacobean Portraits*, I, p. 124.

248 John Stow, writing in 1598, relates how Alice Knevit, née Gibson, founded a school and almshouse in Radcliffe near London and that 'A fayre paynted Table of hir picture' was placed in the chapel and later taken down; Charles Lethbridge Kingsford, ed., *A Survey of London by John Stow, Reprinted from the Text of 1603* (2 vols, Oxford, 1908), I, p. 116.

249 Heinz Archive, *vide* Leman, Sir John; Harding, 'List', II, p. 123; on-site observation.

250 Preston, *Christ's Hospital, Abingdon*, pp. 44–5.

251 *Ibid.*, pp. 38–9.

252 *Ibid.*, pp. 47–8.

253 This is probably a copy of the Brewers' Company portrait of Platt, for which, see above. Heinz Archive, *vide* Platt, Richard.

254 Nicholas Carlisle, *A Concise Description of the Endowed Grammar Schools of England and Wales* (2 vols, 1818), I, p. 434; on-site observation; information provided by Ms Rhona Mitchell, Curator, Christ's Hospital.

255 G.S. Davies, *Charterhouse* (1921), p. 179; *ODNB*, *vide* Sutton, Thomas, and information kindly provided by Dr Stephen Porter.

256 Preston, *Christ's Hospital, Abingdon*, pp. 46–7.

Appendix B

The cost of civic portraits, 1500–1640

	Date	Subject	Institution	Price	Painter
1	1511–12	Lady Margaret Beaufort	Camb., Christ's	60s	M. Vewicke
2	1586	Lady Godiva	Coventry	3s 6d	A. van Noort (?)
3	1596	William of Wyckham	Oxford, New College	£6	S. Strong
4	1597	Sir Thomas White	Oxford City	£3	S. Strong
5	1598	Elizabeth I	Dover	25s	
6	1598(?)	Bishop John Alcock	Cambridge, Jesus	26s 8d	
7	1599	Lawrence Atwell	Exeter	£1	
8	c. 1608	Sir Thomas White	Canterbury	£6 11s 8d	
9	1609	Archbishop Henry Chichele	Oxford, All Souls	£5	S. Strong
10	1609–10	Martin Heton, Bishop of Ely	Oxford, Christ Church	13s	
11	1609–10	Thomas Ravis, Bishop of London	Oxford, Christ Church	13s	
12	1610–11	Cardinal Thomas Wolsey	Oxford, Christ Church	£3	S. Strong
13	1610–11	Bishop Tobias Matthew	Oxford, Christ Church	15s	
14	c. 1612	Prince Charles	Cambridge Univ.	£13 6s 8d	R. Peake
15	1612–13	Lady Elizabeth Pope	Oxford, Trinity	40s	
16	1616	James I	Bury St Edmunds	£11	Mr Fenn
17	1616	T. Bright, and J. Smyth	Bury St Edmunds	£3 6s 8d	Mr Fenn
18	1617	John Blythe	Camb., Peterhouse	20s	J. Newman (?)
19	1618–19	Bodley Frieze	Oxford, Bodley	£155 for 202	Clarke & Knight
20	1624	N. and R. Thorne	Bristol	44s for 2	'Dutch Painter'
21	1625	N. and R. Thorne	Bristol	44s for 2	'Dutch Painter'
22	1626–7	Arthur Lake	Oxford, New College	£4	R. Greenbury
23	1636	Thomas Jesson	Coventry	£3	
24	1636–7	Sir Thomas Bodley	Oxford, Bodley	£2	'French Painter'
25	1638	Baron John Mordaunt	Oxford, Brasenose	£3 5s	G. Jackson
26	1638	William of Wainfleet	Oxford, Magdalen	£5 15s	
27	1640	Thomas Mitchell	Ironmongers	£3 5s	Cooke
28	1640	Thomas Lewin	Ironmongers	£3 5s	Cooke

NOTES

1 J.W. Goodison, ed., *Catalogue of the Portraits in Christ's, Clare and Sidney Sussex Colleges* (Cambrdige, 1985), pp. 35–6.

2 Thomas Sharp, *Illustrative Papers on the History and Antiquities of the City of Coventry* (Birmingham, 1871), p. 218; Ron Aquila Clarke and P.A.E. Day, *Lady Godiva: Images of a Legend in Art and Society* (Coventry, 1982), p. 30.

3 Jane Turner, ed., *The Dictionary of Art* (34 vols., 1996), 29, p. 781.

4 *Ibid.*, 29, p. 81.

5 E. Wollaston-Knocker, *An Account of the Corporation Insignia, Seals and Corporate Plate* (Dover, 1898), p. 46.

6 Communication from Ms Frances Willmoth, Jesus College Library.

7 Devon County Record Office (Exeter Branch), Exeter Corporation Act Book no. 5, p. 432.

8 Edward Hasted, *The History and Topographical Survey of the County of Kent* (12 vols., Canterbury, 1797–1801), XII, p. 642.

9 R.L. Poole, ed., *Catalogue of Portraits in the Possession of the University Colleges, City and County of Oxford* (3 vols, Oxford Historical Society Publications, vols 57, 1912; 81, 1926; and 82, 1926), II, p. 181.

10 *Ibid.*, III, p. 17.

11 *Ibid.*, III, p. 17.

12 *Ibid.*, II, pp. 211–12.

13 *Ibid.*, III, pp. 20–1.

14 Henry Bradshaw, 'On the Collection of Portraits Belonging to the University before the Civil War' [1872], *Collected Papers of Henry Bradshaw* (Cambridge, 1889), p. 292.

15 Poole, ed., *Catalogue of Portraits*, III, pp. 122–3.

16 Margaret Statham, ed., *Accounts of the Feoffees of the Town Lands of Bury St Edmunds, 1569–1622* (Suffolk Record Society 46, 2003), p. 239.

17 *Ibid.*, p. 239.

18 Robert Willis, ed., *The Architectural History of the University of Cambridge* (3 vols., Cambridge, 1886, ed. John Willis Clarke, repr. 1988), I, p. 68.

19 J.N.L. Myres and E. Clive Rouse, 'Further Notes on the Painted Frieze and Other Discoveries in the Upper Reading Room and the Tower Room', *Bodleian Library Record*, 5 (Oct., 1956), pp. 307–8.

20 Bristol Record Office MS. F/Au/1/19, p. 296.

21 Bristol Record Office MS. F/Au/1/20, p. 25.

22 Poole, ed., *Catalogue of Portraits*, II, p. 153.

23 J.C. Lancaster, *St Mary's Hall, Coventry* (n.d.), p. 26.

24 Poole, ed., *Catalogue of Portraits*, I, p. 29.

25 *Ibid.*, II, p. 247.

26 *Ibid.*, II, p. 209.

27 Quarter Court Minutes, Ironmongers' Company, Guildhall Library MS. 16967/2, p. 306.

28 *Ibid.*, p. 306.

Bibliography

(NB: Place of publication is understood to be London unless otherwise indicated.)

UNPUBLISHED PRIMARY SOURCES
Berkshire County Record Office

MS D/EP 7/55.
MS W/AC1/1, Wallingford Borough Archives.

Birmingham Public Library

Aylesford Collection, vols, I–VI.

Bristol City Museum and Art Gallery

Breckonridge Topographical Collection.
'Catalogue of the Braithwaite Topographical Collection' reference E 183, 'Alderman Haythorne's MS'.

Bristol Record Office

MS 04720(1), Robert Ricart, 'The Maire of Bristowe is Kalendar'.
MSS F/Au/1/12–20, Bristol Corporation Audit Books.

British Library

Additional MSS, 8937, 28,330.
Egerton MS 868.
Harleian MSS 1920–2177, 5955, and 7568–9, Holme Papers.
Harleian MS 6115, 'A List or Catalogue of all the Mayors of the City of York'.
Lansdowne MS 207(a).

Cambridge University

Jesus College Audit Book, MS ACC 1.2.
University Library, MS Dd.VII.3.

Bibliography

Chester Record Office

MS AB/1.
MS CR63/2/131 (1624–51), Minute Book of the Company of Painters, Glasiers, Embroiderers and Stationers.
MSS ZG 17/1–2, Records of the Company of Painters, etc.
MS ML/6/166.

Courtauld Institute of Art

Witt Archive, various files.

Coventry City Record Office

MS A7, 'Book of Yearly Accounts'.

Devon County Record Office, Exeter

Exeter Corporation Act Book no. 5.
MS 1579/A/7/3, Totnes Borough Archives.

Folger Shakespeare Library

MS VA 318, Anon., 'A Caveatt for the City of London'.

London, Corporation of London Record Office

Repertories of the Court of Aldermen (Rep. Books).

London, Guildhall Art Gallery

Ref. 11068, Portrait of Thomas Exmewe.

London, Guildhall Library

Brewers' Company, MS 5458, Ordinances.
Carpenters' Company, MS 4329A, Memorandum Book.
Cutlers' Company, MS 7147/1, 'Accounts and Minutes'.
Grocers' Company, MSS 11571/6, 8, 10, 11 and 12, and 11588/2, Wardens' Accounts.
Haberdashers' Company, MSS 15842/1–2, Court Minutes.
Ironmongers' Company, MS 16988/5, Freemen's Registers and Inventories; MS 16967/2, Quarter Court Minutes.
Merchant Taylors' Company; MS 34048/9, Masters' and Wardens' Account Book, vol. 9; MS 34010/9, Court Records; microfilm, 328/7, Court Minutes.
Painter-Stainers Company; MS 5667/1, Court Minutes.
Print Collection, London Alderman Series, nos. 32132–52, and 32170–3.
Saddlers' Company, MS 5384, Wardens' Accounts.

National Archives, Kew

MSE. 319, 'Particulars for Grants'.

National Archives, Family Records Centre

PROB 11/121, will of Warden Raves, Magdalen College, Oxford.

National Portrait Gallery, Heinz Archive

Various files.

Norwich Castle Museum, Norwich

Various portrait files.

Oxford, St John's College

Compotus Animus for 1583–84.

Shrewsbury School Library

'Dr Taylor's History of Shrewsbury', uncatalogued manuscript.
'Escutcheons of the Bailiffs and Mayors of Shrewsbury', uncatalogued manuscript.

Wiltshire County Record Office

MS G23/1/3, Salisbury Borough Ledger Book.
MS G23/1/235, Salisbury Borough Archives.

SECONDARY SOURCES

Airs, Malcolm, *The Making of the English Country House, 1500–1640* (1975).
Aleci, Linda Klinger, 'Images of Identity: Italian Portrait Collections of the Fifteenth and Sixteenth Centuries', in Nicholas Mann and Luke Syson, eds, *The Image of the Individual: Portraits in the Renaissance* (1998), pp. 67–80.
Alford, B.W.F., and T.C. Barker, *A History of the Carpenters' Company* (1968).
Allen, Marion E., ed., *The Wills of the Archdeaconry of Suffolk, 1625–1626* (Suffolk Record Society 37, 1995).
Ames-Lewis, Francis, *The Intellectual Life of the Early Renaissance Artist* (London and New Haven, 2000).
Anderson, J.J., ed., *Records of Early English Drama, Newcastle upon Tyne* (Toronto and Buffalo, 1982).
Anglo, Sidney, *Images of Tudor Kingship* (1992).
Anglo, Sidney, *Spectacle, Pageantry and Early Tudor Policy* (2nd edn, 1997).
Anon., *A Glance at the Pictures in the Hall of the Worshipful Company of Ironmongers* (1847).

Bibliography

Anon., *Exeter and West Country Silver*, Exeter Museums Publication no. 86 (Exeter, 1978).

Anon., *Portraits of the Sixteenth and Early Seventeenth Centuries* (Oxford, 1952).

Anon., *The Worshipful Company of Barbers: Some Descriptive Notes on the Company's Treasures* [1990].

Archer, Ian, 'The Arts and Acts of Memorialization in Early Modern London', in J.F. Merritt, ed., *Imagining Early Modern London* (Cambridge, 2001), pp. 89–113.

Archer, Ian, 'The Nostalgia of John Stow', in D. Smith, R. Strier and D. Bevington, eds, *The Theatrical City* (Cambridge, 1995), pp. 17–34.

Archer, Ian W., *The History of the Haberdashers' Company* (Chichester, 1991).

Archer, Ian W., *The Pursuit of Stability: Social Relations in Elizabethan London* (Cambridge, 1991).

Arnold, A.P., and Arthur G. Ingram, *The History of the Painter-Stainers' Company of London* (2 vols, 1988).

Aston, Margaret, *England's Iconoclasts, I, Laws Against Images* (Oxford, 1988).

Aston, Margaret, 'English Ruins and English History: The Dissolutions and the Sense of the Past', *Journal of the Warburg and Courtauld Institutes*, 36 (1973), pp. 231–55.

Aston, Margaret, 'Puritanism and Iconoclasm', in Christopher Durstan and Jacqueline Eales, eds, *The Culture of English Puritanism, 1500–1700* (Basingstoke, 1996), pp. 92–121.

Atkinson, Tom, *Elizabethan Winchester* (1963).

Auerbach, Erna, *Nicholas Hilliard* (Boston, 1961).

Auerbach, Erna, *Tudor Artists: A Study of Painters in the Royal Service and of Portraiture on Illuminated Documents from the Accession of Henry VII to the Death of Elizabeth* (1954).

Backhouse, Janet, 'Lady Margaret Beaufort', in Richard Marks and Paul Williamson, eds, *Gothic Art for England, 1400–1547* (2003), pp. 246–53.

Bailey, John F. ed., *Transcription of the Minutes of the Corporation of Boston* (3 vols, Boston, 1980–83).

Barker, Emma, Nick Webb and Kim Woods, *The Changing Status of the Artist* (London and New Haven, 1999).

Bateson, Mary, ed., *Records of the Borough of Leicester*, III (1905).

Beaven, Alfred B., *The Aldermen of the City of London* (2 vols, 1903).

Beck, W.S., *Gloves: Their Annals and Associations, a Chapter of Trade and Social History* (1883, repr. Detroit, 1969).

Berger, Karol, 'The Hand and Art of Memory', *Musica Disciplina*, 35 (1981), pp. 87–120.

Bermingham, Ann, *Learning to Draw: Studies in the Cultural History of a Polite and Useful Art* (London and New Haven, 2000).

Bindoff, S.T., ed., *The House of Commons 1509–1558* (History of Parliament Trust, 3 vols, 1982).

Blatchly, John, *The Town Library of Ipswich, provided for the Use of the Town Preachers in 1599: A History and Catalogue* (Woodbridge, Suffolk, 1989).

Bold, John, 'Privacy and the Plan', in John Bold and Edward Chaney, eds, *English Architecture, Public and Private: Essays for Kerry Downs* (1993), pp. 107–19.

Bossy, John, 'The Mass as a Social Institution, 1200–1700', *Past and Present*, 100 (Aug., 1983), pp. 29–61.

Boulton, Jeremy, 'London, 1540–1700', in Peter Clark, ed., *The Cambridge Urban History of Britain*, II (Cambridge, 2000), pp. 315–46.

Bradshaw, Henry, 'On the Collection of Portraits Belonging to the University before the Civil War' [1872], *Collected Papers of Henry Bradshaw* (Cambridge, 1889), pp. 286–96.

Brigden, Susan, 'Religion and Social Obligation in Early Sixteenth Century London', *Past and Present*, 103 (May, 1984), pp. 67–112.

Bromley, J.S. and E.H. Kossman, eds, *Britain and the Netherlands, IV, Metropolis, Dominion and Province* (The Hague, 1971).

Brooke, C.N.L., ed., *A History of the University of Cambridge* (4 vols, 1988–2004).

Brown, Sarah, and David O'Connor, *Glass Painters* (Toronto and Buffalo, 1991).

Browne, A.D., and C.T. Stedman, *A Pictorial History of the Queens' College of Saint Margaret and Saint Bernard, commonly called Queens' College, Cambridge, 1448–1948* (Cambridge, 1951).

Browne, A.L., 'Richard Pates, MP for Gloucester', *Transactions of the Bristol and Gloucestershire Archeological Society* 56 (1935 for 1934), pp. 201–25.

Brunskill, R.W., *Traditional Buildings of Britain: An Introduction to Vernacular Architecture* (1981).

Bryson, Anna, *From Courtesy to Civility: Changing Codes of Conduct in Early Modern England* (Oxford and New York, 1998).

Bullard, M.R.A., 'Talking Heads: The Bodleian Frieze, its Inspiration, Sources, Design and Significance', *Bodleian Library Record*, 14:6 (Apr., 1994), pp. 461–83.

Burbage, F. Bliss, *Old Coventry and Lady Godiva* (Birmingham, n.d.).

Burke, Peter, *The Renaissance Sense of the Past* (1969).

Caius, John, *De Antiquitate Cantabrigiensis Academiae* (1568).

Calendar of Patent Rolls, Edward VI (6 vols, 1924–29).

Campbell, Lorne, *Renaissance Portraits: European Portrait-Painting in the 14th, 15th and 16th Centuries* (London and New Haven, 1990).

Carlisle, Nicholas, *A Concise Description of the Endowed Grammar Schools of England and Wales* (2 vols, 1818).

Carpenter, Christine, 'Henry VII and the English Polity', in Benjamin Thompson, ed., *The Reign of Henry VII* (1993), pp. 11–31.

Carruthers, Mary, *The Book of Memory: A Study of Memory in Medieval Culture* (Cambridge, 2000).

Carruthers, Mary, *The Craft of Thought: Meditation, Rhetoric and the Making of Images, 400–1200* (Cambridge, 1998).

Carruthers, Mary, and Jan M. Kiokowski, eds, *The Medieval Craft of Memory: An Anthology of Texts and Pictures* (Philadelphia, 2002).

Clark, Andrew, ed., *Historical Register of the University of Oxford* (2 vols, Oxford, 1887).

Clark, Peter, 'Visions of the Urban Community: Antiquarians and the English City before 1800', in D. Fraser and A. Sutcliffe, eds, *The Pursuit of Urban History* (1983), pp. 105–13.

Clark, Peter, and Paul Slack, eds, *Crisis and Order in English Towns, 1500–1700* (1972).

Clark, Peter, and Paul Slack, eds, *English Towns in Transition, 1500–1700* (1976).

Clarke, Ronald Aquila, and P.A.E. Day, *Lady Godiva: Images of a Legend in Art and Society* (Coventry, 1982).

Bibliography

Clinch, George, *English Costume from Prehistoric Times to the end of the Eighteenth Century* (1909, repr. Wakefield, 1975).

Clopper, Lawrence M., ed., *Records of Early English Drama, Chester* (Toronto, 1979).

Clough, Cecil H., 'Late Fifteenth Century Monarchs Subject to Italian Renaissance Influence', in John Mitchell and Matthew Moran, eds, *England and the Continent in the Middle Ages: Studies in Memory of Andrew Martindale* (Proceedings of the 1996 Harlaxton Symposium, Stamford, 2000), pp. 298–317.

Collins Baker, C.H., 'John Souch of Chester', *Connoisseur*, 130 (1928), pp. 131–3.

Collinson, Patrick, *The Birthpangs of Protestant England: Religious and Cultural Change in the Sixteenth and Seventeenth Centuries* (1988).

Collinson, Patrick, *The Elizabethan Puritan Movement* (1967).

Collinson, Patrick, 'Foreword' to Ian Gadd and Alexandra Gillespie, eds, *John Stow (1525–1605) and the Making of the English Past* (2004), pp. xiii–xiv.

Collinson, Patrick, 'John Stow and Nostalgic Antiquarianism in Early Modern London', in J.F. Merritt, ed., *Imagining Early Modern London: Perceptions and Portrayals of the City from Stow to Strype, 1598–1720* (Cambridge, 2001), pp. 27–51.

Collinson, Patrick, *The Religion of Protestants: The Church in English Society, 1559–1625* (Oxford, 1982).

Collinson, Patrick, and John Craig, eds, *The Reformation in English Towns, 1500–1640* (1998).

Colvin, Howard, ed., *A History of the King's Works* (6 vols, 1963–82).

Cooper, C.H., *Memoir of Margaret, Countess of Richmond and Derby* (1874).

Cooper, Nicholas, *Houses of the Gentry, 1480–1680* (London and New Haven, 1999).

Cooper, Tarnya, '*Memento Mori* Portraiture: Painting, Protestant Culture and the Patronage of Middle Elites in England and Wales' (Ph.D thesis, University of Sussex, 2001).

Cooper, Tarnya, 'A Painting with a Past', in S. Nolan, *Searching for Shakespeare* (2006), pp. 229–42.

Corley, Brigett, 'Historical Links and Artistic Reflections: England and Northern Germany in the Late Middle Ages', in John Mitchell and Matthew Moran, eds, *England and the Continent in the Middle Ages: Studies in Memory of Andrew Martindale* (Proceedings of the 1996 Harlaxton Symposium, Stamford, 2000), pp. 189–202.

Coward, Barry, *The Stanleys: Lords Stanley and Earls of Derby, 1385–1672; The Origins, Wealth and Power of a Landowning Family* (Chetham Society, 3rd series, 30, 1983).

Cozens-Hardy, Basil, and E.A. Kent, eds, *The Mayors of Norwich* (Norwich, 1938).

Croft-Murray, Edward, *Decorative Painting in England, 1537–1837* (1962).

Cust, Lionel, 'The Lumley Inventories', *Walpole Society*, 6 (1918), pp. 15–35.

Damet, Thomas, *Greate Yermouthe: A Book of the Foundacion and Antiquitye of the Saide Towne* ..., ed., Charles James Palmer (Great Yarmouth, 1847).

Davies, Gerald S., *Charterhouse In London, Monastery, Mansion, Hospital, School* (1921).

Davies, Matthew, and Ann Saunders, *The History of the Merchant Taylors' Company* (Leeds, 2004).

Davis, Cecil T., *The Monumental Brasses of Gloucestershire* (Bath, 1899, repr. 1969).

Dean, David, *Law-Making and Society in Late Elizabethan England: The Parliament of England, 1584–1601* (Cambridge, 1996).

Dobson, Jessie, and R. Milnes Walker, *Barbers and Barber-Surgeons: A History of the Barbers and Barber-Surgeons Company* (Oxford, 1979).

Doolittle, Ian, *The Mercers' Company, 1579–1959* (1994).

Doran, Susan, ed., *Elizabeth: The Exhibition at the National Maritime Museum* (Greenwich, 2003).

Duffy, Eamon, *The Stripping of the Altars: Traditional Religion in England, c. 1400–1580* (London and New Haven, 1992).

Dutton, Hugh T., *Chester Town Hall and its Treasures* (Chester, 1928).

Dyer, Alan, 'English Town Chronicles', *Local Historian*, 12:6 (May, 1977), pp. 285–91.

Earle, John, *Microcosmographie, or a Peece of the World Discovered* (STC 7439, 1622).

Edmond, Mary, 'Bury St. Edmunds, a Seventeenth Century Art Centre', *Walpole Society*, 43 for 1987 (1989), pp. 106–18.

Edmond, Mary, 'Limners and Picture-makers: New Light on the Lives of Miniaturists and Large-scale Portrait Painters Working in London in the Sixteenth and Seventeenth Centuries', *Walpole Society*, 47 (1978–80), pp. 60–242.

Edmond, Mary, 'Sampson Strong', in Jane Turner, ed., *The Dictionary of Art* (34 vols, 1996), 29, p. 781.

Elliott, John R., Alan H. Nelson, Alexandra F. Johnston and Diana Wyatt, eds, *Records of Early English Drama, Oxford* (2 vols, Toronto, 2004).

Ellis, Steven G., 'Centre and Periphery in the Tudor State', in Robert Tittler and Norman Jones, eds, *A Companion to Tudor Britain* (Oxford, 2004), pp. 133–50.

Elton, G.R., *The Parliament of England, 1559–1581* (Cambridge, 1986).

Elyot, Thomas, *The Book Named the Governor* (1531), ed., S.E. Lehmberg (New York, 1962).

Englefield, W.A.D., *The History of the Painter-Stainers' Company of London* (1923).

Esdaile, K.A., *English Church Monuments, 1510–1640* (1946).

Eustace, G.W., *Arundel: Borough and Castle* (1922).

Evans, Nesta, ed., *Wills of the Archdeaconry of Sudbury, 1636–1638* (Suffolk Record Society 35, 1993).

Ferguson, Arthur B., *The Articulate Citizen and the English Renaissance* (Durham, North Carolina, 1965).

Filipczak, Zirka Zaremba, *Picturing Art in Antwerp, 1550–1700* (Princeton, NJ, 1987).

Finch, Isabelle, 'Portrait of an Ironmonger' (BA Hons. thesis, University of East Anglia, 2000).

Fincham, Kenneth, 'Oxford and the Early Stuart Polity', in Nicholas Tyacke, ed., *The History of the University of Oxford*, IV, *Seventeenth Century Oxford* (Oxford, 1997).

Flenley, Ralph, ed., *Six Town Chronicles of England* (Oxford, 1911).

Fletcher, John, 'Tree Ring Dates for some Panel Paintings in England', *Burlington Magazine*, 116:854 (May, 1974), pp. 250–8.

Foister, Susan, 'Foreigners at Court: Holbein, Van Dyck, and the London Painter-Stainers' Company', in David Howarth, ed., *Art and Patronage in the Caroline Court: Essays in Honour of Sir Oliver Millar* (Cambridge, 1993), pp. 32–50.

Foister, Susan, *Holbein and England* (London and New Haven, 2004).

Foister, Susan, 'Paintings and Other Works of Art in Sixteenth Century English Inventories', *Burlington Magazine*, 123:938 (May, 1981), pp. 273–82.

Foister, Susan, 'The Production and Reproduction of Holbein's Portraits', in Karen Hearn, ed., *Dynasties: Painting in Tudor and Jacobean England, 1530–1630* (1995), pp. 21–6.

French, Katherine L., 'The Legend of Lady Godiva and the Image of the Female Body", *Journal of Medieval History*, 18 (1992), pp. 3–19.

Frith, Brian, *Twelve Portraits of Gloucester Benefactors* (Gloucester, 1972).

Fry, Frederick M., ed., *A Historical Catalogue of the Pictures, Herse-Cloths and Tapestry at Merchant Taylors' Hall* (1907).

Fussner, F. Smith, *The Historical Revolution: English Historical Writing and Thought, 1580–1640* (1962).

Ganz, Paul, *The Paintings of Hans Holbein* (1950).

Geertz, Clifford, *The Interpretation of Cultures* (New York, 1973).

Gent, Lucy, *Picture and Poetry, 1560–1620: Relations between Literature and the Visual Arts in the English Renaissance* (Leamington Spa, 1981).

Gent, Lucy, ed., *Albion's Classicism: The Visual Arts in Britain, 1550–1660* (London and New Haven, 1995).

Gibson, Gail McMurray, *The Theatre of Devotion: East Anglian Drama and Society in the Late Middle Ages* (Chicago, 1989).

Girouard, Mark, *Life in the English Country House: A Social and Architectural History* (London and New Haven, 1978).

Gloag, John, *The Englishman's Chair: Origins, Design and Social History of Seat Furniture in England* (1964).

Glover, Elizabeth, *A History of the Ironmongers' Company* (1981).

Goldring, Elizabeth, 'The Earl of Leicester and the Portraits of the Duc d'Alençon', *Burlington Magazine*, 146 (Feb., 2004), pp. 108–11.

Goldring, Elizabeth, 'An Important Early Picture Collection: The Earl of Pembroke's 1561/62 Inventory and the Provenance of Holbein's "Christina of Denmark"', *Burlington Magazine*, 144 (Mar., 2002), pp. 157–160.

Goodison, J.W., ed., *Catalogue of Cambridge Portraits, I, The University Collection* (Cambridge, 1955).

Goodison, J.W., ed., *Catalogue of the Portraits in Christ's, Clare and Sidney Sussex Colleges* (Cambridge, 1985).

Goodison, J.W., *Portraits and other Pictures at King's College, Cambridge* (Cambridge, 1933).

Gransden, Antonia, *Historical Writing in England* (2 vols, 1982).

Grant, Alexander, *Henry VII* (1985).

Grassby, Richard, *The Business Community of Seventeenth Century England* (Cambridge, 1995).

Greenslade, M.W., ed., *Victoria History of the County of Stafford*, 14 (1990).

Gribble, Joseph B., ed., *Memorials of Barnstaple: A History of that Ancient Borough* (Barnstaple, 1830).

Griffiths, Antony, *The Print in Stuart Britain, 1603–1689* (1998).

Grossmann, F., 'Holbein, Torrigiano and Portraits of Dean Colet', *Journal of the Warburg and Courtauld Institutes*, 13 (1950), pp. 202–36.

Gunn, S.J., *Early Tudor Government, 1485–1558* (Basingstoke and New York, 1995).

Gunn, S.J., and P.G. Lindley, eds, *Cardinal Wolsey: Church, State and Art* (Cambridge, 1991).

Harding, G.P., *A List of Portraits in Christ's Hospital* (2 vols, 1804).

Harding, George Perfect, 'A List of Portraits, Pictures in Various Mansions of the

United Kingdom', unpublished manuscript, Heinz Archive, National Portrait Gallery (3 vols, 1804).

Harding, Vanessa, 'The Population of London, 1550–1700: A Review of the Published Evidence', *London Journal*, 15 (1990), pp. 111–28.

Harlow, C.G., 'Robert Ryece [*sic*] of Preston, 1555–1638', *Proceedings of the Suffolk Institute of Archaeology*, 32 (1973), pp. 43–70.

Harris, Mary Dormer, ed., *The Register of the Guild of the Holy Trinity, St Mary, St John the Baptist and St. Katherine of Coventry* (Dugdale Society 13, 1935).

Hartopp, Henry, ed., *Register of the Freemen of Leicester, 1196–1770* (Leicester, 1927).

Hartopp, Henry, ed., *Roll of the Mayors of the Borough and Lord Mayors of the City of Leicester, 1209–1935* (Leicester [1935]).

Haskins, Charles, *The Salisbury Corporation Pictures and Plate* (Salisbury, 1910).

Hasler, P.W., ed., *The House of Commons, 1558–1603* (History of Parliament Trust, 3 vols, 1981).

Hasted, Edward, *The History and Topographical Survey of the County of Kent* (12 vols, Canterbury, 1797–1801).

Hazlitt, W. Carew, *The Livery Companies of the City of London* (2 vols, 1892, repr. 1969).

Heal, Felicity, *Hospitality in Early Modern England* (Oxford, 1990).

Hearn, Karen, *Marcus Gheeraerts II: Elizabethan Artist in Focus* (2002).

Hearn, Karen, *Nathaniel Bacon: Artist, Gentleman and Gardener* (2005).

Hearn, Karen, ed., *Dynasties: Painting in Tudor and Jacobean England 1530–1630* (1995).

Hepburn, Frederick, 'The Portraiture of Lady Margaret Beaufort', *Antiquaries Journal*, 72 (1992), pp. 118–40.

Heywood, Thomas, *The Dramatic Works of Thomas Heywood* (6 vols, 1874, repr. New York, 1964).

Hill, C.P., *A History of Bristol Grammar School* (Gloucester, 1951).

Hill, J.W.F., 'Three Lists of the Mayors, Bailiffs and Sheriffs of the City of Lincoln', *Associated Architectural Societies' Reports and Papers*, 39 (1928–29), pp. 217–56.

Hind, Arthur M., *Engraving in England in the Sixteenth and Seventeenth Centuries* (3 vols, Cambridge, 1952–64).

Historical Manuscripts Commission, *Report on the Manuscripts of the Corporation of Lincoln* (1895).

Historical Manuscripts Commission, *Report on the Manuscripts of the Borough of Reading* (1888).

Hobson, M.E. and H.E. Salter, eds, *Oxford Council Acts, 1626–1665* (Oxford Historical Society Publications, 1933).

Hooker, John Vowell, alias, *The Description of the Citie of Excester ...* [c. 1575], eds, W.J. Harte, J.W. Schopp and H. Tapley-Soper (Devon and Cornwall Record Society, 3 vols, 1919–47).

Hoskins, W.G., *The Age of Plunder: The England of Henry VIII, 1500–1547* (1976).

Housez, Janis C., 'The Impact of the Dissolution of the Monasteries on Patronage Structures in Yorkshire and East Anglia' (Ph.D thesis, McGill University, 1997).

Howard, Maurice, *The Early Tudor Country House: Architecture and Politics, 1490–1550* (1987).

Hudson, Winthrop S., *The Cambridge Connection and the Elizabethan Settlement of 1559* (Durham, NC, 1982).

Hunting, Penelope, *The Leathersellers' Company: A History* (1994).

Imray, Jean, *The Mercers' Hall* (London Topographical Society Publication no. 143, 1991)

Ingamells, John, *The English Episcopal Portrait, 1559–1835: A Catalogue* (1981).

Jaggard, William, *A View of all the Right Honourable the Lord Mayors of this Honourable City of London* (STC 14343, 1601).

James, M.E., 'The Concept of Order and the Northern Rising 1569', *Past and Present*, 60 (Aug., 1973), pp. 49–83.

James, M.E., *Family, Lineage and Civil Society: A Study of Society, Politics and Mortality in the Durham Region, 1500–1640* (Oxford, 1974).

James, Mervyn, 'Ritual, Drama and Social Body in the Late Medieval English Town', *Past and Present*, 98 (Feb., 1983), pp. 3–29.

Jewitt, Llewellyn and W.H. St John Hope, *The Corporation Plate and Insignia of the Office of the Cities and Corporate Towns of England and Wales* (2 vols, 1895).

Johnson, A.H., *The History of the Worshipful Company of Drapers of London* (5 vols, Oxford, 1914–22).

Johnston, Alexandra F., and Margaret Rogerson, eds, *Records of Early English Drama, York* (2 vols, Toronto, Buffalo and London, 1979).

Jones, Ann Rosalind and Peter Stallybrass, *Renaissance Clothing and the Materials of Memory* (Cambridge, 2000).

Jones, Norman, *The English Reformation: Religion and Cultural Adaptation* (Oxford, 2002).

Josselin, J., *Historiola Collegii Corporis Christi*, ed., J.W. Clark (Cambridge Antiquarian Society, 17, 1880).

Journal of the Architectural, Archaeological and Historic [sic] *Society for Chester and North Wales*, NS, 20 (1914).

Kemp, Brian, *English Church Monuments* (1930).

King, David, 'Medieval Glass Painting', in Carole Rawcliffe and Richard Wilson, eds, *Medieval Norwich* (2 vols, London and New York, 2004), I, pp. 121–36.

Kingsford, Charles Lethbridge, ed., *A Survey of London by John Stow, Reprinted from the Text of 1603* (2 vols, Oxford, 1908).

Kirby, Jo, 'The Painters' Trade in the Seventeenth Century', *National Gallery Technical Bulletin*, 20 (1999), pp. 5–49.

Knight, Vivien, ed., *The Works of Art of the Corporation of London* (1986).

Knowles, David, *Bare Ruined Choirs: the Dissolution of the English Monasteries* (Cambridge, 1976).

Knowles, James, 'The Spectacle of the Realm: Civic Consciousness, Rhetoric and Ritual in Early Modern England', in J.R. Mulryne and Margaret Shewing, eds, *Theatre and Government under the Early Stuarts* (Cambridge, 1993), pp. 157–89.

Kuchler, Suzanne and Walter Melion, eds, *Images of Memory: On Remembering and Representation* (Washington, DC, 1991).

Lancaster, J.C., *St. Mary's Hall, Coventry* (n.d.).

Lander, J.R., *Conflict and Stability in Fifteenth Century England* (1977).

Lasko, Peter and N.J. Morgan, eds, *Medieval Art in East Anglia 1300–1520* (1974).

Latimer, John, *The Annals of Bristol in the Seventeenth Century* (Bristol, 1900).

Laynesmith, J.L., *The Last Medieval Queens: English Queenship, 1445–1503* (Oxford, 2004).

Leach, A.F., *English Schools at the Reformation* (1896).

Leach, A.F., *Schools of Medieval England* (1915).

Leggatt, Alexander, *Citizen Comedy in the Age of Shakespeare* (Toronto, 1973).

Leicester Museum and Art Gallery, *Catalogue of Local Portraits* (Leicester, [1956]).

Levy, F.J., *Tudor Historical Thought* (San Marino, California, 1967).

Little, Francis, *A Monument of Christian Munificence, or An Account of the Brotherhood of the Holy Cross, and of the Hospital of Christ in Abingdon* [1627], ed., Claude Delaval Cobham (Oxford and London, 1871).

Llewellyn, Nigel, *Funeral Monuments in Post-Reformation England* (Cambridge, 2000).

Lloyd, Christopher, and Simon Thurley, *Henry VIII: Images of a Tudor King* (1990).

Lloyd Parry, Hugh, *The History of the Exeter Guildhall and the Life Within* (Exeter, 1936).

MacCaffrey, Wallace T., *Exeter, 1540–1640: The Growth of an English County Town* (2nd edn, Cambridge, Mass., and London, 1975).

MacLean, Sally-Beth, *Chester Art: A Subject List of Extant and Lost Art Including Items Relevant to Early Drama* (Kalamazoo, Michigan, 1982).

Man, John, *The History and Antiquities of the Borough of Reading* (Reading, 1816).

Manley, Lawrence, *Literature and Culture in Early Modern London* (Cambridge, 1995).

Mansfield, Alan, *Ceremonial Costume: Court, Civil and Civic Costume from 1660 to the Present Day* (1980).

Manship, Henry, *The History of Great Yarmouth* [c. 1619], ed. Charles John Palmer (Great Yarmouth, 1854).

Marks, Richard, 'An Age of Consumption: Art for England c. 1400–1547', in Marks and Williamson, *Gothic Art for England*, pp. 12–25.

Marks, Richard, *Stained Glass in England During the Middle Ages* (London, Buffalo and Toronto, 1993).

Marks, Richard, and Nigel Morgan, *The Golden Age of British Manuscript Painting, 1200–1500* (New York, 1981).

Marks, Richard, and Paul Williamson, eds, *Gothic Art for England 1400–1547* (2003).

Martens, Maximilian, and Natasja Peeters, '"A Tale of Two Cities": Antwerp Artists and Artisans in London in the Sixteenth Cenury', in Juliette Roding, Eric Jan Sluiter, Bart Westerweel, Marijke van der Meiji-Tolmsa and Eric Domela Nieuwenheis, *Dutch and Flemish Artists in Britain, 1550–1800* (Leiden, 2002), pp. 31–42.

Masson, André, *The Pictorial Catalogue: Mural Decoration in Libraries* (1981).

Matthews, J.H., *A History of the Parishes of St. Ives, Lelant, Towednack and Zennor in the County of Cornwall* (1892).

McRee, Ben, 'Charity and Gild Solidarity in Late Medieval England', *Journal of British Studies*, 32:3 (July, 1993), pp. 195–225.

McRee, Ben, 'Religious Guilds and the Regulation of Behaviour in Late Medieval Towns', in Joel Rosenthal and Colin Richmond, eds, *People, Politics and Community in the Late Middle Ages* (Gloucester, 1987), pp. 108–22.

McVeagh, John, *Tradeful Merchants: The Portrayal of the Capitalist in Literature* (1981).

Mercer, Eric, *English Art, 1553–1625* (Oxford, 1962).

Mercer, Eric, *English Vernacular Houses* (1975).

Millar, Oliver, *The Age of Charles I: Painting in England, 1620–1649* (1972).

Miller, Helen, *Henry VIII and the English Nobility* (Oxford, 1986).

Mitchell, John, 'Painting in East Anglia around 1500: The Continental Connection', in John Mitchell and Matthew Moran, eds, *England and the Continent in the Middle Ages: Studies in Memory of Andrew Martindale* (Proceedings of the 1996 Harlaxton Symposium, Stamford, 2000), pp. 365–80.

Moody, Joanna, ed., *The Private Correspondence of Jane Lady Cornwallis Bacon, 1613–1644* (Madison and Teaneck, New Jersey, 2003).

Moore, Andrew, and Charlotte Crawley, eds, *Family & Friends, A Regional Survey of British Portraiture* (1992).

Moran, JoAnn Hoeppner, *Education and Learning in the Diocese of York, 1300–1500* (York, 1979).

Moran, JoAnn Hoeppner, *The Growth of English Schooling, 1340–1548* (Princeton, 1985).

Morgan, Victor, 'The Dutch and Flemish Presence and the Emergence of an Anglo-Dutch Provincial Artistic Tradition in Norwich, c. 1500–1700', in Juliette Roding, Eric Jan Sluiter, Bart Westerweel, Marijke van der Meiji-Tolmsa and Eric Domela Nieuwenheis, *Dutch and Flemish Artists in Britain, 1550–1800* (Leiden, 2002) pp. 57–72.

Morgan, Victor, 'The Norwich Guildhall Portraits: Images in Context', in Andrew Moore and Charlotte Crawley, eds, *Family & Friends: A Regional Survey of British Portraiture* (1992), pp.21–30.

Morrill, J.S., *Cheshire 1630–1660: County Government and Society during the English Revolution* (Oxford, 1974).

Morris, A.R., 'The Effect upon Schooling in Sussex of the Legislation Dissolving the Religious Houses and Chantries', *Sussex Archeological Collections*, 199 (1981), pp. 149–56.

Myres, J.N.L., 'The Painted Frieze in the Picture Gallery', *Bodleian Library Record*, 3 (1950–51), pp. 82–90.

Myres, J.N.L., 'Thomas James and the Painted Frieze', *Bodleian Library Record*, 4 (1952–53), pp. 30–51.

Myres, J.N.L., and E. Clive Rouse, 'Further Notes on the Painted Frieze and Other Discoveries in the Upper Reading Room and the Tower Room', *Bodleian Library Record*, 5 (Oct., 1956), pp. 290–308.

National Gallery, *The British School* (1998).

Nelson, Alan H., ed., *Records of Early English Drama, Cambridge* (2 vols, Toronto, 1989).

Nicholl, John, *Some Account of the Worshipful Company of Ironmongers* (1851).

Nicholls, J.F., *The Free Grammar School of Bristol and the Thorns [sic], its Founders* (St Peter's Port, Guernsey, 1984).

Nichols, John, *The History and Antiquities of the County of Leicester* (4 vols, 1804–15).

Nichols, John, *The Progresses and Public Processions of Queen Elizabeth* (3 vols, 1823).

Nichols, J.G., ed., *The Chronicle of Queen Jane and Two Years of Queen Mary* (Camden Society 48, 1850).

Nora, Pierre, 'Between Memory and History: *Les Lieux de Memoire*', *Representations*, 26 (Spring, 1989), pp. 7–25.

North, Thomas, ed., *The Accounts of the Churchwardens of St. Martin's Leicester* (Leicester, 1884).

Norton-Kyshe, J.W., *The Law and Custom Relating to Gloves* (1901).

O'Connell, Laura Stevenson, 'Anti-Entrepreneurial Attitudes in Elizabethan Sermons and Political Literature', *Journal of British Studies* 15:2 (Spring, 1976), pp. 2–20.

Ogden, J., *A Descriptive List of the Pictures ... of the Corporation of the City of Canterbury* (2nd edn, 1912).

Oliver, George, *History of the City of Exeter* (1861).

Orme, Nicholas, *Education in the West of England, 1066–1548* (Exeter, 1976).

Orme, Nicholas, *English Schools in the Middle Ages* (1973).

Ormerod, Richard, and Malcolm Rogers, eds, *Dictionary of British Portraiture* (4 vols, 1979–81).

Osborne, James M., ed., *The Autobiography of Thomas Whythorne* (Oxford, 1961).

Owen, Hugh, and John Brickdale Blakeway, *A History of Shrewsbury,* (2 vols, 1825).

Oxford Dictionary of National Biography, eds H.C.G. Matthew and Brian Harrison (2004).

Painter, William, *Chaucer Newly Painted* (1623 edition, STC, 2nd edn, no. 19125.5).

Palliser, D.M., *The Age of Elizabeth: England Under the Later Tudors, 1547–1603* (2nd edn, London and New York, 1992).

Patterson, Catherine F., *Urban Patronage in Early Modern England: Corporate Boroughs, the Landed Elite and the Crown, 1580–1640* (Stanford, 1999).

Peacham, Henry, *The Art of Drawing* (1606).

Peele, Michael, 'Medieval Deeds of the Shrewsbury Drapers Company', *Transactions of the Shropshire Archeological Society*, 52 (1947–48), pp. 238–40.

Phillips, John, *The Reformation of Images: Destruction of Art in England, 1535–1660* (Berkeley, Los Angeles and London, 1973).

Phythian-Adams, Charles, 'Ceremony and the Citizen', in Peter Clark and Paul Slack, eds, *Crisis and Order in English Towns* (1972), pp. 57–85.

Phythian-Adams, Charles, *Desolation of a City: Coventry and the Urban Crisis of the Late Middle Ages* (Cambridge, 1979).

Piper, David, *The English Face* (2nd edn, 1992).

Pollard, A.W., and G.R. Redgrave, eds, *A Short-Title Catalogue of Books Printed in England, Scotland and Ireland and of English Books Printed Abroad, 1475–1640* (2nd edn, 2 vols, 1976).

Poole, R.L., ed., *Catalogue of Portraits Exhibited in the Reading Room and Gallery of the Bodleian Library* (Oxford, 1920).

Poole, R.L., ed., *Catalogue of Portraits in the Possession of the University, Colleges, City and County of Oxford* (3 vols, Oxford Historical Society Publications, vols, 57, 1912; 81, 1926; and 82, 1926).

Preston, Arthur E., *Christ's Hospital, Abingdon: The Almshouses, the Hall and the Portraits* (Oxford, 1929).

Prideaux, Sir Walter Sherburne, *Memorials of the Goldsmiths' Company* (2 vols, 1896).

Quick, Richard, ed., *Catalogue of the Second Loan Collection of Pictures held in the Bristol Art Gallery* (Bristol, 1905).

Rabb, T.K., 'Play not Politics: Who Really Understood the Symbolism of Renaissance Art?', *Times Literary Supplement* (10 Nov., 1995), pp. 18–20.

Rackham, Bernard, 'The Glass Paintings of Coventry and its Neighbourhood', *Walpole Society*, 19 (1930–31), pp. 89–110.

Ransome, David R., 'Artisan Dynasties in London and Westminster in the Sixteenth Century', *Guildhall Miscellany*, 6 (1964), pp. 236–47.

Ransome, David R., 'The Struggle of the Glaziers Company with the Foreign Glaziers,

1500–1550', *Guildhall Miscellany*, 2 (1960), pp. 12–20.

Rappaport, Steve, *Worlds within Worlds: Structures of Life in Sixteenth-Century London* (Cambridge, 1989).

Rastell, John, *The Pastyme of People: The Cronycles of Dyvers realmys and most specyally of the realme of Englond brevely co[m]pylyd* (*STC*, 20724, [1529]).

Rees Jones, S., 'Five Portraits from Peterhouse, Cambridge' (Courtauld Institute of Art Research Report no. 152 [typescript] 1951).

Ricart, Robert, *The Maire of Bristowe Is Kalendar* [c. 1484], ed. Lucy Toulmin Smith (Camden Society, NS, 5, 1872).

Richardson, W.C., *A History of the Court of Augmentations* (Baton Rouge, Louisiana, 1961).

Ridgway, Maurice H., 'Chester Goldsmiths from Earliest Times to 1726', *Journal of the Chester and North Wales Architectural, Archeological and Historic [sic] Society*, 53 (1966), pp. 1–198.

Rostenberg, Leonie, *English Publishers in the Graphic Arts, 1599–1700: A Study of the Printsellers, Publishers and Engravers* (New York, 1963).

Rutledge, Paul, 'Thomas Damet and the Historiography of Great Yarmouth', *Norfolk Archaeology*, 33 (1965), pp. 119–30.

Rutledge, Paul, '"Thomas Damet and the Historiography of Great Yarmouth"', *Norfolk Archaeology*, 34 (1969), pp. 332–4.

Salter, H.E., ed., *Oxford Council Acts, 1583–1626* (Oxford Historical Society Publications, 1928).

Saunders, Ann, and Matthew P. Davies, *History of the Merchant Taylors' Company* (2 vols, 2004).

Scarisbrick, J.J., *The Reformation and the English People* (1984).

Scott, Kathleen L., *Later Gothic Manuscripts, 1390–1490* (2 vols, 1996).

Seaver, Paul S., *The Puritan Lectureships: The Politics of Religious Dissent, 1560–1662* (Stanford, 1970).

Selwood, Jacob, '"English-Born Reputed Strangers": Birth and Descent in Seventeenth Century London', *Journal of British Studies*, 44:4 (Oct., 2005), pp. 728–53.

Sharp, Thomas, *Illustrative Papers on the History and Antiquities of the City of Coventry* (Birmingham, 1871).

Sharpe, Kevin, *Remapping Early Modern England: The Culture of Seventeenth-Century Politics* (Cambridge, 2000).

Shaw, David Gary, *The Creation of a Community: The City of Wells in the Middle Ages* (Oxford, 1993).

Shaw, William A., 'The Early English School of Portraiture', *Burlington Magazine*, 61 (Oct., 1934), pp. 171–84.

Simon, Joan, *Education and Society in Tudor England* (Cambridge, 1967).

Skaer, R.J., 'The Panel Portrait of Andrew Perne', *Peterhouse: a Record* (volume for 1997–98, published 1999), pp. 38–41.

Slack, Paul, *From Reformation to Improvement: Public Welfare in Early Modern England* (Oxford, 1999).

Slack, Paul, 'Social Policy and the Constraints of Government, 1547–58', in J. Loach and R. Tittler, eds, *The Mid-Tudor Polity, c. 1540–1560* (1980), pp. 94–115.

Sommer, William, *Antiquities of Canterbury* (1640).

Stanford, Maureen, ed., *The Ordinances of Bristol, 1506–1598* (Bristol Record Society 41, 1990).

Statham, Margaret, ed., *Accounts of the Feoffees of the Town Lands of Bury St Edmunds, 1569–1622* (Suffolk Record Society 46, 2003).

Stevenson, W.H., and H.E. Salter, *The Early History of St. John's College* (Oxford Historical Society Publications, 1939).

Stewart-Brown, R., 'Notes on the Chester Hand or Glove', *Journal of the Architectural, Archaeological and Historic* [sic] *Society for Chester and North Wales*, NS, 20 (1914), pp. 122–47.

Stocks, Helen, and W.H. Stevenson, eds, *Records of the Borough of Leicester* (Cambridge, 1923).

Stone, Lawrence, *The Crisis of the Aristocracy, 1558–1641* (Oxford, 1965).

Strong, Roy, *Artists of the Tudor Court: The Portrait Miniature Rediscovered, 1520–1620* (1983).

Strong, Roy, *The Cult of Elizabeth: Elizabethan Portraiture and Pageantry* (Berkeley and Los Angeles, 1977).

Strong, Roy, *The Elizabethan Image: Painting in England, 1540–1620* (1970).

Strong, Roy, *The English Icon: Elizabethan and Jacobean Portraiture* (1969).

Strong, Roy, *Holbein and Henry VIII* (1967).

Strong, Roy, 'Holbein in England I and II', *Burlington Magazine*, 109 (Dec., 1967), pp. 276–81.

Strong, Roy, 'A Preliminary Cartoon for the Barber-Surgeons' Group Rediscovered: A Preliminary Report', in *The Tudor and Stuart Monarchy*, I (1995), pp. 55–71.

Strong, Roy, *Tudor and Jacobean Portraits* (2 vols, 1969).

Strong, Roy, *The Tudor and Stuart Monarchy* (Woodbridge, Suffolk, 3 vols, 1995–98).

Stubbings, Frank, *A Catalogue of Portraits at Emmanuel College* (Cambridge, n.d. [1988]).

Surry, L.M.N., *The Portraits of Edward VI* (Portsmouth, n.d.).

Thirsk, Joan, ed., *The Agrarian History of England and Wales, IV, 1500–1640* (Cambridge, 1967).

Thompson, F., *Newport Free Grammar School: A Brief History* (Newport, 1987).

Thompson, James, 'The Herrick Portraits in the Guild Hall, Leicester', *Transactions of the Leicestershire Architectural and Archaeological Society*, 2 (1870), pp. 43–54.

Tillyard, Virginia, 'Civic Portraits Painted for, or Donated to, the Council Chamber of Norwich Guildhall before 1687 with Documentary Evidence relating to the Artistic Background of the City' (MA thesis, Courtauld Institute, 1978).

Tillyard, Virginia, 'Painters in Sixteenth and Seventeenth Century Norwich', *Norfolk Archaeology*, 37 (1980), pp. 315–19.

Tittler, Robert, *Architecture and Power: The Town Hall and the English Urban Community, c. 1500–1640* (Oxford, 1991).

Tittler, Robert, 'Civic Portraiture and Political Culture in English Provincial Towns, ca 1560–1640', *Journal of British Studies*, 37:3 (July, 1998), pp. 306–29.

Tittler, Robert, 'Freemen's Gloves and Civic Authority: The Evidence from Post-Reformation Portraiture', *Costume*, 40 (2006), pp. 13–20.

Tittler, Robert, 'Henry Hardware and the Face of Puritan Reform in Chester', in *Townspeople and Nation: English Urban Experiences, 1540–1640* (Stamford, 2001), pp. 140–55.

Tittler, Robert, 'Henry Manship: Constructing the Civic Memory in Great Yarmouth', in *Townspeople and Nation*, pp. 121–39.

Tittler, Robert, 'The Incorporation of Boroughs, 1540–1558', *History*, 62:204 (Feb., 1977), pp. 24–42.

Tittler, Robert, 'John and Joan Cooke: Civic Portraiture and Urban Identity in Gloucester', in *Townspeople and Nation*, pp. 81–99.

Tittler, Robert, *Nicholas Bacon: The Making of a Tudor Statesman* (London and Athens, Ohio, 1976).

Tittler, Robert, *The Reformation and the Towns in England: Politics and Political Culture, c. 1540–1640* (Oxford, 1998).

Tittler, Robert, '"Seats of Honour, Seats of Power": The Symbolism of Public Seating in the English Urban Community, c. 1560–1620', *Albion*, 24:2 (Summer, 1992), pp. 205–23.

Tittler, Robert, 'Sir Thomas White of London: Civic Philanthropy and the Making of the Merchant Hero', in *Townspeople and Nation*, pp. 100–20.

Tittler, Robert, 'Three Portraits by John de Critz for the Merchant Taylors' Company', *Burlington Magazine*, 147:1228 (July, 2005), pp. 491–3.

Treuherz, Julian, 'New Light on John Souch of Chester', *Burlington Magazine*, 139:1130 (May, 1997), pp. 299–307.

Turner, Jane, ed., *The Dictionary of Art* (34 vols, 1996).

Tyacke, Nicholas, ed., *The History of the University of Oxford*, IV, *Seventeenth Century Oxford* (Oxford, 1997).

Underdown, David, *Fire From Heaven: Life in an English Town in the Seventeenth Century* (London and New Haven, 1992).

Unwin, George, *The Gilds and Companies of London* (4th edn, New York, 1963).

Vanes, Jean, *Education and Apprenticeship in Sixteenth Century Bristol* (Bristol, 1982).

Victoria History of the Counties of England, Staffordshire, XIV (1990).

Victoria History of the Counties of England, Wiltshire V (1957).

Walker, T.A., *A Biographical Register of Peterhouse Men* (2 vols, Cambridge, 1927 and 1930).

Ward, Joseph P., 'Godliness, Commemoration, and Community: The Management of Provincial Schools by London Trade Guilds', in Muriel McClendon, Joseph P. Ward and Michael MacDonald, eds, *Protestant Identities: Religion, Society and Self-Fashioning in Post-Reformation England* (Stanford, 1999), pp. 141–57.

Waterhouse, Ellis, *Dictionary of Sixteenth and Seventeenth Century British Painters* (1988).

Waterhouse, Ellis, *Painting in Britain, 1530 to 1790* (4th edn, 1978).

Watson, J. Steven, *History of the Salters' Company* (1963).

Webster, Charles, *The Great Instauration: Science, Medicine and Reform, 1626–1660* (London, 1975).

Webster, John, *Monuments of Honour* (1624), in F.C. Lucas, ed., *The Complete Works of John Webster* (6 vols, 1927), III.

Weever, John, *Ancient Funeral Monuments* (1631).

Welch, Charles, *History of the Cutlers' Company of London and of the Minor Cutlery Crafts* (2 vols, 1916–23).

Wells-Cole, Anthony, *Art and Decoration in Elizabethan and Jacobean England: The Influence of Continental Prints, 1558–1625* (London and New Haven, 1997).

Weston, Francis, 'Some Account of the Barbers' Company and the Plate, Pictures and Charters at Barber-Surgeons' Hall', *Journal of the British Archaeological Association*, NS, 21 (1915), pp. 17–56.

Wheatley, H.B., *Historical Portraits: Some Notes on the Painted Portraits of the Celebrated Characters* (London, 1897).

Whitburn, Thomas, *Local Pictures as Landmarks of History* (Guildford, 1888).

Whiting, Robert. '"Abominable Idols": Images and Image-breaking under Henry VIII', *Journal of Ecclesiastical History*, 33:1 (Jan., 1982), pp. 30–47.

Whiting, Robert, *The Blind Devotion of the People: Popular Religion and the English Reformation* (Cambridge, 1989).

Willis, Robert, ed., *The Architectural History of the University of Cambridge* (3 vols, Cambridge, 1886, ed. John Willis Clark, repr. 1988).

Withington, Phil, *The Politics of Commonwealth: Citizens and Freemen in Early Modern England* (Cambridge, 2005).

Wollaston-Knocker, E., *An Account of the Corporation Insignia, Seals and Corporate Plate* (Dover, 1898).

Wolsey, S.W., and R.W.P. Luff, *Furniture in the Age of the Joiner* (1968).

Woodall, Joanne, ed., *Portraiture: Facing the Subject* (Manchester and New York, 1997).

Woodforde, Christopher, *English Stained and Painted Glass* (Oxford, 1954).

Woodforde, Christopher, *The Norwich School of Glass Painting in the Fifteenth Century* (Oxford, 1950).

Wolffe, B.P., *The Crown Lands, 1461–1536* (1970).

Woolf, D.R., 'Genre into Artefact: The Decline of the English Chronicle in the Sixteenth Century', *Sixteenth Century Journal*, 19:3 (Fall, 1988), pp. 321–54.

Woolf, D.R., *The Idea of History in Early Stuart England* (Toronto, 1990).

Woolf, Daniel, 'Senses of the Past in Tudor Britain', in Robert Tittler and Norman Jones, eds, *A Companion to Tudor Britain* (Oxford, 2004), pp. 407–29.

Woolf, Daniel, *The Social Circulation of the Past: English Historical Culture, 1500–1730* (Oxford, 2003).

Woolgar, C.M., *The Great Household in Late Medieval England* (London and New Haven, 1999).

Wrightson, Keith, *Earthly Necessities: Economic Lives in Early Modern Britain* (London and New Haven, 2000).

Wrightson, Keith, *English Society, 1580–1680* (1982).

Wrigley, E.A., 'A Simple Model of London's Importance in Changing English Society and Economy, 1650–1750', *Past and Present*, 37 (July, 1967), pp. 44–70.

Yates, Frances, *The Art of Memory* (1966).

Young, Sidney, *The Annals of the Barber-Surgeons of London* (London, 1890).

Yungblut, Laura Hunt, *'Strangers Here Amongst Us': Policies, Perceptions, and the Presence of Aliens in Elizabethan England* (1996).

Zeeveld, W. Gordon, *Foundations of Tudor Policy* (Cambridge, Mass., 1948).

Index

NB: *Page numbers in italics refer to figures. Sitter and painters mentioned only in the Appendices are not indexed; see Appendices for those names. Livery companies are of London unless indicated.*

Index

Mildmay, Sir Walter 42, 79, 99, 171
Milles, William 89n.12, 154
monarchy
    Stuart 44
    Tudor 2, 27, 95–6, 158, 166
morality, civic 23, 56, 59, 102–6, 134
Muscovy Company 54
Myddleton, Sir Hugh 56, 87, 175, 185n.222
Mytens, Daniel 56, 67, 82, 86–7, 136,
    146n.79, 171, 174

Newbury 119
Newcastle upon Tyne 83
Newman, John 44, 75, 79, 82, 84, 170–1,
    187
Newport (I.o.W.) 127, 131
Norwich 48–51, 52, 70, 73, 76, 150
    portraiture in 6, 10, 23–4, 31, 48–52,
        73, 124, 125, 126, 127, 150, 152, 167,
        172, 173, 174
    see also individual names
Nowell, Alexander 104, 112n.41, 125, 149,
    151–2, 171

oligarchy 99–100
Orpwood, Robert 59, 135, 146n.71, 152, 175
Oxford, city of 51, 80, 119, 172, 174, 187
Oxford University 12, 37–47, 81–2, 87,
    100, 171
    All Souls College 80, 170, 187
    Balliol College 61n.23, 170
    Bodleian Library and Frieze 44–6,
        79–80, 141, 153, 170–1, 187
    Brasenose College 43, 61n.23, 125, 127,
        170–1, 187
    Christ Church College 80, 100, 170–2,
        187
    Corpus Christi College 41, 80, 170–1
    Exeter College 158, 171
    Jesus College 100, 171
    Lincoln College 43, 127, 153, 170
    Magdalen College 21, 80, 171–2, 187
    New College 80, 153, 171–2, 187
    Pembroke College 43, 100
    Queens' College 172
    St John's College 51, 100, 122, 126, 153,
        154, 171–2
    Trinity College 100, 169, 171–2, 187

University College 170
Wadham College 43, 100, 136, 170–2
Worcester College 124, 170

Paddy, Sir William 126, 127, 171
painters 69–94, 116
    foreign-born 8, 11, 15–6, 26–31, 56,
        70–2, 78–9, 81–4, 116–17
    terminology 28–9, 35n.31, 72–3
    see also individual painters, Painter-
        Stainers
Painter-Stainers 11, 16, 28–32, 70–1, 82–5,
    175
Painter-Stainers' Company of London 3,
    28–9, 56, 83, 100, 156, 174, 175
paintings, narrative 56, 85, 160–1
    see portraiture
Pargeter, Clement 56, 175
Parker, John 42
Parker, Archbishop Matthew 21, 42, 79,
    86, 124, 149, 171
Parkins, John 59, 152, 175
parliament 99–101
Pate, Richard 59, 63n.45, 76, 116, 127,
    171, 173
patronage 27, 37–68, 70, 72, 76, 82
    civic 3–4, 15, 23–4, 31–2, 37–68, 72–6,
        78–9, 86–7, 96–7, 115, 136
    personal 4–6, 23, 27–8, 30–2, 76, 87,
        95–6, 115
Peacock, William 56, 175
Peake, Robert 79, 86, 87, 91, 170, 187
Percy, Alan 50, 55, 173
Perkins, William 42, 117, 171
Perne, Andrew 42, 43, 171
Pettus, Sir John 127, 173
Platt, Richard 57, 58, 59, 100, 124, 175
playwrights 103–04, 111n. 34, 122
    see also individual names
Plymouth 72, 172
political culture 2, 26, 96–101, 105–9,
    137–9, 150–1, 157–62
    see also identity; legitimacy
Poole, Rachel 12, 37, 79, 81
population 1, 8
Portington, William 122, 160, 175
portraiture
    chronological development 2–3, 6, 8,

210